The Independent Hostel Guide 2026

England
Wales
Scotland
Northern Ireland

Edited by

Sam Dalley and Penny MacGregor

Independent Hostels UK

ISBN 978-1-7398832-4-9

Independent Hostel Guide 2026: 34th Edition.

Editors: Sam Dalley and Penny MacGregor.

British Library Cataloguing in Publication Data. A catalogue record for this book is available at the British Library **ISBN 978-1-7398832-4-9**

Published by: Independent Hostels UK, Speedwell House, Upperwood, Matlock Bath, Derbyshire, DE4 3PE. Tel: +44 (0) 1629 580427.

© Independent Hostels UK, 2026

Printed by: Zenith zenithprint.co.uk

Distributed in the UK by: Cordee Ltd, Unit 11 Dodwells Bridge Industrial Estate, Hinckley, Leicestershire, LE10 3BS. Tel : 01455 611 185

Cover Artwork: Jen Jacobs, THE POPTARTIST, 07891 986690 thepoptartist.com

LinkedIn and X Logos: (pg 6) by Vecteezy

Internal Photographs: Photo on page 205 credited to Brian Sutherland. Photo on page 208 credited to Ike Gibson. Photo on page 159 credited to Mike Emmett. Photo on page 153 credited to Mick Garratt. Photos on page 107 credited to Elliott Simpson. **Other photos were supplied by the accommodation featured. All copyright is retained.**

CONTENTS

Independenthostels.co.uk

SYMBOLS

Dormitories

Private rooms

Sleeping bags required

Hostel fully heated

Some areas heated

Drying room available

Cooking facilities available

Meals provided or available locally

WiFi available

Simple accommodation: basic, clean and friendly

Dogs welcome by prior arrangement

Bike shed

Affiliated to Hostelling International

Accommodation for groups only

pp   per person

Visit our website to explore more symbols

WELCOME TO
INDEPENDENT HOSTELS

Gardiesfauld Hostel, pg 215b

The UK's largest hostel network.

- Friendly accommodation in amazing locations.

- Over 340 hostels, bunkhouses, camping barns and group accommodation centres.

The adventure begins with where you stay

IF YOU LIKE THIS GUIDE
YOU'LL LOVE OUR WEBSITE

- Online availability and booking.

- Powerful searches

- Special offers

- Discover hostels by route and activity

DIRECT BOOKINGS

Elterwater Hostel, pg 100a

- On our website you book directly on the hostels' own booking system, paying no commission or booking fees.

- Everything you say and everything you pay goes direct to your hosts.

- Compare this with platforms like booking.com, Airbnb or Hostelworld which can cost up to 20% in commission.

Ethical Consumer has awarded Best Buy status to the Independent Hostels booking platform.

Book Direct - be kind to your host

WHAT IS AN
INDEPENDENT HOSTEL?

Shining Cliff Hostel, pg 67b

- An independent hostel is a privately or community owned hostel.

- Hostels have shared areas, with self catering kitchens, lounges and gardens.

- They have private bedrooms and occasionally there are beds in dorms. Bunkbeds are commonly used.

- Book the whole hostel for a group get together, or book a room and meet new people.

Privately or community owned

IN THIS GUIDE AND WEBSITE
YOU WILL FIND

Check out our **Perfect for You** pages to see hostels grouped by facility, activity and ethos.

A range of hostel-style accommodation

MONEY SAVING TIPS

Elterwater Hostel, pg 100a

- BYO food to cook breakfast and dinner in the hostel
  - a great opportunity to meet other guests.

- You can make packed lunches too.

- Check out the free acivitities nearby: walks, beaches, waterfalls, visitor centres, parks, museums.

- Hostel staff and your fellow guests are a great source of information about local acivitities.

The great outdoors is free to use

WHAT TO EXPECT

Rookhow Bunkbarn, pg 98a

- Expect to meet people of all ages.

- Expect to chat and exchange stories.

- You will probably need your own towel.

- Often your bed is ready for you to jump into.

- Sometimes you need to BYO sleeping bag or hire bed linen. Best check when you book!

- There is often tea & coffee to help yourself to in the hostel kitchen. Sometimes even a DIY breakfast.

A relaxed and friendly atmosphere

HOSTELS WELCOME
EVERYONE

People use hostels at all stages of their lives:

- Teenagers on their first adventures.

- Families with children.

- Octogenarians who've hostelled all their life.

Maybe this is why multi-generation families love to gather together in a hostel.

People of all ages stay in hostels

MYTH BUSTING

Ocean Backpackers, pg 42a

Myth: I have to share a dorm.
Busted: Love or hate sleeping in dorms, it doesn't actually matter, most hostels have private rooms too.

Myth: Hostels are just for the young.
Busted: All ages, from all walks of life, stay at hostels.

Myth: Hostels are old fashioned and basic.
Busted: Each hostel is unique and run by people who enjoy the same activities that you do. They provide a warm welcome with all the comfort and facilities you need.

Hostels are unique and amazing

FAMILY ROOMS

Radcliffes Lodge, 118b

- Large private rooms are good for families of all sizes.

- Choose a private room of 2,3,4,5,6 beds or more.

- Many rooms have a mix of bunks and beds.

- Some are en suite.

Look for this symbol **P.** in the guide. On the website look for the private family room symbol **F.**

For families of all sizes

PRIVATE ROOMS

Ulva Hostel, pg 198a

Many hostels have private rooms:

- Doubles for couples.

- Twins for friends.

- Larger rooms for families or small groups.

- Some are en suite.

Look for this symbol in the guide and website. 

Privacy at night, social in the daytime

SHARED SLEEPING ROOMS
DORMS

Fort William Backpackers, pg 194b

- Low cost dorms allow individuals to have longer or more frequent holidays.

- Bunks often have individual reading lights and USB sockets.

- Some dorms have private lockers - so bring a padlock (and earplugs if you are a light sleeper).

Look for this symbol in the guide and website. 

Great value for solo travellers

COMMUNAL KITCHENS

Gardiesfauld Hostel, pg 215b

- Hostel kitchens are great places to chat while you cook.

- Share a cup of tea with the people you meet.

- Cook locally bought and foraged food.

- Large pans ideal for cooking for groups

- Save your money on eating-out for other adventures.

Look for this symbol in the guide and website. 

The kitchen is the heart of the hostel

EQUIPMENT STORAGE
BIKE SHEDS

Ballater Hostel, pg 186b

- Many hostels have secure spaces for storing your equipment.

- Often large enough to store bikes for a whole group.

- Some have wash-down areas and workshops for bike repairs.

Look for this symbol in the guide and website. 

On the website the extra symbol indicates that the shed is secure.

Relax knowing your bike is secure

DRYING ROOMS

Ocean Backpackers, pg 42a

- Many hostels have drying and boot rooms

- Go out in all weathers, confident of a dry start the next day.

Look for this symbol in the guide and website 

Don't let the weather stop you

EXCLUSIVE USE

HIRE THE WHOLE HOSTEL

Capel Tanrallt, pg 166a

- Hostels large or small can be hired for sole use.

- Perfect for friends and family get togethers.

- Great for clubs and youth groups.

- Ideal for schools and universities.

- Popular for team building and training

Use our search tool to find the ideal place for your group.

Hire the whole hostel for your group

DOG FRIENDLY

- A third of the hostels welcome dogs.

- There may be an extra fee.

- Often sole use of the hostel or a smaller unit is required.

- Be sure to mention your dog when you book.

Look for this symbol in the guide and website. 

Dogs can stay too

ACCESSIBILITY

Mount Cook Adventure Centre, pg 68a

- Hostels have varying levels of accessibility.

- Some offer fully accessible accommodation including outdoor activities.

- For each hostel with some accessible features, you will find details of what they offer on our website.

- You can also talk directly with your host via our website, to make sure that your needs can be properly met.

Look for this symbol on the website. 

Accessible adventures

ECO HOSTELS

Chartners Farm, pg 118a

- Hostels lead the way in sustainable tourism.

- Shared accommodation means lower CO_2 footprints.

- Many hostels go further with solar panels, heat pumps, wind turbines and EV charging.

- Hostels use 82% less carbon per overnight guest, than hotels. *Bureau Veritas March 2024*

In 2022 Ethical Consumer awarded Best Buy status to the Independent Hostels booking platform.

Sustainable holidays

FAMILY HOLIDAYS

Hillside Farm Bunkbarn, pg 113a

- Hostels are great for family holidays.

- They have family-friendly facilities like kitchens, gardens and games rooms.

- You can cook what you like, when you like.

- Hostel bedrooms come in all sizes, ideal for small and large families.

- Great locations for active holidays.

Fresh air family holidays

FRIENDS AND FAMILY
GET TOGETHERS

Capel Tanrallt, pg 166a

- Hostels are perfect for groups of friends and family.

- Large kitchens for cooking.

- Large tables for eating.

- Mix of private rooms of all sizes for sleeping.

- Great locations for exploring.

Holidays with friends and family

OUTDOOR ACTIVITIES
IDEAL FOR SCHOOLS

Hagg Farm Outdoor Centre, pg 80a

- Lots of outdoor centres provide hostel-style accommodation.

- And many hostels have connections with local activity providers.

- Some provide outdoor activities on-site.

- Ideal for schools, team building and groups.

Ideal for Schools

LARGE HOSTELS FOR
LARGE GROUPS

Ardentinny Outdoor Centre, pg 178b

- Don't worry if your group is large.

- There are plenty of independent hostels with beds for 50 plus people.

- Some sleep over 100.

- A choice of catering is provided.

- Activities are often available too.

Great value for large groups

UNIVERSITY GROUPS

- Get away with your uni friends and explore the UK.

- Hostels are great for socialising, with big rooms, big pans and tables for sharing meals.

- Great value, leaves a bit left over for the pub!

- Great for training, outdoor challenges and summer camps.

- Sports clubs find hostels ideal for overnight accommodation on a tour.

Hostels are great for every group

SCHOOL RESIDENTIALS

- Exclusive use of the whole property.

- Large dining rooms and plenty of safe space.

- Bunkrooms and separate leaders' bedrooms.

- A choice of catered packages or self catering.

- Risk assessments, outdoor activities and learning packages.

- Great locations for field studies.

The best value school residentials

INTER HOSTELS
WALKING ROUTES

Hostels, in all their diversity, offer new perspectives on oft forgotten corners of the British countryside, their situations engendering a desire to explore in new and inventive ways. But they don't have to be seen in isolation, frequently there is another hostel over the horizon to expand walking ambition. So, you may spend several nights in a first hostel and a day walking to that near-neighbour hostel, crafting your very own inventive mini-break walking adventure. In a bid to nurture this sense of connection this QR code takes you to a model Inter-Hostel Walking Route linking Alston and Ninebanks Hostels.

Mark Richards

We would love hostellers to send us GPX files of their own hostel linking walking routes.

stay@independenthostels.co.uk

Join the project- send us your GPX routes

ACCOMMODATION ON
LONG DISTANCE ROUTES

Mounthooly Bunkhouse on the Ravenber Way,   pg 68a

Our website shows the locations of hostels along over 60 of the most popular walking and cycling routes.

Specialising in accommodating walkers and cyclists, these hostels offer:

- Drying rooms
- Secure bike storage
- Breakfast & packed lunches
- Single night stop-overs
- Camaraderie with others on the route

Hostels mapped on over 60 routes

YHA
PAST AND PRESENT

Skidaw House, pg 105b

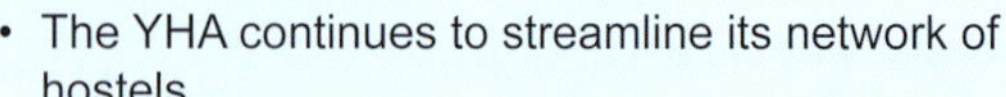

- The YHA continues to streamline its network of hostels.

- Over 50 former youth hostels are featured in this guide and website (see the QR code for details).

- A few remain affiliated to the YHA. Look out for this symbol in the guide and our website.

Over 50 former YH's are on our website

HOSTELS ARE
GOOD FOR SOCIETY

- Hostels provide affordable accommodation.

- Hostels are naturally sustainable.

- Hostel provide low-impact access to protected landscapes. Often subsidised for the young.

- Hostels promote contact with others and independent travel. Good for mental and physical well-being.

- Hostels welcome everyone

Hostelling for fresh air, and adventure

Liverpool
Manchester
81b
WALES
64b
Oswestry
Shrewsbury
63a
63b
64a
62a
Ludlow
61b
62b
65a
61a
60b
Ross on
Wye
60a
59b
Bristol
48b
48a
47b
Bath
47a
Minehead
42a
42b
44b
44a
43a
43b
Barnstaple
Yeovil
41b
46b
Bude
Okehampton
41a
45a
Exeter
40a
45b
40b
Newquay
Torquay
Plymouth
39b
39a
38b
Penzance
Falmouth
Isles of
Scilly
0 miles 50
0 kilometres 80
Guernsey
Jersey 38a

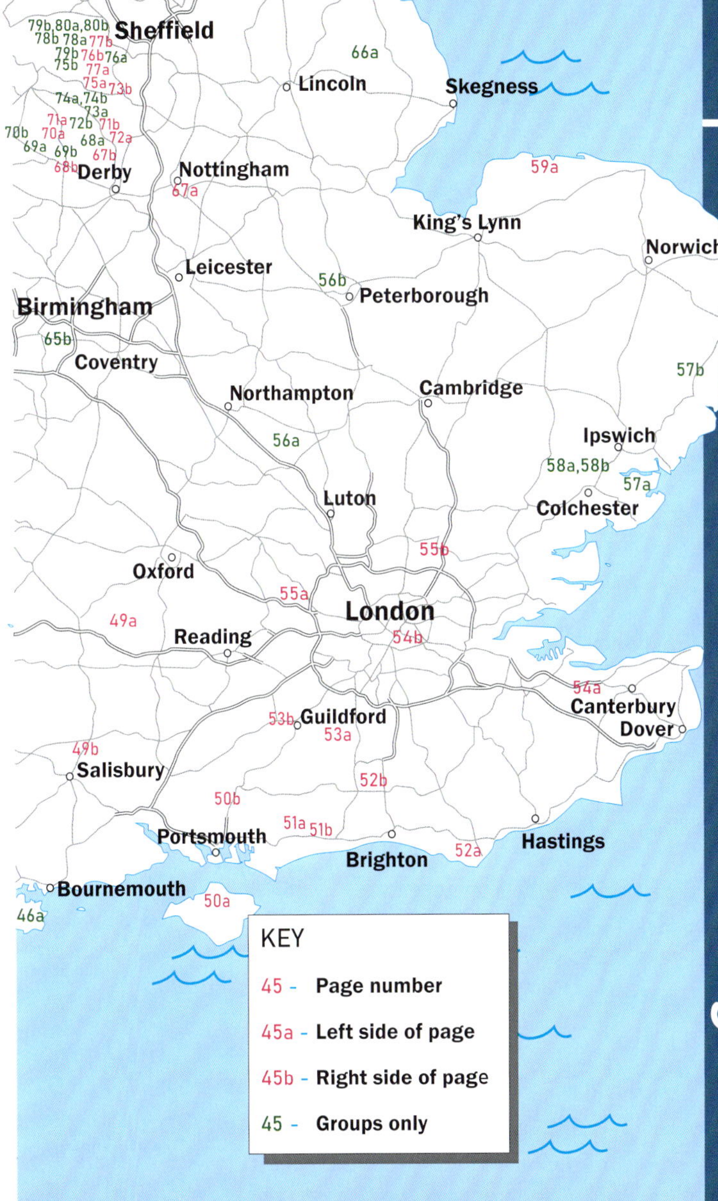
81b
79b,80a,80b
78b 78a 77b
79b 76b 76a
75b 77a
75a 73b
74a,74b
73a
71a 72b 71b
70b 70a 68a 72a
69a 69b 67b
68b Derby
Sheffield
66a
Lincoln
Skegness
59a
King's Lynn
Norwich
Nottingham
67a
Leicester
56b
Peterborough
Birmingham
65b
Coventry
57b
Northampton
Cambridge
56a
Ipswich
58a,58b
57a
Luton
Colchester
55b
Oxford
55a
49a
London
54b
Reading
54a
53b Guildford
Canterbury
53a
Dover
49b
52b
Salisbury
50b
51a 51b
52a
Portsmouth
Hastings
Brighton
Bournemouth
50a
46a
South England
35
KEY
45 - Page number
45a - Left side of page
45b - Right side of page
45 - Groups only

North England

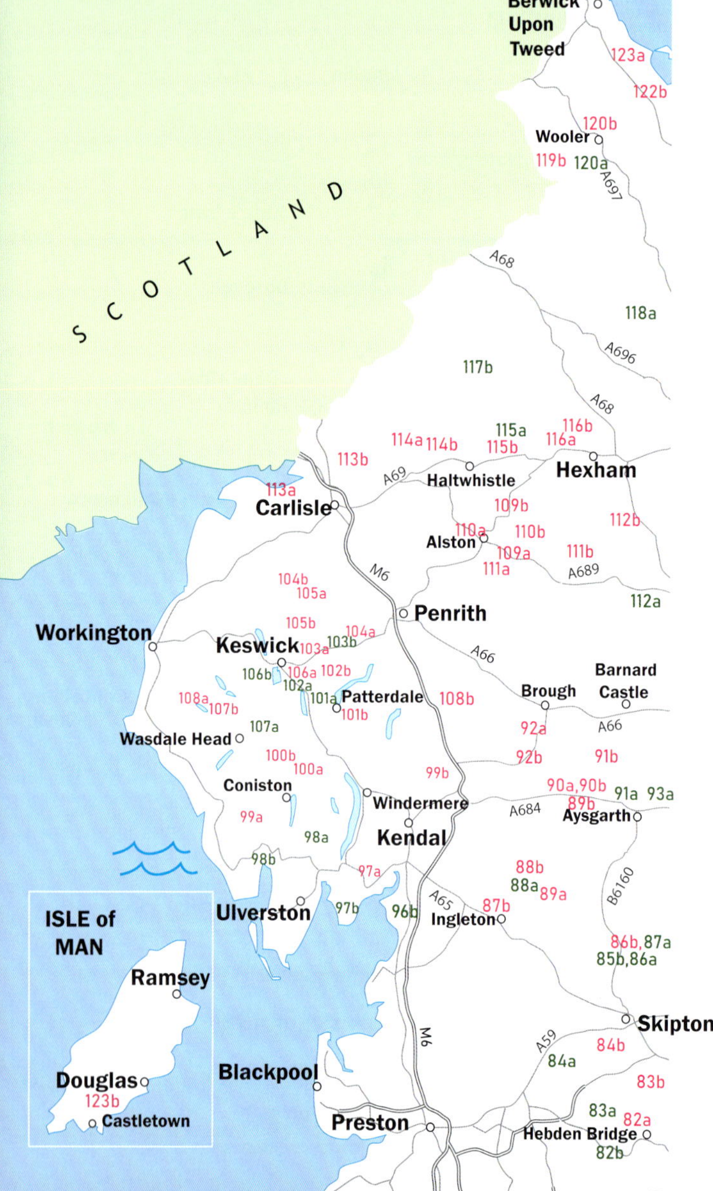

122a, 121b
121a
A1
Alnwick
119a
118b
117a
Newcastle upon Tyne
Durham
A1(M)
0 miles 50
0 kilometres 80
KEY
45 - Page number
45a - Left side of page
45b - Right side of page
45 - Groups only
Middlesborough
Whitby
93b
94a
94b
95a
95b
Richmond
A1
96a
Scarborough
Thirsk
Pickering
85a
York
Harrogate
Leeds
Hull
66b
Huddersfield

North England

JERSEY
ACCOMMODATION CENTRE
38a

LANDS END
HOSTEL
38b

Close to the fishing village of Gorey in St Martin, JAAC offers flexible accommodation for individuals, families, and groups. Options include private en suite rooms, multi-bed dormitories, and a scenic camping field. Guests enjoy shared lounges, dining areas, and outdoor recreation spaces. On-site activities include bushcraft, archery, and low-velocity paintball, with catering, transport, and group support services available for a seamless stay in Jersey.

Land's End Accommodation, in the hamlet of Trevescan, is 1/2 mile from Land's End. Double glazed & centrally heated, it has a fully equipped kitchen & dining areas inside & out. Modern bathrooms & bedrooms with TVs & WiFi. New bunk beds with USB ports & LED lights. Bedding/towels supplied. Bike storage with CCTV, parking & small honesty shop.

DETAILS

- **Open** - All year
- **Beds** - 84: Bunks: 5×8, 1×6, 4×4 Doubles: 3×2 Singles: 4×1
- **Price/night** - Groups: £40 to £62pp (full board). Single(B&B) from £47pp.

DETAILS

- **Open** - All year. Self check-in from 2:00pm via key code.
- **Beds** - 14: 1x2 1x2 with private bathroom, 1x4, 1x4 en suite
- **Price/night** - Private rooms from £69, continental breakfast £9.50, cooked breakfast £11.50, packed lunch £10

CONTACT: Ina
Tel: 01534 498636
info@jerseyhostel.co.uk
www.jerseyhostel.co.uk
La Rue de la Pouclee et des Quatre Chemins, St Martins, Jersey, JE3 6DU

CONTACT: Niko
Tel: 07585 625774
hello@landsendholidays.co.uk
www.landsendholidays.co.uk
Mill Barn, Trevescan, Sennen, Nr Land's End, Penzance, TR19 7AQ

LOWER PENDERLEATH
FARM HOSTEL
39a

Just three miles from St Ives' beaches & 5 miles from Penzance, Lower Penderleath Farm Hostel provides self-catering accommodation in four twin rooms and one alpine dormitory for 12. Plus a self contained family maisonette with small kitchen and private shower & toilet. BYO sleeping bags.

Pub food in two local villages is within walking distance. Bedding not provided.

DETAILS

■ **Open** - May-Sept. Arrive between 9am-6pm, depart by 10am.
■ **Beds** - 24: 4x2 + dorm platform of 12, 1x4 self contained maisonette
■ **Price/night** - £23 dormitory. £48 private room sleeping 2. £128 Maisonette sleeping 4. Minimum of 2 nights stay.

CONTACT: Russell Rogers
rusrogers60@gmail.com
stivescampingandhostel.com
Lower Penderleath Farm, Towednack,
St.Ives, Cornwall, TR26 3AF

BOSWINGER
HOSTEL
39b

In a tiny hamlet on the Cornish coast, with secluded coves, coastal paths & cycle routes on the doorstep. Popular with walkers, cyclists, families & schools. The perfect stop-over on the South West Coast Path and the Cornish Way cycle route. Close to The Eden Project & The Lost Gardens of Heligan, both of which offer excellent programmes ideal for schools (catering available). Book by the room up to 2 months in advance, or book exclusive use of the whole hostel.

DETAILS

■ **Open** - All year (except January). Check-in: 5pm to 8.30pm.
■ **Beds** - 40 (incl one dbl): 3x6, 3x4, 1x4 (family with a double bed), 3x2
■ **Price/night** - From £32pp. Enquire for sole use prices.

CONTACT: Charlotte Parry
Tel: 03453 719107
charlotteparry@btinternet.com
yha.org.uk/hostel/yha-boswinger
Gorran, St Austell, Cornwall, PL26 6LL

DOLPHINS
BACKPACKERS
40a

Dolphins Backpackers provides affordable accommodation just ten minutes from the South West Coast Path in the centre of the scenic coastal village of Tintagel. It is just five minutes' walk from the castle, famous for King Arthur's legends, myth and folklore.

The hostel sleeps up to 4 in a barn bunkhouse dorm room. There is a welcoming atmosphere in the shared kitchen, the communal areas and the large covered garden.

DETAILS
- **Open** - All year
- **Beds** - 4: 1x4
- **Price/night** - From £25

CONTACT: John Richardson
Tel: 07740 976326
hello@dolphinsbackpackers.co.uk
www.dolphinsbackpackers.co.uk
Fore Street, Tintagel, Cornwall, PL34 0DB

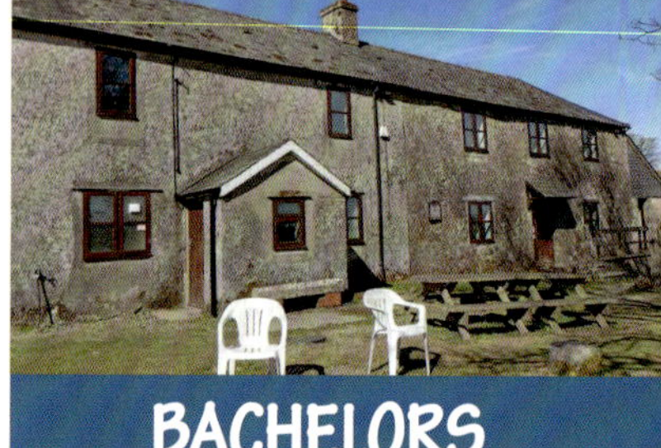

BACHELORS
HALL
40b

Set in a beautiful secluded valley in Dartmoor National Park, Bachelors Hall offers groups of all kind the chance to experience the freedom of the moor and the vastness of the landscape.
Formerly run as a traditional youth hostel, it was completely refurbished in 2019. Sleeping 60 across 6 rooms and 2 pods in the garden. The building is centrally heated with a commercial kitchen and large separate dining room/classroom.

  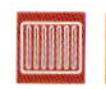    
GROUPS ONLY

DETAILS
- **Open** - All year (Closed over the Christmas Period).
- **Beds** - 56 beds in 6 rooms: 1x14, 1x10, 2x6, 2x4. Pods: 2x6
- **Price/night** - £420 for up to 35 guests and then £12pp up to 60 max

CONTACT: Paula Bullen
Tel: 01237 429501
pbullen@athenalearningtrust.uk
www.bachelorshall.co.uk
Princetown, Yelverton, Devon. PL20 6SL

EXETER GLOBE
BACKPACKERS

41a

Globe Backpackers offers clean, comfortable, self-catering accommodation for up to 30.

Book a bed, a room or the whole place.

It is just a few minutes' walk from Exeter's city centre with its cathedral, picturesque historic waterway, quay and wide range of shops, pubs, clubs, cafés and restaurants.

DETAILS

■ **Open** - All year (phone for Xmas). Check in 3.30 - 7.30pm (earlier or later by arrangement only).
■ **Beds** - 30: 3 private rooms and 5 dormitories.
■ **Price/night** - See our online booking.

CONTACT: Duty Manager
Tel: 01392 215521
info@exeterbackpackers.co.uk
www.exeterbackpackers.co.uk
71 Holloway Street, Exeter, EX2 4JD

ELMSCOTT
HOSTEL

41b

Elmscott Hostel is surrounded by unspoiled coastline with sea views of Lundy Island. Great for walking, cycling, surfing and bird watching. The South West Coast Path is just a few mins' walk away. The hostel is well equipped for all your self-catering needs and has a games room and shop. In winter it is only available for sole use bookings.

DETAILS

■ **Open** - All year, (groups only in winter).
■ **Beds** - 32 (35 in winter): 1 unit of 20: 2x6, 2x4; 1 unit of 12: 1x6, 1x4, 1x2. Extra 3 bed room for sole use in winter.
■ **Price/night** - Adult from £30, under 16s from £23. Discounts for groups or longer stays.

CONTACT: Hostel Reception
Tel: 01237 441367 or John & Thirza
01237 441276
enquiries@elmscott.org.uk
www.elmscott.org.uk
Elmscott, Hartland, Bideford, Devon, EX39 6ES

OCEAN
BACKPACKERS

42a

Situated in the picturesque harbour area of Ilfracombe in North Devon, this cosy, cool, clean and friendly hostel offers fantastic facilities for groups, families and solo travellers. There is storage and a drying room for wetsuits, bikes & boards. Plenty of books, games & USB ports. A well equipped self-catering kitchen and a spacious living room with free WiFi. A real home from home. Close to beach, restaurants & bars.

DETAILS

- **Open** - All year (Nov-Easter exclusive hire only). Check in 4pm to 7pm.
- **Beds** - 37: mix of dorms / family rooms
- **Price/night** - Dorms from £25pp. Double/twin rooms from £66. Contact by email/phone for group bookings.

CONTACT: Alex
Tel: 07775 501878 or 01271 867835
info@oceanbackpackers.co.uk
www.oceanbackpackers.co.uk
29 St James Place, Ilfracombe, Devon, EX34 9BJ

CALVERT DEVON
LODGES

42b

Calvert Devon's lodges offer affordable accommodation in the heart of rural Devon, just ten minutes from Exmoor and the North Devon coast. Sleep in modern lodges for groups of 4 to 40 (up to 106 for Schools groups) with options for onsite catering, a heated pool, and outdoor activities. It's the perfect base for groups of families and friends and schools. Whether you want a peaceful countryside retreat or an action-packed holiday, Calvert Devon makes group getaways easy, fun, and unforgettable.

DETAILS

- **Open** - All year
- **Beds** - 46: 4 lodges sleep up to 10 guests, the fifth sleeps 6 people.
- **Price/night** - See website.

CONTACT:
Tel: 01598 763221
hello@calvertdevon.org.uk
calvertdevon.org.uk
Calvert Devon, Wistlandpound, Kentisbury, Barnstaple EX31 4SJ

ROCK AND RAPID
BUNKHOUSE
43a

Perfect for an adventurous or relaxing break. The Rock and Rapid Adventure Centre offers activities such as climbing (climbing wall on-site for lessons or use by experienced climbers) coasteering, raft building and canoeing. The bunkhouse can be rented out for sole use, or an activity package can be put together for your group. This can vary from a few activities to a full programme, including food. Just 20 mins from the North Devon coastline. Hen and stags, family and school groups all welcome.

DETAILS

■ **Open** - All year. 24 hours.
■ **Beds** - 40: 2x18, 2x2
■ **Price/night** - Sole use £350 for single nights and £300 for multiple nights. £10 per dog per stay.

CONTACT: Keith Crockford
Tel: 01769 309003
climb@rockandrapidadventures.co.uk
www.rockandrapidadventures.co.uk
Hacche Mill, South Molton, EX36 3NA

NORTHCOMBE
CAMPING BARNS
43b

A mile outside the town of Dulverton on Exmoor, Northcombe Camping Barns nestle in the Barle river valley with good canoeing, walking and bridleways. A perfect base for groups on Exmoor. The barns sleep 16 and 28 in partitioned dormitories. Smaller groups can be catered for. Heated by wood-burning stoves with a well equipped kitchen, you just need to bring your own pillows, sleeping bags or duvets.

DETAILS

■ **Open** - All year. Arrive after 4pm, depart before 10.30am
■ **Beds** - 44: Barn16: 1x6, 1x10. Barn28: 1x6, 1x10, 1x12
■ **Price/night** - Sole use: Barn16 from £200. Barn 28 from £300. Showers 20p. Electric meter £1 coins.

CONTACT: Sally Harvey
Tel: 01398 323602
sallyeharvey17@gmail.com
www.northcombecampingbarns.co.uk
Hollam, Dulverton, Somerset, TA22 9JH

EXMOOR
BUNKBARN

44a

Formerly a granary on a working farm, this eco-friendly bunkbarn is close to Winsford Hill and Wimbleball Lake. Perfect for exploring Exmoor on foot, bike or canoe. Hot water, central heating & WiFi included in price. Well equipped, open-plan kitchen/diner with seating for all. Large drying room. Outside BBQ area and small field with campfire. BYO bedding & towels. Sleeps max 25 - sole use only. Free logs for the stove and camp fire. Enjoy Exmoor's dark skies.

DETAILS

- **Open** - 1st March to 31st Oct.
- **Beds** - 25: 1x14, 1x8, 1x3
- **Price/night** - Whole barn only:- 2 nights minimum- Weekend £400 per night. Weekdays £350 per night.

CONTACT: Julia or Guy Everard
Tel: 07967 114331
bookings@exmoorbunkbarn.co.uk
www.exmoorbunkbarn.co.uk
Week Farm, Bridgetown, Dulverton
TA22 9JP

BOSSINGTON
BUNKHOUSE

44b

Bossington Bunkhouse, (part of Bossington Hall luxury B&B), sleeps 7 (2 x twin, 1x king, 1 x single). There's a small shared kitchen and shared bathroom, and the ground floor rooms are self contained. Perfect for walkers, cyclists, couples & solo visitors, the South West Coast Path is just a 10 min walk away. The picturesque town of Porlock is 1 mile away & the stunning Exmoor coast is a 15 min stroll. Packed breakfast, ready meals & supplies available. All bedding & towels provided.

DETAILS

- **Open** - March 1st to November 30th
- **Beds** - 7: 2x twin, 1x king, 1 x single
- **Price/night** - £55pp based on two people. £60 single occupancy.

CONTACT: Guy or Annie
Tel: 01643 862800 or 07375 676830
bunkhouse@bossingtonhall.co.uk
bossingtonhall.co.uk
Bossington Hall, Selworthy, Porlock, Minehead, Somerset. TA24 8HJ

MONKTON WYLD
COURT

45a

This Victorian neo-Gothic mansion in the Dorset National Landscape has easy access to the Jurassic Coast at Lyme Regis as well as the Wessex and Monarch's Way long distance footpaths. Guests can use the vegetarian self-catering kitchen to prepare their own meals or vegetarian meals can be pre-booked. There is also camping in the grounds. Run by a charity that promotes sustainable living. Fruit and vegetables are grown in the organic garden.

- **Open** - All year. Office opening hours: 9am-5pm.
- **Beds** - 38: bed spaces (various rooms)
- **Price/night** - B&B £55 per person, Exculsive use £1250.

CONTACT: Office Team
Tel: 01297 560342
info@monktonwyldcourt.org
www.monktonwyldcourt.co.uk
Elsdon's Lane, Monkton Wyld, Nr Charmouth, Dorset, DT6 6DQ

THE BUNKER
PORTLAND

45b

The Bunker is on the South West Coastal Path, with Chesil Beach on its doorstep and world class sport climbing, diving sites and water-sports a short distance away. Sleeping up to 18 in 6 private bunk rooms, each with a shower and sink, The Bunker offers affordable accommodation for groups and individuals. It has a large communal area, kitchen with tea and coffee and free WiFi. Breakfast and packed lunches available when booked in advance.

- **Open** - All year. Check in from 3pm, check out by 10am.
- **Beds** - 18: 3x4,3x2, private bunkrooms
- **Price/night** - Ranging from £41 - £82 per room. Exclusive hire available.

CONTACT: Tony or Sally
Tel: 07846 401010
stay@thebunkerportland.com
www.thebunkerportland.com
Victoria Square, Portland, Dorset, DT5 1AL

CUMULUS OUTDOORS
RESIDENTIAL CENTRE

46a

Cumulus Outdoor Residential Centre is situated in the small seaside town of Swanage on Dorset's Jurassic Coast. The purpose built centre sits in 6 acres of private grounds and has units sleeping 16, 32, 32 or 47 which can be hired individually or together. The centre is popular with groups of friends/families, schools, youth groups, DofE & corporate groups. A range of outdoor activities are available if required. Dogs welcome with arrangement.

DETAILS

- **Open** - All year.
- **Beds** - 133: Bungalow 16, Studland 47, Durlston 32, Peveril 32,
- **Price/night** - Bungalow - £256, enquire for other buildings.

CONTACT: Julia Munn
Tel: 01929 422480
sam@cumulusoutdoors.com
www.cumulusoutdoors.com
Cobbler's Lane, Swanage, Dorset,
BH19 2PX

MILTON ABBEY
SCHOOL

46b

Milton Abbey School, near Blandford Forum, is an historic, private boarding school in the heart of the Dorset National Landscape. During school holidays 5 self contained boarding houses are available on a catered basis. Each house sleeps up to 50 in a mix of single, twin, triple & quad rooms. Book one or more of the houses or book exclusive use of the site. All the school's leisure facilities can be hired, including swimming pool, sports hall, tennis courts and a theatre.

DETAILS

- **Open** - School holidays only.
- **Beds** - 230: 5 separate boarding houses each sleeping 50 in a mix of single, twin, triple and quad rooms.
- **Price/night** - Please enquire.

CONTACT: Edward Brayshaw
Tel: 01258 882246 or 01258 880484
events@miltonabbey.co.uk
www.miltonabbey.co.uk
Milton Abbas, Blandford Forum, Dorset.
DT11 0BZ

MENDIP
BUNKHOUSE

47a

Larkshall (Mendip Bunkhouse) is the Cerberus Spelaeological Society's HQ. It offers well appointed comfortable accommodation on The Mendips, perfect for caving, walking, cycling, climbing, diving at Vobster Quay and for exploring the Somerset countryside. Local attractions include Wells, Wookey Hole, Cheddar Gorge, Glastonbury & Bath. Camping available. Ample parking.

DETAILS

- **Open** - All year. All day.
- **Beds** - 30+: 1x5, 1x6, 1x8, 1x14 (plus camping).
- **Price/night** - £15pp + 50% for single nights. Min 2 nights at weekends. Enquire for sole use of a bunkroom.

CONTACT: Bookings Officer
Tel: 07723 006520
hostelbookings@cerberusspeleo.org.uk
www.cerberusspeleo.org.uk
Cerberus Spelaeological Society,
Larkshall, Fosse Rd. Oakhill, Somerset,
BA3 5HY

BATH YMCA

47b

Bath YMCA offers great value accommodation. Centrally located, all the sights of this World Heritage city are easily reached on foot.
With 210 beds, Bath YMCA specialises in making guests feel comfortable. Fully air conditioned lounge with TV, laundry, lockers, football table and WiFi. Couples, families, groups and backpackers all welcome.

DETAILS

- **Open** - All year. All day.
- **Beds** - 210: Dorms: 1x10, 3x12, 1x15, 1x18. Rooms: 7 x quad, 6 x triple, 29 x twin, 5 x double, 9 x single
- **Price/night** - Dorm from £20pp (£25 at weekends), Private rooms from £34 (£38 at weekends). Includes breakfast.

CONTACT: Reception
Tel: 01225 325900
stay@ymca-bg.org
www.ymcabath.org.uk
International House, Broad Street Place,
Bath, BA1 5LH

GOBLIN COMBE
LODGE

48a

In the heart of North Somerset, 10 miles outside Bristol, this Eco timber framed building is set in12 acres of private grounds. Including an 8 acre camping field, wildflower meadow, 18ft yurt, covered outdoor classroom and a Grade II listed cottage. Run on a not-for-profit basis and surrounded by SSSI woodlands, it offers flexible accommodation for groups with the option of activities and classes.

DETAILS

■ **Open** - All year
■ **Beds** - 98: Lodge 38: 4x2, 4x4, 4x6 + 60 camping
■ **Price/night** - Youth/Charity Groups £22pp (min 16 people). Private Groups £24pp (min 17 people). Plus VAT.

CONTACT: Hannah Baker
Tel: 07702 532710
goblin.combe@groundwork.org.uk
www.goblincombe.org.uk
Cleeve Hill Road, Cleeve, North Somerset. BS40 5PP

THE BRISTOL
WING

48b

The Bristol Wing provides unique accommodation for independent travellers, groups and tourists.

This iconic former police headquarters provides chic accommodation in the heart of Bristol.

A mix of private, en suite and dorm rooms with communal spaces and cafe.

Close to the bus station, and perfectly located for Bristol's best attractions and shopping from big names to quirky markets.

DETAILS

■ **Open** - All year.
■ **Beds** - 84
■ **Price/night** - Enquire for price

CONTACT: Sarah Bradicich
Tel: 0117 428 6199
info@thebristolwing.co.uk
www.thebristolwing.co.uk
9 Bridewell Street, Bristol, BS1 2QD

COURT HILL
CENTRE
49a

STONEHENGE
HOSTEL
49b

Only a few steps from the historic Ridgeway National Trail, Court Hill Centre enjoys breathtaking views over the Vale of the White Horse.

Reclaimed barns surround a courtyard garden. Providing accommodation for schools, families, groups and individuals, the centre offers evening meals, breakfasts and picnic lunches. There is a beautiful high-roofed dining room which retains the atmosphere of the old barn. A meeting/class-room, camping and self-catering kitchen are also available.

Welcome to Stonehenge Hostel, family farm & vineyards, where the perfect overnight accommodation awaits!

Set in over 40 acres of stunning Wiltshire countryside, vineyards, farm & woodlands, the hostel is located just 8 miles from the historic city of Salisbury and is only 5 miles from the iconic Stonehenge. Come along and enjoy the rare breed farm animals, vineyards and over 70 beds in the fantastic Stonehenge Hostel.

DETAILS

- **Open** - All year. To check availability please call 01235 760253.
- **Beds** - 45 1x13,1x5, 6x4,1x3
- **Price/night** - From £22.50. U18 £15.50

CONTACT: Reception
Tel: 01235 760253
courthillcentre@hotmail.com
www.courthill.org.uk
Letcombe Regis, Wantage, OX12 9NE

DETAILS

- **Open** - All year
- **Beds** - 70: 2x2, 1x3, 5x4, 1x5, 1x6 + dorms
- **Price/night** - Enquire for prices.

CONTACT: Reception
Tel: 01980 629438
marketing@choldertonrarebreedsfarm.com
www.stonehengehostel.co.uk
Beacon House, Amesbury Road, Cholderton, Salisbury, Wilts, SP4 0EW

COWES BASE CAMP
UKSA

50a

UK Sailing Academy's 4-acre waterfront site in Cowes on the Isle of Wight can accommodate groups of 10 to 100+. Dormitory style blocks contain self-contained 4-8 berth bunk rooms with separate leader rooms. UKSA offers catered holidays by the sea with optional activities for families & groups of all sizes. Facilities include indoor heated swimming pool & full-sized sports hall.

  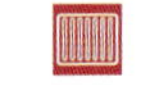    

DETAILS

- **Open** - All year (except Xmas)
- **Beds** - 335: 12x8,5x6,41x4,14x2,10x1
- **Price/night** - Accommodation with activities: 4 nights/5 days from £299pp, 2 nights/3 days from £220pp. Accommodation £50pp (full board). Get in touch for family and group rates.

CONTACT: Schools and Groups Team
Tel: 01983 203045
schools@uksa.org
uksa.org
Arctic Road, Cowes, Isle of Wight,
PO31 7PQ

SOUTH DOWNS
ECO LODGE

50b

An award-winning eco-renovation in the heart of the South Downs National Park right on the South Downs Way. Perfect base for walkers, cyclists, business away-days and family get-togethers. The Lodge offers well-appointed self-catering accommodation. There are also B&B rooms and a campsite with yurts, shepherds hut and secluded pitches. Large grounds with woodland trails and a café. Pubs, shops & take-aways, 2 miles.

DETAILS

- **Open** - Hostel, B&B and Campsite are open all year. Yurts from Apr to Oct.
- **Beds** - 73: Hostel 39: 14 rooms. B&B 24: 11 rooms. Shepherds Hut: 1 Double. Yurts 10: 3 yurts + Camping 34: 9 pitches
- **Price/night** - See website.

CONTACT: Reception
Tel: 01730 823549 or 01730 823166
accommodation@sustainability-centre.org
southdownsecolodge.com
The Sustainability Centre, East Meon,
Hampshire, GU32 1HR

GUMBER BOTHY
AND CAMPSITE

51a

Gumber Bothy Camping Barn is a converted Sussex flint barn on a working sheep farm within the National Trust's Slindon Estate. There is no access by car. It provides simple overnight accommodation and camping for walkers, horse riders, and cyclists, just off the South Downs Way. A tranquil and remote location, to get away from it all. Only a 5-minute walk from Stane Street, the Roman road that crosses the South Downs Way at Bignor Hill. NO CARS.

DETAILS

- **Open** - All year
- **Beds** - 25: 1x16, 1x5, 1x4 + camping
- **Price/night** - Bothy: £20pp, under 12's £10. Camping: £15pp, under 12's £7.50. Discounts for groups (DoE/Scouts etc)

CONTACT: Lisa Tupper
Tel: 01798 869259 or 07834 524452
lisahayes1@hotmail.co.uk
www.bignorromanvilla.co.uk
Gumber Farm, Slindon, West Sussex,
BN18 0RN

SOUTH DOWNS
BUNKHOUSE

51b

Perfect for walkers, cyclists, runners etc wanting to stay in the South Downs National Park. This beautifully converted barn on a working farm is on the South Downs Way. Equipped with 2 ovens, microwave, fridge/freezer toasters, kettles, dishwasher, washing machine & tumble dryers. Courtyard with BBQ. Pubs & cafes within walking distance. Secure bike storage & bike wash. A function room can be hired separately, with a kitchenette and loo.

DETAILS

- **Open** - All year. All day
- **Beds** - 20: 3x4, 1x8 (optional 3 extra beds). B&B in the farmhouse: 2x dbl/twin
- **Price/night** - From £36pp. BYO sleeping bag, or hire linen&towel £7pppn.

CONTACT: Kate Lock
Tel: 01798 831100 or 07710 630219
kate@southdownsbunkhouse.co.uk
www.southdownsbunkhouse.co.uk
Houghton Farm, Houghton, Arundel,
West Sussex, BN18 9LW

SOUTH DOWNS
CLUB HOUSE

52a

Offering affordable, comfortable stays for up to 21 guests in 7 ensuite rooms. South Downs Club house is set in woodland on the edge of Eastbourne in the South Downs National Park, directly on a footpath leading to Beachy Head.

Fully refurbished, it features a modern kitchen, spacious communal area, outdoor seating, a fire pit, secure bike racks, and ample parking—perfect for groups, walkers, cyclists, and families

DETAILS

- **Open** - All year
- **Beds** - 21: 3x2, 1x3, 3x4 all ensuite
- **Price/night** - Exclusive hire from £480 to £910. Beds from £18, Private Rooms from £35. Prices vary with Season.

CONTACT: Kim
Tel: 07946 265073
kim@southdownsclubhouse.fun
southdownsclubhouse.fun
1 East Dean Road, Eastbourne, East Sussex, BN20 8ES

GAVESTON
HALL

52b

A former boarding school nestling in beautiful countryside, Gaveston Hall accommodates groups of all sizes. The 85 beds are spread across dorms, private single/twin rooms & chalets.

Set in magnificent grounds with a football field, tennis court, woodland walks and fishing lake. Inside there are table tennis & pool tables and an indoor swimming pool. Room for coach parking.

DETAILS

- **Open** - Closed January.
- **Beds** - 85: Hall: 1x18,1x16 1x14 2xdbl, 1xtwin, 1xsgl. Chalets: 2x10, 1x13, 1x14
- **Price/night** - From £30pp. Small extra charge for bedding hire or BYO.

CONTACT: Rita Barclay
Tel: 07957 440 781 or 07432 897 193
gavestonhall@outlook.com
www.gavestonhallsussex.com
Nuthurst, Horsham, West Sussex
RH13 6RF

HURTWOOD
HIDEOUT

53a

Formerly YHA Holmbury St Mary, now independently owned, Hurtwood Hideout sits within 2,000 acres of open-access countryside & woodland in the Surrey Hills National Landscape.

A perfect rural retreat, only 30 miles from central London, with great walking, cycling & mountain biking routes on the doorstep. Ideal for families, couples, individuals & groups of up to 49 people.

DETAILS

- **Open** - All year
- **Beds** - 49: 10x4, 3x2, 1x3 (dbl+sgl).
- **Price/night** - From £45pp. £540 for "Group Rooms" (up to 26 beds). Sole use £1500 (up to 40 people).

CONTACT: Josh Belshaw
Tel: 01306 730777
info@hurtwoodhostel.com
www.hurtwoodhostel.com
Radnor Lane, Holmbury St Mary,
Dorking, Surrey, RH5 6NW

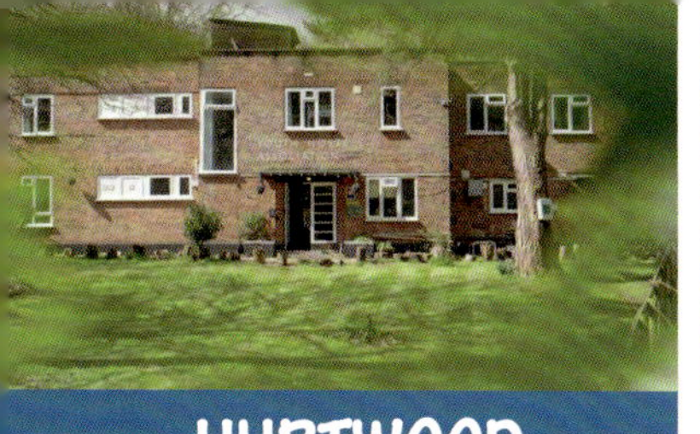

PUTTENHAM BARN
BUNKHOUSE

53b

Puttenham Barn Bunkhouse, on the North Downs Way/Pilgrims Way, offers simple accommodation for walkers & cyclists in the Surrey Hills National Landscape. A converted historic barn with volunteer wardens to welcome you. Pub food in the village. Garden, picnic benches & secure cycle shed. Sleeping bag hire available. No cars allowed on site but limited street parking nearby. Railway stations: Wanborough (3.5 km) & Guildford (7 km).

DETAILS

- **Open** - Open from April to October. No access 10am-5pm.
- **Beds** - 11: 2x4 (bunk beds), 1x3 (sleeping platform).
- **Price/night** - See website.

CONTACT: Bookings
Tel: 01483 811001
book@puttenhambarn.uk
puttenhambarn.uk
The Street, Puttenham, Nr Guildford,
Surrey, GU3 1AR

PALACE FARM
HOSTEL
54a

Palace Farm Hostel is a relaxing, flexible 4* hostel on a family run farm.

Situated in the village of Doddington, (which has a pub!), in the North Kent Downs AONB. The area is great for walking, cycling & wildlife. There are ten fully heated en suite rooms sleeping up to 39 people. Duvets, linen and continental breakfast included.

DETAILS

■ **Open** - All year. 8am to 10pm. Flexible, please ask.
■ **Beds** - 39: 1x8, 1x6, 2x5 (family room), 1x4, 1x3 and 4x2
■ **Price/night** - From £18-£40pp (all private en suite rooms). Group reductions.

CONTACT: Graham and Liz Cuthbert
Tel: 01795 886200
info@palacefarm.com
www.palacefarm.com
Down Court Road, Doddington,
Sittingbourne / Faversham, Kent,
ME9 0AU

THE WALRUS
HOSTEL
54b

The Walrus Hostel is London's most central hostel. Just outside Waterloo station it is only a 10 minute walk to Big Ben, The London Eye and The Houses of Parliament.

This prime position, the friendly, helpful staff and the competitive prices have meant that it steadily ranks among the top 5 budget accommodation in London. Book direct for free early check in, towel hire + 10% off at the bar!

DETAILS

■ **Open** - Open all year. Check in from 2:30pm
■ **Beds** - 68: 3x2, 2x4, 3x6, 1x8, 1x28
■ **Price/night** - Dorms: £24.50 - £42.75. Enquire for private rooms.

CONTACT: Reception
Tel: 07545 589214
thewalrushostel@gmail.com
www.thewalrusbarandhostel.co.uk
172 Westminster Bridge Road, London,
SE1 7RW

JORDANS
HOSTEL
55a

Jordans offers accommodation in a tranquil rural location yet with quick train connections to central London.

Accommodation for up to 18 guests. Welcomes solo travellers, families with children and groups, all year round.

Lovely walking and cycling from the doorstep in to the beautiful Chilterns countryside. YHA Jordans is the oldest purpose built Youth Hostel in England and Wales.

DETAILS

- **Open** - All year (camping May-Sept)
- **Beds** - 18: 2x4, 2x5
- **Price/night** - See website for details..

CONTACT: Nicola
Tel: 01494 873135
YHA 0345 371 9523
nickjordans1@hotmail.com
yha.org.uk/hostel/yha-jordans
Welders Ln, Jordans, Beaconsfield,
Buckinghamshire HP9 2SN

HARLOW
INTERNATIONAL
55b

Harlow International Hostel,in the centre of a landscaped park, is one of the oldest buildings in Harlow. The town of Harlow is your ideal base for exploring London, Cambridge and the best of South East England. The journey time to central London is only 35 minutes from the hostel door and it is the closest hostel to Stansted Airport. National Cycle Route 1 passes the front door. Meals can be provided for groups. There's a children's zoo, orienteering course and outdoor pursuits centre in the park.

DETAILS

- **Open** - All year. 8am - 10.30pm (check in 3-10.30pm).
- **Beds** - 30: 2x1, 5x2, 1x4, 1x6, 1x8
- **Price/night** - Please see the website.

CONTACT: Richard Adams
Tel: 01279 421702
mail@h-i-h.co.uk
www.h-i-h.co.uk
13 School Lane, Harlow, Essex,
CM20 2QD

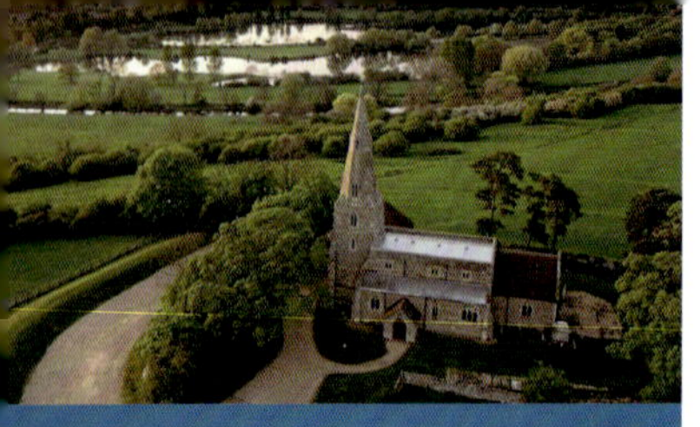

CHELLINGTON
CENTRE

56a

Award winning, eco-friendly, residential youth centre - an inspirational space popular with school and youth groups. Sleeps 36 in 8 bunkrooms (+36 camping for youth groups). Modern facilities, self-catering kitchen & breakout rooms. Amazing views of stunning Bedfordshire countryside. Easy access from M1/A1. Disabled access. Youth discounts.

DETAILS

- **Open** - All year. Arrive 5pm, exit 12pm.
- **Beds** - 72: 36 in bunkrooms (2x5, 5x4, 1x6) + 36 youth campers
- **Price/night** - From £17pp (full occupancy). W/end 2 night min. School/youth groups: week night £495-£660, w/end night £585-700. Other groups: week night £660-780, w/end night £785-1,025.

CONTACT: Debbie Holloway
Tel: 01234 720726
admin@chellington.org
www.chellington.org
St Nicholas Church, Felmersham Road,
Carlton, Bedford MK43 7NA

GARDEN
HOUSE

56b

Luxury 42 bed hostel in the charming market town of Stamford in rural Lincolnshire. Sleeping up to 42 across 20 en suite rooms (no bunks), Garden House is offered on a sole use basis to groups of 16-42 at weekends. Couples, families & smaller groups can book by the room midweek. Beautifully appointed with communal rooms, a large walled garden & parking for 20 cars.

DETAILS

- **Open** - All year
- **Beds** - 42: 2x4, 1x3, 11x double/twin, 3x double, 2x twin, 1x1 (all ensuite)
- **Price/night** - Sole use: W/e £1,400 (min 2 nights). M/w £1,100 (no min nights). Full week from £6,250. Discounts for longer stays. Twin room from £75.

CONTACT: Graham Starmer
Tel: 01780 430310
info@gardenhousestamford.co.uk
stamford.holiday/garden-house
High Street, St. Martins, Stamford,
Lincolnshire, PE9 2LP.

1912 CENTRE

57a

DARSHAM
COUNTRY CENTRE

57b

The 1912 Centre is the former Harwich fire station with views across the harbour. The centrally heated hostel offers a large dining / recreational area, with bunk beds in cabin style rooms. Two ground floor rooms suitable for disabled. Facilities include a fully equipped kitchen, showers & drying room. BYO sleeping bag. Close to town amenities, Harwich Town railway station and just 50m from the promenade and a sandy beach.

Darsham Country Centre is in the old railway station. Affiliated with the Woodcraft Folk, the Centre provides self-catering accommodation for groups of up to 30.
Perfectly situated for exploring the stunning Suffolk countryside & its many tourist attractions. Heritage Coast & seaside town of Southwold 10 miles away. Overflow camping for up to 15. Shop and garage nearby.

DETAILS

- **Open** - All year.
- **Beds** - 26: 3x6, 2x2, 1x4.
- **Price/night** - 1 night £295, 2 nts £590, 3 nts £860, 4 nts £1150 then £150 per extra night. Discounts for scout, guide, brownie & youth groups. Ask for a quote.

CONTACT: Debbie Hill
Tel: 01255 552010
info@harwichconnexions.co.uk
www.harwichconnexions.co.uk
Cow Lane, Off Kings Quay Street,
Harwich Essex CO12 3ES

DETAILS

- **Open** - All year.
- **Beds** - 30: 1x1, 1x2, 3x5, 2x6
- **Price/night** - Voluntary groups £170 (24 people+£7.50/extra pers). Statutory groups £250 (24 ppl+£10/extra pers). Priv groups £385 (24 ppl+£20/extra pers).

CONTACT: Annette Day
Tel: 07941 640796 or 01728 668736
darsham@woodcraft.org.uk
www.darshamcountrycentre.org.uk
Old Station House Main Road Darsham
Saxmundham, Suffolk. IP17 3PL

OLD BROODER
BUNKHOUSE
58a

Comfortable, rural farm-stay accommodation in train-accessible Suffolk. Sleeps 22 across five bedrooms, including a beautifully restored Shepherd's Hut. Mix of oak bunks & beds. Relax in cosy sitting room; croquet, BBQ, ping-pong & badminton; explore the farm, picnic in a meadow. 20+ bikes included in hire or kayak down the River Stour. Go Ape, visit castles, coast, historic towns. Larger groups can also book the Tudor Barn (58b).

DETAILS
- **Open** - Check booking arrangements
- **Beds** - 22: 2x2, 2x8, 1x2 (hut)
- **Price/night** - W/ends: From £40-£62pppn. 2 nights m/week from £30 pppn. Contact us for further information.

CONTACT: Juliet Hawkins
Tel: 01787 247235
gfhawkinsltd@outlook.com
www.thehall-milden.co.uk
The Hall, Milden, Lavenham, Sudbury, Suffolk CO10 9NY

TUDOR BARN
58b

The Tudor Barn offers atmospheric group accommodation on an environmentally friendly working farm in rural Suffolk. Sleeping 25+ (singles/doubles/4 posters) in 4 private rooms plus the huge space of the Tudor Barn where you also feast & relax. The perfect base for group celebrations, reunions or activity breaks. Bikes & Tudor costumes are included. Larger groups can sometimes also hire the Old Brooder Bunkhouse 58a (sleeping 22) 100m down the track.

DETAILS
- **Open** - Check booking arrangements
- **Beds** - 25+: 3x2, 1x3, 1x16 (plus cots)
- **Price/night** - W/ends: From £40-£60 pppn. Midweek from £30 pppn. Contact us for further information.

CONTACT: Juliet Hawkins
Tel: 01787 247235
gfhawkins@btconnect.com
www.thehall-milden.co.uk
The Hall, Milden, Lavenham, Sudbury, Suffolk CO10 9NY

DEEPDALE
ROOMS AND CAMPING
59a

CAMP HILLCREST
BUNKHOUSE
59b

Deepdale Rooms offers a range of comfortable, private, self-catering rooms. Choose from double, twin, triple, quad, family & larger rooms for small groups. Most rooms are en suite. All bedding is provided, BYO towels, but can be provided. Facilities include a large well equipped kitchen, communal dining area & living room, underfloor heating throughout & laundry/drying facilities. There's also an adjoining campsite. Large groups by arrangement.

DETAILS

■ **Open** - All year. All day. Collect key from Deepdale Visitor Information Centre
■ **Beds** - 60: 13 x dbl, 3 twin, 4 triple, 5 quad, 4 family quad, 2 small group
■ **Price/night** - Private rooms from £42.

CONTACT: Deepdale Rooms & Camping
Tel: 01485 210256
stay@deepdalecamping.co.uk
deepdalecamping.co.uk
1 Deepdale Granary, Burnham
Deepdale, Norfolk, PE31 8DD

Quirky bunkhouse in the Wye Valley just off Offa's Dyke. Sleeping 16 in 3 rooms, it can be booked by the bed, the room or for sole use. The perfect base for walkers, cyclists, outdoor enthusiasts & the young at heart. Enjoy the pool table, cinema screen and 2 acres of grounds with hot tub, skate park, high rope course, fire pit, pizza oven and animals. Camping, flat & horse box also available.

DETAILS

■ **Open** - All year
■ **Beds** - 28: B/house 16: 1x8,1x5,1x3. Flat 8. Horsebox 4. Plus camping.
■ **Price/night** - B/house: Weekends from £350, midweek from £25pp. Horsebox: w/e £100, m/w £60. Flat: w/e £100, m/w £60 (2 guests), extra guests £25pp,

CONTACT: Corinna
Tel: 01594 531220 or 07919 385886
corinna.seaton@yahoo.co.uk
camphillcrest.co.uk
Camp Hillcrest, The Common, St Briavels, Gloucestershire GL15 6SH

CROFT FARM
WATERPARK

60a

Croft Farm Waterpark sits just outside Tewkesbury in the scenic River Avon Valley, with it's own lake.

Accommodation is in cabins, a pod village, chalets & camping. Great for touring the Cotswolds, Malverns, Bredon Hill & the Forest of Dean. A wide range of watersports, activities & tuition are on offer. A footpath meanders through the meadow to the River Avon and free river fishing is available to guests.

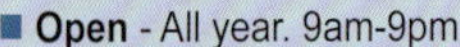

DETAILS

■ **Open** - All year. 9am-9pm.
■ **Beds** - 216: Chalets: 32x4, 8x twin. Cabins: 5x8. Pods: 8x4.
■ **Price/night** - Chalets - £55. Pods £65 Cabins £140. Min stay of two nights.

CONTACT: Martin Newell
Tel: 01684 772321 or 07736 036967
info@croftfarmwaterpark.com
www.croftfarmwaterpark.com
Bredons Hardwick, Near Tewkesbury, Gloucestershire GL20 7EE

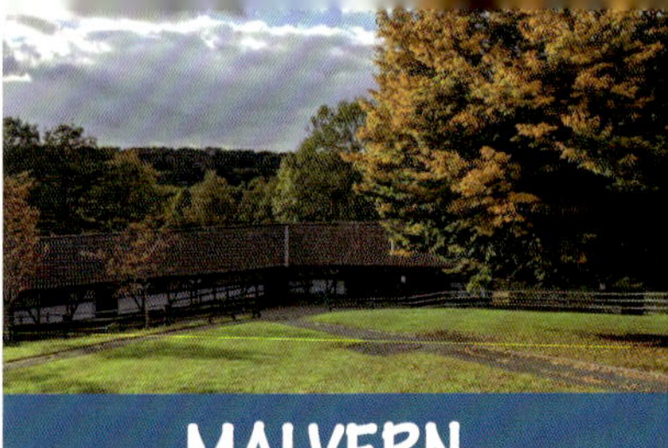

MALVERN
CENTRE

60b

Run by Boundless Events, the Malvern Centre nestles in the picturesque Malvern Hills ANOB.

South Block sleeps 55, North Block sleeps 43 and the self contained Chalet sleeps 18. Book by the unit or book the whole site. There is a large commercial kitchen, a dining room with seating for 100 and plenty of classrooms & break out spaces.
Outdoor activities are available.

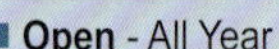
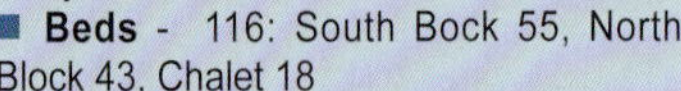

DETAILS

■ **Open** - All Year
■ **Beds** - 116: South Bock 55, North Block 43, Chalet 18
■ **Price/night** - From £36pp with a minmum group size. Please enquire for Chalet.

CONTACT: Reception
Tel: 01684 574546
enquiries@boundlessoutdoors.co.uk
boundlessevents.co.ukOld Hollow, Malvern, Worcestershire WR14 4NR

DUNFIELD
HOUSE
61a

Standing in 15 acres of gardens & parkland, Dunfield House is the ideal rural location for your group to meet together as a community. The centre offers a fully catered service for 12-27 in the Stable accommodation and 25-74 in the House accommodation. Groups of up to 120 can be accommodated with camping. You can also book the Stables as self-catering. Dunfield House has the LOtC Quality Badge for learning.

DETAILS

- **Open** - All year, except closed for two weeks over Christmas.
- **Beds** - 120. Main house:73. Stables:23 + 5 pull-out beds. Camping.
- **Price/night** - Main House £1,764 + £32pp full board. Stables £754 self-catering. (All prices include VAT).

CONTACT: Nicole
Tel: 01544 230563
info@dunfieldhouse.org.uk
www.dunfieldhouse.org.uk
Kington, Herefordshire. HR5 3NN

LUDLOW MASCALL
CENTRE
61b

A beautiful Victorian building in the heart of Ludlow, providing en suite accommodation within walking distance of restaurants, shops and pubs. Close to the Shropshire Hills and Mortimer Forest with miles of stunning landscapes to explore. Fresh towels, bed linen, complimentary toiletries, tea and coffee making facilities, parking and WiFi included. Residents also have access to a lounge, dining area, kitchen, and courtyard garden. Breakfasts available.

DETAILS

- **Open** - All year except NY and Xmas.
- **Beds** - 19: 1x family room (sleeps 4), 7x twin, 1x single.
- **Price/night** - Family room (4 beds) from £84. Twin from £66. Single from £47.

CONTACT:
Tel: 01584 873882
info@ludlowmascallcentre.co.uk
www.ludlowmascallcentre.co.uk
Lower Galdeford, Ludlow, Shropshire
SY8 1RZ

CLUN MILL
HOSTEL

62a

YHA partner hostel in rural Shropshire. Clun Mill is a restored 18th century stone water mill with many original features including some original machinery. Available for sole use, Clun Mill sleeps groups of up to 23 across 4 rooms. With a large enclosed grassy area, plenty of space inside and well away from neighbours, perfect for young children & gatherings of friends or families.

DETAILS

■ **Open** - All year.
■ **Beds** - 23: 2x4 (en suite), 1x7, 1x8 (en suite).
■ **Price/night** - £840 w/ends & school holidays, £665 w/days including Sun. Min 2 nights. 1 night stays considered but prices are higher.

CONTACT: Manager
Tel: 07725 426450 or 01244 255440
clunmill@yha.org.uk
yha.org.uk/hostel/yha-clun-mill
The Mill, Clun, Craven Arms, Shropshire. SY7 8NY

HAYE FARM
SLEEPING BARN

62b

This bunkhouse on a working farm has a fully equipped self-catering kitchen, dining room and lounge. Enjoy the quiet rural location on the covered decking, patio (with BBQ) and lawn. The nearby Wye Forest is one of the largest remaining ancient forests in England. On the Worcestershire Way and close to the Severn Way and Mercian Way (NCN route 45) at Bewdley (1 mile). The West Midland Safari Park and Severn Valley Railway are also very close.

DETAILS

■ **Open** - All year. 24 hour access.
■ **Beds** - 15: 1x2, 1x3, 1x4, 1x6
■ **Price/night** - Exclusive use from £300/night. Smaller groups/private rooms may be available. Visit website for prices.

CONTACT: Stuart Norgrove
Tel: 07732 489195
haye-farm@outlook.com
www.haye-farm.co.uk
Haye Farm, Ribbesford, Bewdley, Worcestershire, DY12 2TP

BRIDGES
YOUTH HOSTEL
63a

In the Shropshire Hills, close to Long Mynd & Stiperstones, Bridges Hostel is perfect for walkers. The Shropshire Way, the End to End cycle route & mountain bike routes pass close by.

The hostel has a self-catering kitchen, lounge with wood fire, drying room, shop & large garden. Camping available.

DETAILS

■ **Open** - All year. Reception:8-10am & 5-10pm. Hostel closes at 11pm.
■ **Beds** - 28: 2x4 en suite, 2x6, 1x8 plus camping
■ **Price/night** - 4-bed ensuite: £125, £105 2+ nights. 6-bed: £150, £130 2+ nights. 8-bed: £190, £150 2+ nights. Sole use from £440.

CONTACT: Bridges Youth Hostel
Tel: 01588 650656 or 01694 722350 (up to 8pm)
mickandgill@btconnect.com
Ratlinghope, Shrewsbury, Shropshire, SY5 0SP

ALL STRETTON
BUNKHOUSE
63b

All Stretton Bunkhouse offers comfortable, cosy, self-catering accommodation for groups of up to 10. It has easy access to the Long Mynd with walks & bike rides for all levels. The busy town of Church Stretton is a short drive & it's just 10 mins' walk to the local pub. There's a well equipped kitchen, a shower, two toilets & a tumble dryer. Dogs welcome with sole use.

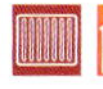

DETAILS

■ **Open** - All year, all day. Arrive after 4pm and leave before 10.30am.
■ **Beds** - 10: 2x4, 1x2
■ **Price/night** - £35pp. Twin Room £70. 4 Bed Room £135. Exclusive use £310 (dogs free). £1 pppn discount if arriving without a vehicle - refunded on arrival.

CONTACT: Frankie or Mike Goode
Tel: 01694 722593 or 07870 147123
info@allstrettonbunkhouse.co.uk
www.allstrettonbunkhouse.co.uk
Meadow Green, Batch Valley, All Stretton, Shrops, SY6 6JW

STOKES BARN
BUNKHOUSES

64a

On top of Wenlock Edge AONB in the heart of Shropshire, Stokes Barn has two bunkhouses with comfortable, centrally heated, dormitory accommodation. Perfect for corporate groups, walkers, field study, schools, stag/hen parties or reunions with friends/family. Ironbridge World Heritage Site is 6 miles away. Much Wenlock is within walking distance with shops, pubs & sports facilities.

  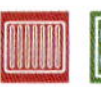      

DETAILS

- **Open** - All year. All day.
- **Beds** - Threshing Barn 28: 1x12,1x10,1x6 Granary 16: 1x10,1x4,1x2
- **Price/night** - Barn: midweek £339, w/end £550. Granary: m/week £242, w/end £375. Both units: w/end £850. Min of 2 nights at all times.

CONTACT: Helen
Tel: 01952 727491
info@stokesbarn.co.uk
www.stokesbarn.co.uk
Stokes Barn, Newtown Farm, Much Wenlock, Shropshire, TF13 6DB

SPRINGHILL
FARM BUNKHOUSE

64b

Part of a Welsh hill farm on the Wales/Shropshire border at 1475ft above sea level, with beautiful views over the Ceiriog Valley and Berwyn Mountains. Great for walking, riding, cycling, team building, meetings, or just to relax . The bunkhouse has under-floor heating, entrance hall, drying room, large self catering kitchen, dining area & lounge. The patio and lawn have a BBQ. Horse riding and archery on site. Good walking from the door. Horses and pets on request. Limited WiFi & mobile.

DETAILS

- **Open** - All year by arrangement.
- **Beds** - 37: B/house: 25, Cottages: 2x6
- **Price/night** - £30pp (including bedding but not towels).

CONTACT: Sue Benbow
Tel: 01691 718406
sue@springhillfarm.co.uk
springhill.farm
Springhill Farm, Glyn Ceiriog, Selattyn, Oswestry, Shropshire, SY10 7NZ

BELL HEATH
CENTRE
65a

Bell Heath Centre, set amidst 20 acres of secluded woodlands, offers the perfect rural escape with excellent transport links to Birmingham. It sleeps up to 92 & outdoor adventures can be organised on site. The spacious centre is perfect for large family groups, reunions, weddings, stag/hen parties, schools, faith groups & corporate events. Facilities include a commercial kitchen, hall (seating 100), lounge & games room.

DETAILS

- **Open** - All year.
- **Beds** - 92: Main Centre: 78: 9x8, 3x2. Cottage: 8. Snug: 6 + glamping/campsite
- **Price/night** - From £30pp with a min group size. Please enquire for holiday cottages, glamping and campsite.

CONTACT: Reception
Tel: 01684 574546
enquiries@boundlessoutdoors.co.uk
boundlessevents.co.uk
Quantry Lane, Belbroughton,
Stourbridge, Worcestershire. DY9 9UU

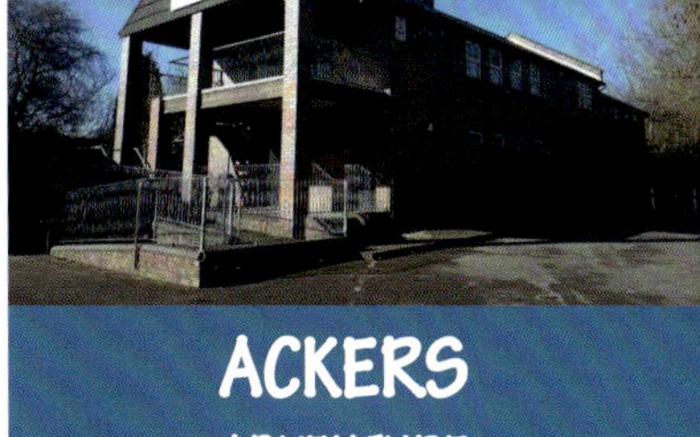

ACKERS
ADVENTURE
65b

Ackers Residential Centre (ARC) is a purpose built accommodation centre set in 70 acres of semi rural land just 2 miles from the centre of Birmingham. Perfect for The Sea Life Centre, Cadbury World, Thinktank, The Bull Ring shopping centre, National Motorcycle Museum & the NEC. With 9 sleeping rooms, a fully equipped self-catering kitchen, dining area and a rec room with TV, DVD, games and comfy seating. Ackers Adventure provide instructor led outdoor activities on site which can be incorporated into your stay.

DETAILS

- **Open** - All year.
- **Beds** - 26: 4x4, 5x2
- **Price/night** - Enquire for price.

CONTACT:
Tel: 0121 772 5111
bookings@ackers-adventure.co.uk
www.ackers-adventure.co.uk
Ackers (ARC), Waverley Canal Basin,
Small Heath, Birmingham, B10 0DQ

VIKING
CENTRE
66a

Situated in the village of Claxby in the Lincolnshire Wolds Area of Outstanding Natural Beauty, this low cost hostel has a well equipped kitchen and good sized communal area. Within easy reach of Lincoln, Gainsborough, Scunthorpe and Grimsby. The perfect location for: walking, cycling, field studies, outdoor pursuits, educational activities and conservation projects. Popular with family groups, schools, scouts, guides, walkers, cycling groups and other organisations.

DETAILS

- **Open** - All year.
- **Beds** - 20: 2x4, 2x6
- **Price/night** - £150. Dogs (max 2) £15 per stay.

CONTACT: David Beer
Tel: 07710 692534 or 01673 847767
vikingcentre48@gmail.com
www.thevikingcentre.com
Pelham Road, Claxby, Market Rasen,
Lincolnshire LN8 3YR

HULL TRINITY
BACKPACKERS
66b

In the heart of historic Hull this hostel is aimed at the individual traveller, groups, cyclists & families. Perfect for Hull's museums & attractions, such as The Deep, Marina, theatres & Connexin Live Arena. Sport fans friendly too. Family en suite, singles & dorms. Self-catering kitchenettte & coffee lounge. Daily ferries to Holland put Europe on the doorstep. Proudly independent.

DETAILS

- **Open** - Open from March-Dec. 5-10pm check in, flexible with notice.
- **Beds** - 20+: 1x6, 2x4, 1x family en suite, 2x single/twin. Flexible.
- **Price/night** - Direct from £22pp (dorm), £36pp (single). £49 (small double). En suite £54.

CONTACT: Glenn Gavin
Tel: 07853 000474 or 01482 223229
hulltrinitybackpackers@gmail.com
hulltrinitybackpackers.com
51/52 Market Place, Kingston Upon Hull.
HU1 1RQ

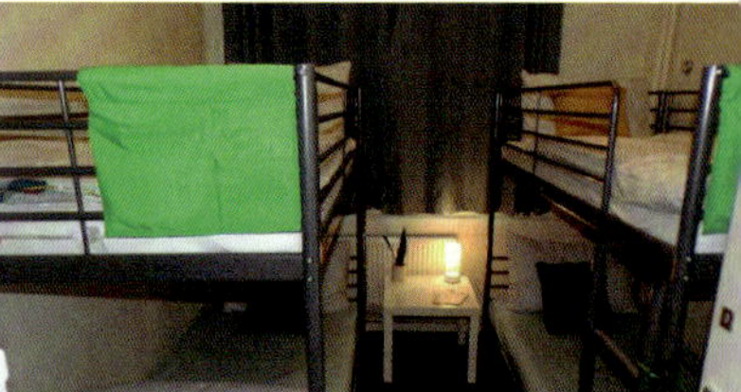

IGLOO
HYBRID

67a

Off Market Square, right in the centre of Nottingham, Igloo Hybrid offers great value and comfort. With dorms, singles, doubles, triples, and family quarters as well as our posh en suite Shed digs. Rooms and communal areas feature up-cycled furniture and street art murals, with a self-catering kitchen, WiFi, power showers, lockers, lounge & courtyard.

DETAILS

- **Open** - Reception open 7am-10pmMon - Sun. Closed late Dec - Early Jan.
- **Beds** - 58: dorms, singles, twins, doubles, triples, quads and family rooms.
- **Price/night** - Dorms: from £29pp. Sleep pods, singles & doubles from £36. Quad Rooms from £90. En suites from £44.

CONTACT: Igloo Hybrid
Tel: 0115 9483822
hybrid@igloohostel.co.uk
www.igloohostel.co.uk
4-6 Eldon Chambers, Wheeler Gate, Nottingham, NG1 2NS

SHINING CLIFF
HOSTEL

67b

With its own crags, streams, lakes & 600-acres of mature woodland, Shining Cliff Hostel has nature on its doorstep. Access is half a mile from the nearest parking area along a woodland footpath. Paths lead through the woods to the A6 at Ambergate (20 mins' walk) which has a food shop, pub, buses and trains to Derby. The hostel is ideal for groups and individuals wishing to enjoy time away in a peaceful woodland setting.

  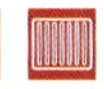        

DETAILS

- **Open** - All year.
- **Beds** - 20: 1x4, 2x6, 2x2
- **Price/night** - Sole use: £325 Fri/Sat (min 2 nights). £200-280 Sun-Thur. Room bookings: £25 per adult, £15 per child (Sun-Thurs only). £10/dog (sole use only).

CONTACT: Kate Tuck
Tel: 07794 268059
shiningcliffhostel@yahoo.com
shiningcliffhostel.co.uk
Jackass Lane, Alderwasley, Derbyshire.
DE56 2RE

MOUNT COOK
ADVENTURE CENTRE
68a

Mount Cook, a purpose built activity centre centre, offers groups of 8 - 180 the perfect base for an exciting weekend or holiday in the Peak District. A whole range of outside activities can be organised on-site or off-site for a minimum of 8 people. Popular with schools, sports clubs, youth groups and corporate team building. B&B, full or half board. Self-catering with sole use bookings. Activities are an optional extra.

DETAILS

- **Open** - All year. Office hours 9-5.
- **Beds** - 180: 140 Beds across 35 bedrooms (including 2 with disabled access), plus 40 beds across 10 Pods.
- **Price/night** - Please contact for prices - prices start at £18.90 pp per night.

CONTACT: The Office
Tel: 01629 823702
Explore@mountcook.uk
www.mountcook.uk
Porter Lane, Middleton-by-Wirksworth, Matlock, DE4 4LS

ASHBOURNE
GATEWAY LODGE
68b

Following a one-year renovation project, Gateway Lodge will open in May 2026. The new hostel will be ideal for family groups, walking & cycling holidays, residential workshops, school, and youth groups. There will be seven ensuite bedrooms sleeping 35 people. The new facilities includes a large comfortable lounge & dining area, well equipped self-catering kitchen, drying room, and cycle storage. The hostel is part of the Link Centre with a café and selection of halls and meeting rooms that can be hired.

 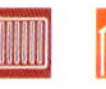    

DETAILS

- **Open** - Planned opening 1 May 2026
- **Beds** - 35: across 7 rooms (2 additional apartments opening later)
- **Price/night** - From £20.00 per person.

CONTACT: Crispin Scott
Tel: 07849 771827
ashbourne.gateway@gmail.com
ashbournegateway.org.uk
Station Road, Ashbourne, Derbyshire DE6 1AE

ALSTONEFIELD
CAMPING BARN

69a

Close to Dovedale, Manifold Cycle Trail, Carsington Water, Alton Towers & Roaches Rocks (great for climbers). Ideal for quiet groups, families, cyclists, walkers, DofE, scouts, schools & team building. Camp in the comfort of a remote cosy barn with log burning stove, toilet & water. No electric & no distractions. In a meadow, off the beaten track with great views. BYO camping equipment. Glamping wagon also available.

       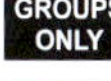 

DETAILS

- **Open** - All year. Not Xmas & New Year.
- **Beds** - 12: BYO sleeping mats & bags
- **Price/night** - £132. Discounts mid-week (term time) when made by email from this website.

CONTACT: Robert or Teresa Flower
Tel: 01335 310349
gateham.grange@btinternet.com
www.gatehamgrange.co.uk
Gateham Grange, Alstonefield,
Ashbourne, Derbys. DE6 2FT

BUTTERTON
CAMPING BARNS

69b

At Fenns Farm guests can choose from a range of accommodation to suit all budgets. There are four properties, Waterslacks Camping Barn sleeping 15, Wills Glamping Barn sleeping 6 and two holiday cottages, Fenns & Foggs Barns both sleeping 7. All the accommodation is situated on the edge of the Peak District village of Butterton, in walking distance of the local pub and the Manifold Valley.

DETAILS

- **Open** - All year for Fenns, Foggs & Wills. Waterslacks is closed in winter.
- **Beds** - 35: Waterslacks:15. Wills:6. Fenns:7. Foggs:7 `
- **Price/night** - Waterslacks from £155, Wills from £85, Fenns & Foggs from £200.

CONTACT: Jason and Michelle
Tel: 07376 489047 or 07708 200282
fennsfarmaccommodation@gmail.com
www.fennsfarmaccommodation.com
Fenns Farm, Wetton Road, Butterton,
Leek, Staffordshire, ST13 7ST

SHEEN
BUNKHOUSE
70a

Sheen Bunkhouse is in a quiet corner of the Peak District, close to the beautiful Dove and Manifold valleys. It has a well equipped self-catering kitchen, lounge, two bunkrooms and separate toilets & showers.

The Manifold Track, Tissington Trail and High Peak Trail give easy access to beautiful countryside, ideal for families and cyclists. Dovedale and the moors offer stunning walking. Buxton, Leek and Bakewell are within 12 miles and Alton Towers is 20 minutes away by car.

DETAILS

- **Open** - All year. 24 hours access. Reception 8am - 9pm.
- **Beds** - 14: 1x8, 1x6
- **Price/night** - From: Adults £20, u16 £15.

CONTACT: Jean or Graham Belfield
Tel: 01298 84501 or 07538932708
grahambelfield11@gmail.com
Peakstones, Sheen, Derbys, SK17 0ES

ROACHES
BUNKHOUSE
70b

Roaches Bunkhouse sits at the foot of The Roaches gritstone edge in the Peak District, amidst some of the best climbing in the country, plus walks & cycling in stunning scenery. Close to local pubs, the historic market town of Leek is 3 miles away, while the white knuckle rides of Alton Towers are a 30 min drive. The bunkhouse has 2 self contained lodges, sleeping 9 & 25. These can be booked separately or can be interconnected.

DETAILS

- **Open** - Open all year
- **Beds** - 34: Peak Lodge 25: 5x5. Stanley's Rest: 9: 1x5, 1x4.
- **Price/night** - Stanley's Rest from £380. Peak Lodge from £790. Min stay 2 nights. Offers for longer stays.

CONTACT: Emma Baines
Tel: 01538 300308
info@roachesbunkhouse.com
roachesbunkhouse.com
Upper Hulme Mill, Roach Road, Upper Hulme, Nr Leek, Staffordshire, ST13 8TY

ROYAL OAK
BUNKBARN
71a

The Royal Oak Bunk Barn offers four private rooms, twin, double, or family-sized, with bed linen provided. Showers and toilets are accessed via an external staircase and shared with the campsite, and there is a communal kitchen. With direct access to the High Peak and Tissington Trails, it's a popular base for exploring limestone gorges, stone circles, and the surrounding scenic countryside. A campsite is also available, dogs are welcome, and you can enjoy great meals in the friendly rural pub.

DETAILS
- **Open** - Open all year.
- **Beds** - 12: 2x2, 2x4
- **Price/night** - From £40, see website. £10 key deposit. Dogs £10 per stay.

CONTACT: The Royal Oak
Tel: 01298 83288
stay@peakpub.co.uk
www.royaloakhurdlow.co.uk
The Royal Oak, Hurdlow, Nr Buxton,
SK17 9QJ

YOULGREAVE
HOSTEL
71b

At the centre of the pretty village of Youlgreave in the heart of the White Peak, this youth hostel has been given a contemporary upgrade under private management. The hostel has an on-site artisan bakery, cafe and a bookshop There is a self-catering kitchen, a patio with picnic tables, cycle storage and nine private bedrooms (7 en suite). Individual travellers are always welcome.

DETAILS
- **Open** - All year. All day
- **Beds** - 34: 1x2, 2x3 family/dbl bed, 2x4, 2x4 en suite, 2x6 en suite.
- **Price/night** - Private 2 bed en suite from £105. Private 4 bed room from £125. 3 bed family en suite from £115. Private 6 bed en suite room from £170.

CONTACT: Colin Trigg
Tel: 07725 426450 or 01244 255440
lou@fountainhouseyoulgreave.co.uk
Fountain Square, Church Street,
Youlgreave, near Bakewell, Derbyshire,
DE45 1UR

COSY COTTAGE
YOULGREAVE

72a

Cosy Cottage is in the Peak District village of Youlgreave, just minutes from the Limestone Way.

Perfect for walkers, couples, and families, it sleeps up to four in two bedrooms. It has a well-equipped kitchen and cosy lounge with log burner.

The thriving village has pubs, shops, cafés, and easy access to walks, cycling, wild swimming and Bakewell.

 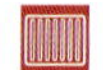       

DETAILS

- **Open** - All Year
- **Beds** - 4: 2x2
- **Price/night** -   £150 per night (two nights minimum stay). Discounts for longer stays. Dog £10 per stay.

CONTACT: Helena
Tel: 07936 067758 or 07843 001224
cosycottagemoorlane@outlook.com
www.cosycottagemoorlane.com
2 Moor Lane, Youlgrave, Bakewell, DE45 1US

THE RECKONING
HOUSE

72b

Renovated to a high standard including double glazing and insulation, the Reckoning House is situated 3 miles from Bakewell. It is on the edge of the Lathkill Dale National Nature Reserve, full of interesting flora and fauna as well as outstanding geological features.

Horse riding, fishing, golf and cycle hire are available locally. Local walks include the Limestone Way. Facilities include: cooking area, 4 calor gas rings (gas supplied), hot water for washing up & showers, storage heaters in all rooms.

DETAILS

- **Open** - All year. By arrangement.
- **Beds** - 12: 2x6 bunk rooms.
- **Price/night** - Sole use £140 per night.

CONTACT: Rachel Rhodes
Tel: 01629 812416 or 07960169777
mandalecampsite@yahoo.co.uk
www.mandalecampsite.co.uk
Mandale Farm, Haddon Grove, Bakewell, Derbyshire, DE45 1JF

THORNBRIDGE
OUTDOORS

73a

Thornbridge Outdoors offers excellent flexible group accommodation for groups from 6 to 136. With its superb location in the heart of the Peak District you have access to countryside, quaint villages, stately homes and the traffic free Monsal Trail, popular with walkers and cyclists.

DETAILS

■ **Open** - All year.
■ **Beds** - 136. Lodge 38: 4x5, 4x3, 1x6. Farm House 38: 2x8, 2x6, 1x5, 1x3, 1x2. Woodlands 10: 1x5, 1x4, 1x1. 9 Bell Tents sleeping 50. Plus camping.
■ **Price/night** - W/end: 2 nights from £1605.10 (Farm House), £2007.90 (Lodge), £641.70 (Woodlands), £1564 (Bell Tents & Basecamp). Ask for w/days, whole-site, longer stays, & activities.

CONTACT: Customer Services and Business Support Team
Tel: 01629 640491
thornbridgeoutdoors@sheffield.gov.uk
www.thornbridgeoutdoors.co.uk
Great Longstone, Bakewell, DE45 1NY

BRETTON
HOSTEL

73b

Bretton Hostel, in the heart of the Peak District near Eyam & Hathersage, feels remote on Bretton Edge. A peaceful space with far-reaching views across the Peak. Excellent walks & cycle rides from the door. Perfect to wind down, for outdoor activities & for gatherings. Fully equipped kitchen, living/dining room, WiFi, secure cycle store & eco-studio. Bottom sheet & pillow provided, but bring your own bedding. Local pubs nearby.

DETAILS

■ **Open** - Sole use March-New Year. Individual beds/rooms May-Sept (Sun-Thu only). Arrive from 4pm, dep by 11am.
■ **Beds** - 17: 1x8, 1x6, 1x3
■ **Price/night** - Sole use w/end from £378 (min 2 nts) more for large grps, less m/week. Beds £30, private rms from £65.

CONTACT: Clare Palmer
Tel: 07792 385134
bookings@brettonhostel.co.uk
brettonhostel.co.uk
Bretton, Eyam, Hope Valley, S32 5QD

NIGHTINGALE
CENTRE
74a

The Nightingale Centre, in the heart of the Peak District, is perfect for conferences, retreats, and group getaways. Surrounded by beautiful countryside, it offers easy access to walking, cycling, and outdoor activities. The charming Victorian building features 30 bedrooms and flexible meeting spaces. There is plenty of parking and fast Wifi. The Centre also provides affordable stays for schools, youth, and community groups.

DETAILS

- **Open** - All Year
- **Beds** - 77: 29 bedrooms and 1 dorm.
- **Price/night** - Packages from £116 per person. Exclusive-use bookings available for groups of 25+ poeple.

CONTACT: Kathryn Breen
Tel: 01298 871218
info@tngc.org.uk
www.thenightingalecentre.org.uk
The Nightingale Centre, Great Hucklow, Nr Buxton,Derbyshire, SK17 8RH

FOUNDRY
ADVENTURE CENTRE
74b

With all of the Peak District National Park within easy access, the centre is an ideal location for activities and tourism and it welcomes a wide range of groups. 31 or 52 bed configurations can be booked. The spacious centre includes; a large lounge with library, TV & wood burning stove, well equipped kitchens, dining areas & 9 bedrooms. There is parking for 20+ vehicles and grass areas for on site activities & camping. An extensive network of paths give access to the countryside.

DETAILS

- **Open** - All year. All day.
- **Beds** - 52 or 31 in 9 bedrooms
- **Price/night** - 31 beds from £880 per night, 52 beds from £1180 per night.

CONTACT: Tim Gould
Tel: 07786 332702
admin@foundrymountain.co.uk
foundryadventurecentre.co.uk
The Old Playhouse, Great Hucklow, Derbyshire, SK17 8RF

PINDALE
OUTDOOR CENTRE

75a

A mile from Castleton in the Peak District, Pindale Farm offers a range of accommodation: B&B in the farmhouse. Six self-catering/self-contained rooms sleeping 8 or 10 people in the Barn. A self-catering unit sleeping 8 people in The Engine House. Plus an AA 3 Pennant campsite. Perfect for D of E expeditions and many outdoor activities. Instruction is available.

DETAILS

■ **Open** - All year (camping March-October). 24 hours.
■ **Beds** - 64: Farmhouse: 4. Engine House: 8. Barn: 4x8, 2x10. + camping.
■ **Price/night** - Camping £11pp, hook up £7, gazebo £10. DofE camping £9.50pp. Barns £21pp + £1 electric tokens.

CONTACT: Alan Medhurst
Tel: 01433 620111 or 07812 638099
info@pindalefarm.co.uk
www.pindalefarm.co.uk
Pindale Road, Hope, Hope Valley, Derbyshire, S33 6RN

BRADWELL

75b

WAR MEMORIAL HALL

Bradwell War Memorial Hall is in the pretty village of Bradwell in the heart of the Peak District, close to the caverns of Castleton and Bakewell. This community run hall offers low cost self-catering accommodation to groups of 6-42. An ideal base for walkers, bikers, DofE, students or climbers who wish to explore this popular area. There are no beds so BYO sleeping mats and bedding. The rooms are centrally heated, there's a well equipped kitchen, hot showers, WiFi and a village full of amenities

DETAILS

■ **Open** - Weekends and school holidays.
■ **Beds** - 42: 1x30, 1x6, 1x4/6
■ **Price/night** - £220. There are no beds. BYO sleeping mat & bedding.

CONTACT: Vanessa Ball
bradwellwarmemorial@gmail.com
bradda.org/village_organisation/
bradwell-war-memorial-hall
Netherside, Bradwell, Hope Valley, Derbyshire S33 9HJ

ST MICHAELS
CENTRE

76a

St Michael's Centre, located in the village of Hathersage, provides high quality family friendly group accommodation, surrounded by the beautiful countryside of the Peak District National Park. There are comfortable dormitory style bunk beds and a lovely central hall which provides a communal kitchen, dining and lounge area for enjoyable shared living. Attached cottage also available separately or for larger groups.

DETAILS

- **Open** - All year. Office open Monday to Friday 8.30 am - 4pm
- **Beds** -   44: Centre 38: 2x2, 1x4, 2x6, 1x8, 1x10. Attached cottage 4/6.
- **Price/night** - From £550 for 20 people, plus £25 per additional person. Min stay 2 nights. Short notice discounts.

CONTACT: Centre Office
Tel: 01433 650309
stmichaels@nottscc.gov.uk
nottsoutdoors.nottinghamshire.gov.uk
Main Road, Hathersage, S32 1BB

BASE CAMP
76b ## HATHERSAGE (YHA PARTNER)

Recently reopened as an independent YHA Partner, the former YHA Hathersage provides a welcoming spot for Peak District adventures.

With excellent walking, cycling and climbing routes nearby, including the iconic Stanage Edge, it's made for outdoor enthusiasts.

In the heart of Hathersage village, cafés, pubs, shops and the outdoor pool offer plenty of ways to unwind.

DETAILS

- **Open** - Open Year Round
- **Beds** - 61: in 2 buildings
- **Price/night** - See website for prices for private bedrooms and whole hostel hire.

CONTACT:
hathersage@basecamphostels.com
basecamphostels.com
Castleton Road, Hathersage, Hope Valley, Derbyshire. S32 1EH

THORPE FARM
BUNKHOUSES

77a

Close to Hathersage and 2 miles west of Stanage Edge, the bunkhouses are on a family-run farm that produces ice cream. Popular areas for climbing and walking from meadows to moorland, with fantastic views & mountain biking. Each bunkhouse is heated and has a living room, kitchen, bathrooms with toilets, showers and washbasins. Sleep in dorms with bunks or The Hayloft with mattresses on the gallery floor. Secure bike storage and free parking.

DETAILS

■ **Open** - All year. No restrictions.
■ **Beds** - 78: Old Shippon 32: 2x12, 2x4. Old Stables 14: 1x8, 1x6. Pondside 14: 1x8, 1x6. Byre 14: 1x6, 1x4. Hayloft: 4
■ **Price/night** - See own website.

CONTACT: Jane Marsden
Tel: 01433 650659
jane@hope-valley.co.uk
www.thorpe-bunk.co.uk
Thorpe Farm, Hathersage, Peak District,
Via Sheffield, S32 1BQ

HOMESTEAD
AND CHEESEHOUSE

77b

In the heart of Bamford these two bunkhouses are on a small farm just 3 miles from the iconic Stanage Edge.

Perfectly located for visiting Castleton, Chatsworth House & Hathersage. Both bunkhouses are centrally heated with hot showers & well equipped kitchens. Sheets & pillows are provided.

BYO sleeping bags.

DETAILS

■ **Open** - All year. Check in after 4pm. Check out by 11am.
■ **Beds** - 26: Homestead 22: 1x10, 2x6. Cheesehouse 4: 1x4
■ **Price/night** - From £25pp. Sole use: Homestead £250, Cheesehouse £60. Min 2 nights for Homestead at weekends. Phone for a quote for single nights.

CONTACT: Helena Platts
Tel: 01433 651298
The Farm, Bamford,
Hope Valley, S33 0BL

CROOKSTONE
BARN
78a

EDALE BARN
COTEFIELD FARM
78b

Run by the Crookstone Adventure Trust, Crookstone Barn offers remote off-grid bunkhouse style accommodation on a Peak District hillside. Ideal for schools, youth groups, families & community projects, this well equipped barn is 3 miles from the nearest road in the village of Hope. It sleeps up to 23 in 5 rooms. Groups are met by the Trust's Land Rover on day of arrival and driven to the barn. With Kinder Scout on the doorstep, it's the perfect place for walking and exploring in this beautiful area.

Overlooking Mam Tor, at the start of the Pennine Way, Edale Barn is a traditional camping barn; a stone tent with a wooden sleeping platform. Close to Kinder Scout, Jacobs Ladder, Kinder Downfall & Hollins Cross. Adjoining the barn, but with external access, is a cooking area with mains water & a chemical toilet. No heating or electricity. BYO sleeping mats/bags, cooking equipment & torches. Pubs serving meals are an easy walk away. NO DOGS

DETAILS

- **Open** - 1 April - 31 October
- **Beds** - 23: in 5 rooms, mostly single beds, some bunkbeds
- **Price/night** - £200 for up to 15 people, plus £10pp. Youth groups £100.

CONTACT: Tim or John (second number)
Tel: 07742 551112 or 07412 020029
crookstonebarn@gmail.com
crookstoneadventuretrust.org.uk
Edale, Derbyshire. S33 7ZA

DETAILS

- **Open** - All year. Arrive after 4pm, depart before 10am.
- **Beds** - 8: 8 in Barn, + 6 camping
- **Price/night** - £80 sole use, min 2 nights in peak season.

CONTACT: Sally Gee
Tel: 01433 670273 or 07507 405161
sallygee52@hotmail.com
www.fb.com/cotefieldfarmcottages
Cotefield Farm, Olllerbrook, Edale, Hope Valley, Derbyshire. S33 7ZG

OLLERBROOK
FARM BUNKHOUSES
79a

JOHN HUNT
BASE
79b

Close to the start of the Pennine Way with easy access to Kinder Scout and the village of Edale via a network of footpaths from the doorstep. Castleton, Buxton, Bakewell and Chatsworth House are all within 40 minutes' drive. There are 2 bunkhouses each with a fully equipped kitchen and available for sole use by groups. Bring your own sleeping bags and personal towels.

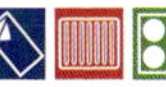

DETAILS

■ **Open** - All year. All day. Arrive after 4pm depart before 10.30am.
■ **Beds** - 32: Nab View 18: 3x6, Stables Bunkhouse 14: 3x4,1x2
■ **Price/night** - Nab View: £800 (2 nights) , £1020 (3 nights). Stables Bunkhouse: £500 (2 nights), £700 (3 nights)

CONTACT: Sheila
Tel: 01433 670235
ollerbrookfarm@gmail.com
www.ollerbrookfarm.co.uk
Ollerbrook Booth, Edale, Hope Valley, Derbyshire, S33 7ZG

The John Hunt Base is situated in the High Peak on the site of Hagg Farm (pg 80a). The base offers comfortable, family friendly accommodation for groups of up to 18. It is ideal for sightseeing, hill walking, trail running and biking as well as quieter pursuits. There is a picnic area, wildlife garden with fire pit and a playing field with climbing boulder. Activities can be arranged including climbing, stream scrambling, caving & on-site high ropes.

DETAILS

■ **Open** - All year. Office: Mon-Thur 8.30am-4.30pm, Fri 8.30-3.30pm
■ **Beds** - 18: 1x8, 1x6, 2x2.
■ **Price/night** - £335-£390 depending on season. 2 nights min stay.

CONTACT:
Tel: 01433 651594
haggfarm@nottscc.gov.uk
nottsoutdoors.nottinghamshire.gov.uk
Hagg Farm OEC, Snake Rd, Bamford, Hope Valley, S33 0BJ

HAGG FARM
OUTDOOR EDU CENTRE
80a

Situated in the Peak District's Woodlands Valley, Hagg Farm offers comfortable accommodation for up to 44 people with an additional 18 beds in the John Hunt Base next door (79b). Part of Nottinghamshire CC's Environmental & Outdoor Education Service, Hagg Farm is available for private hire by groups, families, clubs & charitable organisations. It can be booked on a self-catering or catered basis.

DETAILS

- **Open** - All year. Office: Mon-Thurs 8:30am-4.30pm, Fri 8:30am-3.30pm
- **Beds** - 44: 4x8, 2x4, 2x2
- **Price/night** - £26.50-£31.50pp (depending on season). Min charge for 25 people. Min 2 night stay.

CONTACT: Kirsty Weatherall
Tel: 01433 651594
haggfarm@nottscc.gov.uk
nottsoutdoors.nottinghamshire.gov.uk
Hagg Farm OEC, Snake Rd, Bamford, Hope Valley, S33 0BJ

LOCKERBROOK FARM
OUTDOOR CENTRE
80b

Lockerbrook Outdoor Centre, run by the Woodcraft Folk, is situated in glorious isolation high above Ladybower Reservoir with stunning views across the Upper Derwent Valley. This converted hill farm has two barns, which sleep 38 in 7 rooms, plus 3 extra twin rooms. Self-catering kitchen, dining room, large social space, log burner & drying room. Catering & activities can be booked.

DETAILS

- **Open** - All year.
- **Beds** - 44: Main barn 38 (36 bunks + 2 fold-out beds). 3 x twin rooms
- **Price/night** - Barn: £825-£1,050. Twin rooms: £63-£70. Extra charge PPPN over 30 guests. 2 nights min. Discounts for 5+ nights & for schools & youth groups.

CONTACT: Clare Thompson / Matt North
Tel: 01433 651412
lockerbrook@woodcraft.org.uk
lockerbrook.org.uk
Snake Pass, Bamford, Hope Valley, Derbyshire, S33 0BJ

BOARSHURST
CENTRE
81a

The Boarshurst Centre is situated on the north western edge of the Peak District with easy road and rail links to Manchester (12 miles away).

With 32 beds across 2 dorms and 2 leaders' rooms the centre provides well appointed self-catering accommodation for child, youth, adult and family/friend groups who seek to practice outdoor pursuits. BYO sleeping bags

DETAILS
- **Open** - All year. Check in from 12 noon or earlier by arrangement.
- **Beds** - 32: 2x12, 2x4
- **Price/night** - Sole Use. Adult Groups: £550. Family Groups £500. Child/Youth Groups £450.

CONTACT: Mark Jones
Tel: 07979 864472
theboarshurstcentre@gmail.com
www.boarshurstcentre.org
Boarshurst Lane, Greenfield, Oldham
OL3 7EA

EMBASSIE
LIVERPOOL BACKPACKERS
81b

The Embassie is a majestic terraced house in an unspoilt Georgian square. Until 1986 it was the Consulate of Venezuela! Only 15 minutes' walk from the centre of Liverpool, known for its nightlife, it's in the perfect position. Recently refurbished, there are new kitchen facilities, a brand new shower suite and an all new games room & relax area with Sky Sports and HD television. The hostel is clean, safe and staffed 24 hours. Bedding is provided (including sheets) and free coffee, tea, toast and jam are available 24 hours.

DETAILS
- **Open** - All year. All day.
- **Beds** - 50
- **Price/night** - £19 (Sunday to Thursday), £25 Friday, £32 Saturday

CONTACT: Kevin
Tel: 0151 707 1089
embassie@gmail.com
www.embassie.com
1 Falkner Square, Liverpool, L8 7NU

HEBDEN BRIDGE
HOSTEL
82a

IOU Hebden Bridge Vegetarian Hostel, run by national arts organisation IOU Creation Centre, offers contemporary, comfortable & affordable accommodation at the heart of this vibrant town.

Exclusive use, dorms and private rooms are available, all with en suite facilities. Perfect for solo travellers, families or groups. Everyone is welcome.

DETAILS

- **Open** - All year
- **Beds** - 45: 1x3 (dbl + sgl), 9x4 (all sgl), 1x6 (bunks)
- **Price/night** - Dorm beds from £30, Private rooms from £70. Exclusive use of the whole hostel & facilities from £1000 mid week, excluding Bank Holidays.

CONTACT: Jill
Tel: 01422 553578
info@hebdenbridgehostel.org
hebdenbridgehostel.org
The Birchcliffe Centre, Hebden Bridge, W Yorks, HX7 8DG

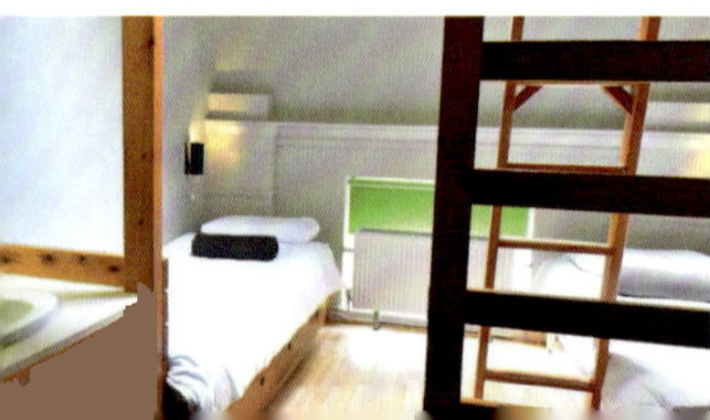

HEIGHT GATE
82b

Bunkhouse for groups, with 32 beds & camping. The 17th-century farmhouse is perfect for larger gatherings. On the Pennine Way with outdoor activities on the doorstep. There's a well-appointed kitchen, large lounge, accessible wet room & indoor barn for activities. Outside there's a fire pit, campfire area, field for games/camping & parking for 8 cars. BYO bedding & towels.

DETAILS

- **Open** - All year: Check in from 12 pm. Check out by 4pm
- **Beds** - 32: 1x2, 1x8, 1x10, 1x12 plus camping
- **Price/night** - Sole use from: £353 (Oct- April), £470 (May-Sept). Enquire for mid-week discounts.

CONTACT: Jack Sheen
Tel: 07481 155292
jack.sheen@woodcraft.org.uk
www.heightgate.org.uk
Stock Hey Lane, Todmorden, West Yorkshire. OL14 6EL

BLAKEDEAN
SCOUT HOSTEL
83a

Blakedean Scout Hostel is available for youth, church and family groups to enjoy. Sleeping groups of up to 24, the hostel provides centrally heated, no-frills, accommodation in the Pennine Hills on the Lancashire/Yorkshire border.

The Pennine Way passes close by, leading to some superb walking over the moors. The area is also great for mountain biking, geo-caching, river walks, bird watching and exploring the great outdoors.

DETAILS
- **Open** - All year
- **Beds** - 24: 2x10, 2x2
- **Price/night** - £160. (2 night min stay Fri & Sat).

CONTACT: Anya Sayer
Tel: 07848 285679
bookings@blakedean.org.uk
blakedean.org.uk
Widdop Road, Hebden Bridge, West Yorkshire. HX7 7AT

HAWORTH YOUTH
83b
HOSTEL (YHA PARTNER)

YHA Haworth is a Victorian Gothic mansion located in the village that was home to the Brontë sisters. It features a sweeping staircase, café, self-catering kitchen, lounge, and private bedrooms. The surrounding moors—which inspired Emily Brontë's Wuthering Heights—offer rugged beauty and stunning views. The hostel is popular with walkers, cyclists, families, and overseas tourists. Available for sole hire by groups of up to 85 people. Catering packages available.

DETAILS
- **Open** - All year
- **Beds** - 85 : 2x1, 2x2, 4x4, 6x6, 4x8
- **Price/night** -   From £35 per person in private rooms. Exclusive hire £1300 midweek, £1500 weekends..

CONTACT: Reception
Tel: 07479 948560 or 07904 058547
yhahaworth@gmail.com
www.thehaworthhostel.com
Longlands Hall, Lees Lane, Haworth, BD22 8RT

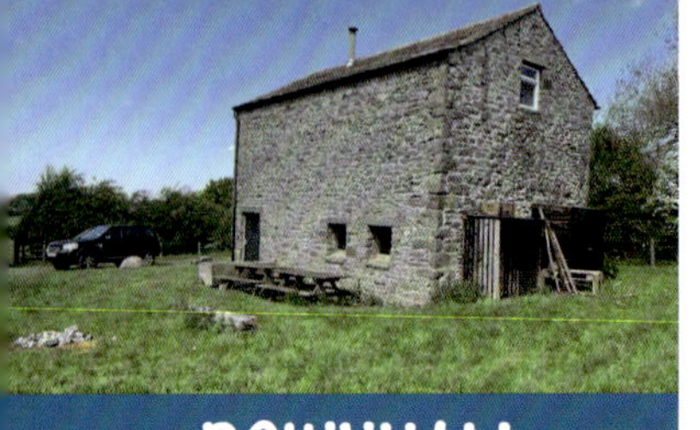

DOWNHAM
CAMPING BARN
84a

Located in the Forest of Bowland Natural Landscape, Downham hugs the skirt of Pendle, an area renowned for Quakers, radicals and witches. This off-grid, simple barn sleeps 12 (BYO camp beds or roll mats). There is a table with benches, WC with basin (cold water), and upstairs sleeping area. Photovoltaic cells provide power for limited LED lighting and there is a wood-burning stove (purchase fuel when booking). Outside there is a portable BBQ, fire pit and camping.

DETAILS

- **Open** - All year. Check out by 11am unless previously agreed.
- **Beds** - 12: 1x12 + camping
- **Price/night** - Barn: £100 per night (min 2 nights). Tents: £10 per unit.

CONTACT: Bookings Secretary
Tel: 07817 725976
mail@cositowneley.co.uk
www.downhamvillage.org.uk
Twiston Lane, Downham, Clitheroe, Lancs. BB7 4DF

EARBY
HOSTEL
84b

Cosy, historic hostel with large kitchen & dining room which can seat all 21 people in one room. Lounge with log burner.

Secure cycle storage for 20 bikes. Large wildlife garden with BBQ. Private parking for 6 cars. Great local pub. Medium sized Co-op supermarket open 7 days 6am to 10pm. Food available with prior request. Good public transport links.

       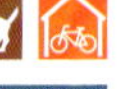

DETAILS

- **Open** - All year.
- **Beds** - 26: Hostel 21: 1x2, 2x6, 1x7. Cottage 5: 1xdbl, 1x3
- **Price/night** - £25pp, or £450 for exclusive use of the whole hostel. Adjoining family cottage (sleeps 5), £75 midweek/£80 weekend.

CONTACT: Matt
Tel: 01282 842349 or 07791 903454
matt@earbyhostel.co.uk
earbyhostel.co.uk
9-11 Birch Hall Lane, Earby, Lancashire, BB18 6JX

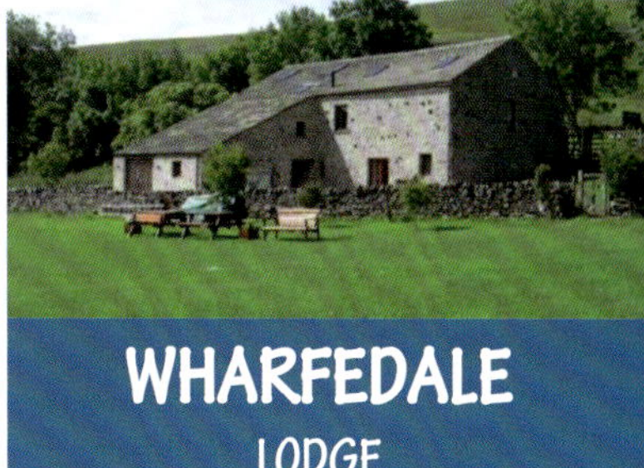

WEST END
OUTDOOR CENTRE

85a

Amidst stunning landscape overlooking Thruscross Reservoir on the edge of the Yorkshire Dales National Park, this self-catering centre offers excellent facilities in bunkrooms plus an en suite leaders' room. Well equipped kitchen, dining, lounge & shower/toilet areas.

Ideal for team building, youth groups & family parties. 12 miles from Harrogate & Skipton. No stag or hen groups.

DETAILS

- **Open** - All year. Flexible.
- **Beds** - 30: 4x2, 3x4, 1x6, 1x4 en suite
- **Price/night** - Fri-Sat £875, Midweek £325 (min 2 nights). 1 night midweek £450. 4 nights midweek: £1100, 7 nights £1600. Fri+Sat+BH £1300. £5 per dog.

CONTACT: Hedley or Jill Verity
Tel: 07811 456430 or 07810 876626
info@westendoutdoorcentre.co.uk
www.westendoutdoorcentre.co.uk
West End, Summerbridge, Harrogate,
HG3 4BA

WHARFEDALE
LODGE

85b

Nestling in the Yorkshire Dales, Wharfedale Lodge offers luxury, hotel quality, accommodation to groups of 6-20 in 8 comfortable twin rooms and a further 4 bed family room (2 x bunks). Groups of friends, families and corporates will enjoy the stunning location and the top quality facilities. With the famous Kilnsey Crag close by, the beautiful market town of Skipton a short drive away, the Dales Way on the doorstep and fishing, golf and pony trekking nearby there will be plenty to keep everyone happy.

DETAILS

- **Open** - All year.
- **Beds** - 20: 8 x twin, 1x4
- **Price/night** - Weekends (Fri/Sat) £1450. Midweek from £350 per night.

CONTACT: Matthew Ramsden
Tel: 07719 200933
contact@wharfedalelodge.com
www.wharfedalelodge.com
Kilnsey, North Yorkshire. BD23 5PT

SKIRFARE
BARN

86a

Skirfare Barn, with its stunning backdrop of Upper Wharfedale & Littondale, nestles in the Yorkshire Dales with the climbers' challenge, Kilnsey Crag, on the doorstep. The area is famous for walking & cycling with many footpaths, including the Dales Way, close by. At nearby Kilnsey you can book day fishing & food at The Kilnsey Park, or bar snacks at The Tennant Arms Hotel. Pony & Llama trekking & many other activities are also nearby. The barn provides warm, comfortable accommodation for walking, cycling, friends or family groups.

DETAILS

- **Open** - All year.
- **Beds** - 20: 2x2 (twin), 2x4, 1x8.
- **Price/night** - From £17.50 per person.

CONTACT:
Tel: 01756 636350
info@skirfarebarn.com
www.skirfarebarn.com
Kettlewell Road, Kilnsey, North Yorkshire, BD23 5PT

KETTLEWELL
HOSTEL

86b

Kettlewell Hostel is a multi award winning stylish Independent Youth Hostel in the the Yorkshire Dales. Serving great value home-made meals & local beer in the large dining room. There's a cosy lounge with woodburner (logs provided), a lovely garden, self-catering kitchen & a secure bike shed. Sleeps 42 in 11 bedrooms. Great walking/cycling from the doorstep.

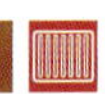

DETAILS

- **Open** - All year. Reception 8-10am, 4-9pm.
- **Beds** - 42: 1 x twin, 1 x double, 4x3, 2x4, 2x6, 1x5/6
- **Price/night** - Beds from £25, private rooms for 2 from £59. Sole use from £560. YHA membership discount on the website.

CONTACT: Saul & Floss Ward
Tel: 01756 760232
hello@thekettlewellhostel.co.uk
www.thekettlewellhostel.co.uk
Whernside House, Kettlewell, Skipton, North Yorkshire, BD23 5QU

WHARFESIDE
HOUSE
87a

In the village of Kettlewell in the Yorkshire Dales National Park, Wharfeside house provides self-catering accommodation for groups. It has a well equipped kitchen with Aga and fridge freezer, showers with male and female toilets, a large communal space, drying area and large indoor bike/equipment store. Onsite parking for 4 vehicles.

DETAILS

■ **Open** - All year round including Christmas and New Year, 24 hours.
■ **Beds** - 32: 2x8, 1x6, 1x4, 3x2
■ **Price/night** - Sole use from £240 depending on group size (25% reduction for midweek - excluding Bank Holidays). Small group/youth group rates available - more details on online booking.

CONTACT: John Yorke
Tel: 07906 871801 or 01484 318328
bookings@wharfeside.org
wharfeside.org
Middle Lane, Kettlewell, Skipton, BD23 5QX

INGLETON
GRETA TOWER
87b

On the edge of the Yorkshire Dales, surrounded by magnificent countryside with caves, waterfalls and mountains, Ingleton is dominated by Ingleborough, the best known of Yorkshire's Three Peaks (this is a great base for The Challenge). Known for its walking routes and waterfall trail, the area has plenty for walkers, climbers, mountain bikers and cavers. Licensed and serving tasty meals there is also a self-catering kitchen. Perfect for families and school trips.

DETAILS

■ **Open** - All year (Nov-Mar exclusive hire only). Reception 8am-10am & 5-10pm.
■ **Beds** - 64: 4x6, 2x5, 7x4, 1x2,
■ **Price/night** - Beds from £30, rooms from £60. Sole use bookings welcome.

CONTACT: Manager
Tel: 015242 41444
info@ingletonhostel.co.uk
www.ingletonhostel.co.uk
Greta Tower, Sammy Lane, Ingleton, North Yorkshire, LA6 3EG

THE OLD SCHOOL
BUNKHOUSE
88a

Situated near Ingleton in the Yorkshire Dales, on the Yorkshire Three Peaks route, The Old School Bunkhouse sleeps up to 26. It has a comfortable lounge, with TV, DVD & WiFi, a large kitchen diner, 4 bathrooms & a drying room with washing machine.

Outside is parking for 12 cars and great views of Ingleborough and Whernside. The pub over the road is ideal for that celebratory drink.

DETAILS
- **Open** - All year.
- **Beds** - Sleeps 26: 2x6, 2x5, 2x2
- **Price/night** - Seasonal pricing available to view on website. Duvet hire £7.50 pp per stay. £10 per dog.

CONTACT: Debbie Bryant
Tel: 07909 223819
oldschoolbunkhouse@gmail.com
www.oldschoolbunkhouse.co.uk
Hawes Road, Chapel le Dale, Ingleton, LA6 3AR

BROADRAKE
BUNKBARN
88b

Broadrake Bunkbarn offers direct access to the Three Peaks Challenge Walk which can be started from the door. It is an ideal stopover on the Pennine Journey or Dales High Way.

This popular accommodation for 20 has an upstairs open-plan living space with excellent self-catering & communal facilities. Perfect for extended family reunions, cyclists, cavers and dark sky enthusiasts. Individuals, couples and small groups welcome mid-week.

DETAILS
- **Open** - All year. All day.
- **Beds** - 20: 1x8, 2x4, 2x twin.
- **Price/night** - Weekends: £1,200 for 2 nights sole use. Mid Week from £30pp.

CONTACT: Mike & Rachel Benson
Tel: 01524 241357 or 07740 434207
info@broadrake.co.uk
www.broadrake.co.uk
Broadrake, Chapel-le-Dale, Ingleton, LA6 3AX

3 PEAKS
BUNKBARN

89a

Situated in Horton in Ribblesdale, the 3 Peaks Bunkbarns are perfect for walking on the Pennine Way and the 3 Peaks. The main barn has 4 rooms each sleeping up to 8. The second barn has 4 rooms each sleeping up to 6, with en suite shower rooms. Both have a kitchen/dining room.

DETAILS

- **Open** - All year. Please try & arrive before 10pm, Check out by 10am.
- **Beds** - 56: Main Bunkhouse 32 : 4x8. New Bunkhouse 24: 4x6.
- **Price/night** - £130 (room of 6). £160 (room of 8). Discounts for: NHS, Military, Schools & Unis. mid-week (even in school holidays) & all bookings Nov-Feb. Bedding/towel hire £15 - book in advance.

CONTACT: Carl & Susan Johnson
Tel: 07870 849419 or 01729 860380
hello@3peaksbunkroom.co.uk
www.3peaksbunkroom.co.uk
Horton in Ribblesdale, Settle, North Yorkshire, BD24 0HB

AYSGILL
CAMPING BARN

89b

A charmingly converted barn for up to 4 guests, with cosy furnishings, a well-equipped kitchen, a log burner, and fully made-up beds.

Set in open grazing land with panoramic views, it's just a short walk from Aysgill Falls and only a mile from the characterful market town of Hawes.

Perfect for walkers, cyclists, or anyone simply looking to unwind and take a break in peaceful countryside.

DETAILS

- **Open** - All year
- **Beds** - 4: 1x4
- **Price/night** - From £140 per night – no minimum stay required.

CONTACT: Amy Allen
Tel: 01969 667477 or 07902 176538
aysgillcampingbarn@gmail.com
www.aysgillcampingbarn.co.uk
Scaurhead Farm, Beggarmans Rd, Gayle, Hawes, Yorkshire Dales, DL8 3SF

CHAPEL GALLERY
BUNKHOUSE
90a

Situated in the market town of Hawes in Wensleydale, Chapel Gallery Bunkhouse offers comfortable accommodation for up to 10 guests.

Book a bed in a dorm, a private room (sleeps 5) or the whole bunkhouse.

With The Pennine Way on the doorstep, and easy access to footpaths and bridleways as well as the famous Yorkshire 3 Peaks, the bunkhouse is perfect for walkers, cyclists and runners.

DETAILS

- **Open** - All year.
- **Beds** - 10: 2x5 (bunks + 1 single bed)
- **Price/night** - Bed £30. Room (sleeps 5) £150. Whole Bunkhouse £300.

CONTACT: Ellie & John
Tel: 07474 138536 or 01969 667584
info@chapelgalleryhawes.com
chapelgalleryhawes.com
Burtersett Road, Hawes, North Yorks, DL8 3NP

HOSTEL AT HAWES
90b

The Hostel at Hawes is your perfect base for enjoying the delights of the Yorkshire Dales. Surrounded by great walking & cycling, with the option of booking outdoor activities. It is popular with schools, clubs, families, couples and groups of friends. Sleeping 58 across 16 rooms, choose from doubles, family rooms & larger rooms for groups Book a room or book the whole hostel. Friendly lounge with bar and big drying room.

DETAILS

- **Open** - All year.
- **Beds** -   56: 1x8, 1x7, 2x6, 1x5, 1x4, 2x3, 5x2, 2xdbl 1 x dbl en suite +camping
- **Price/night** -   £35-£40pp (approx). Larger groups £30pp. Exclusive hire from £950 to £1300 depending on season.

CONTACT: Steve Bussey
Tel: 01969 667368 or 07960 068415
haweshostelmanager@gmail.com
hostelathawes.com
Lancaster Terrace, Turfy Hill, Hawes, Yorkshire. DL8 3LQ

LOW MILL
OUTDOOR CENTRE

91a

Low Mill Outdoor Centre, a not-for-profit charity, lies on the edge of the pretty village of Askrigg in Wensleydale in the Yorkshire Dales.

With good access to many walks, cycle routes, rivers, climbs and caves it is the perfect base for all types of groups; schools, clubs and friend & family get-togethers.

DETAILS

- **Open** - All year
- **Beds** - 42: Main Building: 26: 1x14, 1x6, 1x4, 2x2. The Wing: 14: 1x8, 1x4, 1x2
- **Price/night** - Whole Centre bookings only: W/E: 2 nights £2,500. Mid wk: 3 nights £3,000, 4 nights £3,500

CONTACT: Low Mill
Tel: 01969 650432
info@lowmill.com
www.lowmill.com
Station Road, Askrigg, Leyburn, North Yorkshire DL8 3HZ

CROW TREES
BUNKBARN

91b

Crow Trees Bunkbarn is a beautiful conversion of a stone barn on a working hill farm in Swaledale in the Yorkshire Dales National Park. This luxury bunkbarn sleeps up to 27 people across 4 bedrooms, 3 of which are en suite. Primarily offered to groups on a sole use basis, you can also book by the bed or the room. It's the perfect place for walkers, cyclists and groups to explore the Dales and an Ideal party location.

 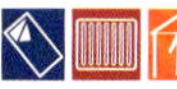    

DETAILS

- **Open** - All year
- **Beds** - 27: 1x2 (dbl/twin), 1x4 (dbl/bunks), 1x5 (dbl/bunks), 1x14 + 2 mattresses.
- **Price/night** - £30pp. Sole use: from £450. Less for 7+ nights.

CONTACT: Leanne or Adam
Tel: 01748 886332
mail@crowtreesbunkbarn.co.uk
crowtreesbunkbarn.co.uk
Gunnerside, Richmond, North Yorkshire. DL11 6JL

KIRKBY STEPHEN
HOSTEL

92a

Former Methodist Church with a great welcome and a range of accommodation for individuals, families and groups. Set amongst beautiful authentic features; stained glass, arches and panels. There's a large dining room & kitchen and a quiet lounge in the gallery.

Kirkby Stephen is a market town in the upper Eden Valley. On Wainwright's Coast to Coast path with easy access to the Pennine Journey, the W2W cycle route, the Howgill Hills, the Yorkshire Dales and the Lake District.

DETAILS

- **Open** - All year.
- **Beds** - 38: 1x8, 3x6, 2x4, 1x2, 1x3.
- **Price/night** - £32 per person

CONTACT: Denise
Tel: 07812 558525
info@kirkbystephenhostel.co.uk
www.kirkbystephenhostel.co.uk
Market Street, Kirkby Stephen, Cumbria, CA17 4QQ

STAY HOWGILLS
BARN

92b

Stay Howgills, a converted stone barn in Ravenstonedale in the rugged Cumbrian Hills. The Barn sleeps 14 in 4 rooms, and the Bothy sleeps 2. Superbly equipped and well heated, guests are sure of a cosy, comfortable stay. Situated down a farm track with stunning views, perfect for walkers and cyclists. Wainwright's Pennine Journey passes by and the Pennine Bridleway is close.

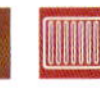

DETAILS

- **Open** - All year
- **Beds** - 16: Barn: 2x2 (dbls), 1x4 (bunks), 1x6 (2 sgls + bunks). Bothy; 1xdbl. Plus camping
- **Price/night** - Barn from £390. Barn & Bothy from £440 (min 2 nights). Enquire for bargain mid week rooms & beds.

CONTACT: Lynda Livesey
Tel: 07767 731387
stayhowgills@gmail.com
www.stayhowgills.co.uk
Murthwaite, Ravenstonedale, Kirkby Stephen, CA17 4LP

REDMIRE
STATION HOUSE
93a

Owned by the Scouts, this former station masters house sits on the Wensleydale heritage railway line near to Leyburn in the beautiful Yorkshire Dales.

The hostel offers sole use accommodation to youth organisations, clubs and groups of friends & families. Sleeping up to 20 in bunks and space for more to camp, Station House is the perfect wallet-friendly base for exploring.

DETAILS

- **Open** - All year. Check in after 4pm, check out by 10am
- **Beds** - 20: 1x2, 1x4, 2x7
- **Price/night** - Sole use. Youth groups: 4 nights (Mon-Fri) £320. 3 nights w/end (Fri-Mon) £330. Other groups: (Mon-Fri) £480. W/end £480. Whole week £700.

CONTACT: Sarah Brogan
bookings@redmirestationhouse.co.uk
redmirestation.house
Hargill Lane, Redmire, Leyburn,
Yorkshire DL8 4ES

ST MICHAELS
LODGE
93b

St Michael's Lodge was the former Church of Hudswell.

Keeping many original features the Church has been transformed into a 16 bed lodge catering for walkers and cyclists,with 6 en suite private bedrooms, a cozy communal area, drying room & kitchen.

Outside, there is a seating area & secure bike store.

DETAILS

- **Open** - All year
- **Beds** - 17: 3x2, 1x3, 2x4
- **Price/night** - From £79 for a private room for 2 people. From £159 for a private room for 4 people.

CONTACT: Melanie
Tel: 01748 343022
melanie.sadler@stmichaelslodge.com
stmichaelslodge.com
St Michael's Lodge, Hudswell,
Richmond, DL11 6BW

BROMPTON ON SWALE
BUNKBARN

94a

Located on a small working farm, just 3 miles east of Richmond. The VisitEngland accredited Brompton on Swale Bunkbarn offers a welcome break from walking or cycling the Coast to Coast. Book a bunk or a private room. It is also available for sole use to outdoor active groups. A pot of tea for weary walkers upon arrival and safe storage for bikes makes this bunkhouse especially welcoming. Close to the Yorkshire Dales, Swaledale, Wensleydale, Easby Abbey, Richmond Castle & Ellerton Lakes. Dogs welcome (on a lead).

DETAILS

- **Open** - February-November
- **Beds** - 12: 3x4
- **Price/night** - £15pp. sleeping bag £2, towel £1. £1 electric meter. Sole use £180

CONTACT: Chris Wilkin
Tel: 01748 818326
chris01748@gmail.com
24 Richmond Road, Richmond, North Yorkshire, DL10 7HE

COTE GHYLL
MILL

94b

With scenic trails right from the doorstep, and the charming village of Osmotherley just a short stroll away, you'll find endless opportunities to explore the great outdoors from Cote Ghyll Mill. It offers top-quality B&B in the summer and exclusive group hire in the winter. Whether it's conquering a section of the Coast to Coast, cycling through rolling countryside, or enjoying a family picnic by the beck, Cote Ghyll Mill provides comfort, convenience, and a warm welcome at the heart of nature.

DETAILS

- **Open** - Rooms Mar-Oct,Groups all year
- **Beds** - 30 : 4x Single, 6 xTwin, 2 x 3, 2 x 4 (Family)
- **Price/night** - Single £95, Twin £125, Triple £160, Family £195

CONTACT: Reception
Tel: 01609 883425
mill@coteghyll.com
www.coteghyll.com
Osmotherley, Northallerton, DL6 3AH

BANK HOUSE
FARM HOSTEL
95a

Luxury bunkbarn and camping loft on an organic farm in beautiful dale of Glaisdale. Stunning views of the North York Moors and just 1 mile from the Coast to Coast route. The bunkbarn (Dorm Cottage) is a modern barn conversion ideal for groups and families enjoying longer stays. The camping loft provides simple, unheated, single-night shelter for walkers and cyclists.

DETAILS

- **Open** - All year. Phone calls 9am-8pm
- **Beds** - Bunkbarn 10: 1x10. Camping Loft 6: 1x6.
- **Price/night** - Bunkbarn: Midweek: £60 (2 people) to £220 (10 people). Weekend nights: £150 (2 people) to £310 (10 people). Camping Loft: £20pp

CONTACT: Chris or Emma Padmore
Tel: 01947 897297
info@bankhousefarmhostel.co.uk
www.bankhousefarmhostel.co.uk
Bank House Farm, Glaisdale, Whitby, North Yorkshire, YO21 2QA

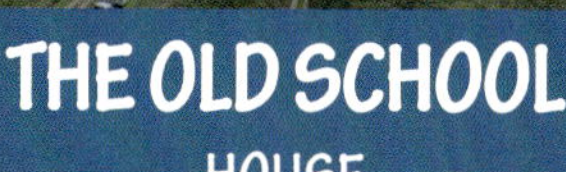

THE OLD SCHOOL
HOUSE
95b

The Old School House welcomes schools, groups, walkers & families to Robins Hood's Bay, home to one of the most unique beaches on Yorkshire's east coast. At the end of the Coast to Coast walk, on The Cleveland Way and just 1 mile from NCN1, Robin Hood's Bay is an historic fishing village with cobbled streets, rockpools, pubs & cafes. The perfect place to explore & unwind.

DETAILS

- **Open** - All year
- **Beds** - 41: 6x4, 1x5, 2x6
- **Price/night** - Sole use: £1300 inc. VAT for 2 nights, extra nights discounted. Self-catering private 6-bed rooms £20pppn (min £40). Schools from £40pppn (plus activities, usually £5pp per activity.)

CONTACT: Helen & Dave
Tel: 07754 168178
dave@oldschoolhouserhb.co.uk
www.oldschoolhouserhb.co.uk
Fisherhead, Robin Hoods Bay, Whitby, Yorkshire YO22 4ST

DALBY FOREST
HOSTEL
96a

Dalby Forest Hostel, is now owned and run independently as a YHA Partner Hostel. Sleeping 21 across 4 rooms, the hostel is available for sole use bookings.

Situated in the south/east of the North Yorks National Park in the sleepy village of Lockton, the hostel is perfect for groups of friends and families and groups of walkers & cyclists.

DETAILS

- **Open** - All year
- **Beds** -   21: 1x3 (accessible), 1x4,1x6,1x8
- **Price/night** - £765 w/ends & school holidays, £595 w/days including Sun. Min 2 nights. One night stays considered but price is higher.

CONTACT: Manager
Tel: 07725 426450 or 01244 255440
colintrigg1@hotmail.co.uk
yha.org.uk/hostel/yha-dalby-forest
Old School, Lockton, Pickering, North Yorkshire. YO18 7PY

YEALAND
OLD SCHOOL
96b

Yealand Old School provides newly refurbished, self-catering accommodation with en suite bedrooms and group dorms. Relax in the grounds of the Quaker Meeting House. A short stroll from Summerhouse Hill and Warton Crag amidst spectacular limestone scenery and nature reserves. LEJOG passes the front door on Route 6. Quiet village location, Local pub open for food on some days.

DETAILS

- **Open** - All year. Check in between 5-8pm or by arrangement.Depart by 11am
- **Beds** - 24: 1x2, 2x4, 10 x stacking beds, plus mats, plus camping
- **Price/night** - Sole use from £310 for 10 people, Over 10 £16 per person.

CONTACT: Warden
Tel: 07783 559484
yealandwarden@yealandoldschool.co.uk
www.yealandoldschool.co.uk
18 Yealand Rd, Yealand Conyers, Carnforth, Lancashire LA5 9SH

WITHERSLACK
CYCLE BARN
97a

HUMPHREY HEAD
GROUP HOSTEL
97b

Between Grange Over Sands and Kendal on the northern shore of Morecambe Bay, within the beautiful Whitbarrow Nature Reserve in the southern Lake District. Built for cyclists and walkers with drying room, laundry, kitchen, diner, lounges, cycle storage, workshop and bike wash. Perfect for groups, families and individuals. Just 500m from the Morecambe Bay Cycle Way, the Lakes & Dales Loop and NCN 700 & 70.

Perched on an outcrop overlooking Morecambe Bay on the edge of the Lake District, Humphrey Head Group Hostel & Outdoor Centre provides accommodation for groups of 20–66.

It's perfect for educational visits, schools, clubs, and privately run groups. Remote and private, surrounded by stunning scenery and wildlife, with on-site outdoor activities, there's something for everyone. Catering & camping available.

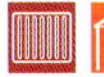

DETAILS

- **Open** - All year
- **Beds** - 14: 2x2 (twin), 1x4 (family),1x6.
- **Price/night** - From £31 including bedding and towel. Please call for exclusive use deals.

CONTACT: Karen Unsworth
Tel: 01539 552223
info@witherslackcyclebarn.co.uk
www.witherslackcyclebarn.co.uk
Beck Head Farm, Witherslack, Grange Over Sands. Cumbria, LA11 6SH

DETAILS

- **Open** - Open all year, all day.
- **Beds** - 66: 3x8,3x6,5x4,1x2,1x2 sgles
- **Price/night** - Sole use: Groups up to 20: Mon-Fri £1860, Fri-Sat £1260. 1 night £900. Please enquire for larger groups.

CONTACT: Elspeth or Kirsty
Tel: 015395 35030
info@meremountains.co.uk
humphreyhead.education
Humphrey Head O.C, Holy Well Lane, Flookburgh, Cumbria LA11 7LY

ROOKHOW

98a

Escape to the heart of the Lake District, leaving the crowds behind. Rookhow is a secluded haven within 12 acres of ancient woodland nestled between Coniston and Lake Windermere. The newly renovated self-catering barn has underfloor heating, log fires and a snug sitting room. Enjoy the campfire, outdoor seating area and yurt in the woods. Hire the Meeting House for extra space.

DETAILS

- **Open** - All year.
- **Beds** - 30: Barn 16: 1x2, 1x6, 1x8. Meeting House 10: on floor (bring mats). Yurt:4. Camping. Maximum of 30 on site.
- **Price/night** - Bunkbarn £410 (min 2 nights). Yurt £50, Meeting House £70. Sole use of whole site £530.

CONTACT: Sue Nicholls
Tel: 07377 971783
contactrookhow@gmail.com
rookhow.org.uk
Rookhow, Rusland, nr Grizedale,
Ulverston, South Lakeland, LA12 8LA

KEPPLEWRAY
CENTRE

98b

A large outdoor centre near Coniston in the unspoilt and remote Duddon Valley on the edge of the southern Lake District World Heritage Site.

The Kepplewray Centre sleeps groups of 12-60. Ideally suited for schools, sports teams, faith groups, friends & family get-togethers and corporate team building, a whole range of outdoor activities can be provided if required.

DETAILS

- **Open** - All year
- **Beds** - 60
- **Price/night** - Self Catering £35 per person with a minimum booking of 12 people. Please enquire for catered options.

CONTACT: The Team
Tel: 01229 716936
stay@kepplewray.org.uk
www.kepplewray.org.uk
Broughton-in-Furness, Cumbria,
LA20 6HE

HIGH WALLABARROW
CAMPING BARN
99a

High Wallabarrow is a traditional hill farm in the Duddon Valley, the Lake District's quiet corner.

The well equipped camping barn sleeps 10+ upstairs. Downstairs is a large living area, wood burner & fully equipped kitchen. Mattresses provided. BYO bedding. WC just outside & shower nearby. Pub 15 mins' walk. Climbing crag 10 mins' walk. No very rowdy groups.

DETAILS

- **Open** - All year. Arrive after 4pm, (possibly earlier by arrangement) vacate by 11am.
- **Beds** - 10: 1x10 with extra possible.
- **Price/night** - £15pp m/week term time. W/ends & school hols sole use: £150 (min 2 nights). £1.50 per dog per night.

CONTACT: Chris Chinn (8am to 10pm)
Tel: 01229 715011 or 07974 822020
camden.chinn@gmail.com
www.wallabarrow.co.uk
High Wallabarrow, Ulpha, Broughton-in-Furness, Cumbria, LA20 6EA

DACRES STABLE
CAMPING BARN
99b

A short drive from Kendal, Dacres Stable Camping Barn is on the eastern edge of the Lake District National Park. On a gated road away from the main A6 it is a perfect base for exploring the Yorkshire Dales, the Lake District and the Eden Valley. Great too for mountain biking, walking, & cycling on quiet tracks and lanes.

The camping barn sleeps up to 8 on a sole use, self-catering basis.

DETAILS

- **Open** - Easter to November inclusive.
- **Beds** - 8
- **Price/night** - Ground floor only (sleeps 2+) £55. Ground floor plus upper bunk room £95. Min 2 nights stay. Reductions for longer stays & mid-week.

CONTACT: Hilary Fell
Tel: 01539 823208 or 07788 633936
dacresstablecampingbarn.blogspot.com
Grisedale Farm, Whinfell, Kendal, Cumbria, LA8 9EN

ELTERWATER
HOSTEL
100a

GREAT LANGDALE
BUNKHOUSE
100b

With direct access to the fells right from the front door and warm, homely accommodation at a great price, Elterwater Hostel is the perfect base for cycling, walking, climbing — or simply enjoying a quiet break, whether on your own or with family and friends. The hostel has been welcoming guests since 1939 and can accommodate up to 38 people in private or shared rooms. Home-cooked meals are also available.

Great Langdale Bunkhouse is situated at the foot of the Langdale fells, amidst some of the finest mountain scenery in England. There's direct access to mountain biking, road cycling, walking, fell running, wild swimming & climbing.

The bunkhouse sleeps 18 across 5 rooms, each with a kettle & free WiFi. There's biomass central heating throughout so it's toasty warm with an endless supply of hot water & powerful showers. Secure bike storage on request. Next to two good pubs. Please note, there is no kitchen.

DETAILS
- **Open** - All year (Nov-Feb groups only). Access 7.30am-11.30pm. Reception 7.30-10am & 5-10pm.
- **Beds** - 38 : 6x2, 1x4, 1x4 ensuite, 3x6
- **Price/night** - From £25pp. Check website for special offers. Call for sole use.

CONTACT: Reception
Tel: 01539 437245
bookings@elterwaterhostel.co.uk
www.elterwaterhostel.co.uk
Elterwater, Ambleside, Cumbria, The Lake District, LA22 9HX

DETAILS
- **Open** - All year. All day.
- **Beds** - 18: 2x6, 3x2
- **Price/night** - From £21.50 per person.

CONTACT: Vicky
greatlangdalebunkhouse@gmail.com
www.greatlangdalebunkhouse.co.uk
Great Langdale Bunkhouse, Great Langdale, Ambleside, LA22 9JU

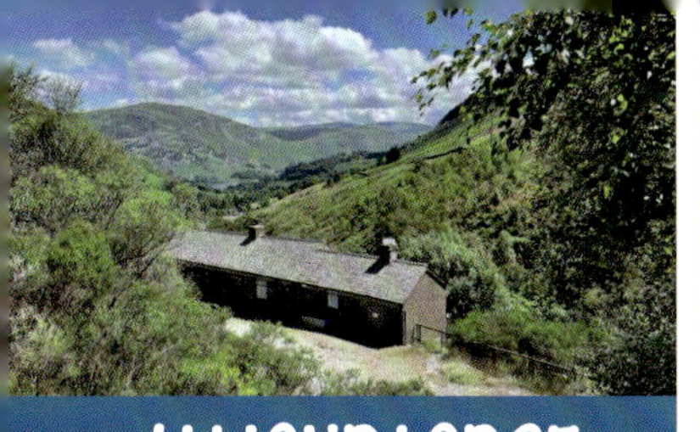

ALMOND LODGE
HELVELLYN
101a

Almond Lodge is a newly refurbished luxury group hostel perched 1/3 of the way up Helvellyn in the Lake District. Sleeping up to 28 across 4 rooms with breathtaking views from every window, the Lodge is perfect for groups of walkers, climbers, cyclists, runners, swimmers or friends and families in need of some mountain therapy. The village of Glenridding with local shops, nice pubs and restaurants and the southern end of Ullswater is just over 1 mile away.

GROUPS ONLY

DETAILS
- **Open** - All year
- **Beds** - 28: 3x8, 1x4
- **Price/night** - Sole use only: £475 weekdays. £650 w/e & bank hols. Plus £60 per stay service charge.

CONTACT: Jon
Tel: 07799 440557
jon@almondlodgehelvellyn.com
almondlodgehelvellyn.com
Almond Lodge Helvellyn, Greenside Road, Glenridding. CA11 0QR

SHEPHERDS
CROOK
101b

Noran Bank Farm lies in Patterdale near Ullswater. The most beautiful of the lakes, it has steamer cruises, private boat hire, paddle boarding & wild swimming.

Shepherd's Crook Bunkhouse is a quality barn conversion on a working hill farm with Herdwick sheep and Galloway & Blue Grey cattle. It sleeps 8 and nestles under Arnison crag. Wainwright loved the area, the Coast to Coast walk & many of his other routes go right past the door.

DETAILS
- **Open** - All year.
- **Beds** - 8: 1x6, 1x2 + B&B.
- **Price/night** - £28pp. Sole use £170. Farmhouse B&B £45pp.

CONTACT: Mrs Heather Jackson
Tel: 01768 482327 or 07833 981504
heathernoranbank@gmail.com
noranbankpatterdale.co.uk
Noran Bank Farm, Patterdale, Penrith, Cumbria, CA11 0NR

STYBECK FARM
FISHER GILL CAMPING BARN
102a

ST JOHNS IN THE VALE
102b
CAMPING BARN

Situated in Thirlmere at the foot of the Helvellyn mountains, close to Sticks Pass & the spectacular Fisher-Gill waterfall, the barn has direct access to walks, hills & rock climbing. There are local & national bus stops at the end of the lane. Accommodation consists of two rooms; a kitchen/diner with all the basic equipment & a 5 bed bunkroom (BYO sleeping bag). A pub serving meals is a short walk away. Perfect for quiet country retreats, but not suitable for noisy groups. No mobile phone signal or WiFi.

St John's-in-the-Vale Camping Barn is an 18th century stable on a peaceful hill farm, with stunning views to Blencathra, Helvellyn & Castle Rock. The Barn has a sleeping area upstairs (mattresses provided) & an equipped kitchen, sitting/ dining area below. A separate toilet & shower are within the building. A wood-burning stove makes it nice & cosy. Outside there is a BBQ & seating area. The star-filled night skies are magical. Self catering hayloft is also available (sleeping up to 4; 2 adults & 2 children).

DETAILS

- **Open** - All year. Check in by 7.30pm.
- **Beds** - 5
- **Price/night** - £27pp. Sole use £135. BYO Sleeping bag. £1 for the shower.

CONTACT: Louise Hodgson
Tel: 07799 403764
stybeckfarm@btconnect.com
www.stybeckfarm.co.uk
Stybeck Farm, Thirlmere, Keswick, Cumbria CA12 4TN

DETAILS

- **Open** - All year. All day.
- **Beds** - Barn 8: 1x8. Hayloft 4
- **Price/night** - Barn: From £16pp, min £50 a night. £128 Fri & Sat. min 2 nights

CONTACT: Sarah
Tel: 01768 779242
info@campingbarn.com
www.campingbarn.com
Low Bridge End Farm, St John's-in-the-Vale, Keswick, CA12 4TS

THE WHITE HORSE
INN BUNKHOUSE

103a

The White Horse Inn has 2 bunkhouses in the converted stables of this traditional Lake District inn at the foot of Blencathra

Guests are welcome in the Inn which has great pub food, open fires, local ales and is open from 11am to 11pm. Each bunkhouse has a basic kitchen, dining area and bunkrooms sleeping between 4 and 6. Paths to the mountains from the garden & the C2C route passes the door.

DETAILS

- **Open** - All year. All day access.
- **Beds** - 48: Bunkhouse 26: 1x6, 5x4. Bunkhouse 22: 3x6, 1x4
- **Price/night** - £16pp. 4 bed room £64. 6 bed room £96. Bedding £5/stay. Enquire for Xmas/New Year.

CONTACT: Phil, Stevie or Adrian
Tel: 017687 79883
info@thewhitehorse-blencathra.co.uk
www.thewhitehorse-blencathra.co.uk
The White Horse Inn, Scales, Nr Threlkeld, Keswick, CA12 4SY

LOWSIDE FARM
CAMPING BARN AND PODS

103b

Nestling at the foot of Blencathra, with paths to the mountains from the doorstep Lowside Farm Camping Barn, Pods & Cottages are your perfect Lake District base. Sleeping groups of up to 14, the newly converted camping barn is modern & comfortable, The six, 4 berth luxury camping pods and the 2 cottages, provide extra accommodation for larger groups, older family members and those with small chilldren. Bedding is provided.

GROUPS ONLY

DETAILS

- **Open** - All year
- **Beds** - 38: Barn 14: 1x12,1x2. Pods 24: 6x4. Herdwick House 12: 2xdbl 1x twin,1x3. Tarn Cottage 6: 2xdbl,1x2.
- **Price/night** - From £36pp. Min 10 people in the Barn. Min 2 nights.

CONTACT:
Tel: 07887 645229
microlodges@btinternet.com
lowsidefarm.co.uk
Lowside Farm, Troutbeck, Penrith, Cumbria CA11 0SX

BLAKEBECK FARM
CAMPING BARN
104a

At the foot of Souther Fell, within easy reach of Blencathra, Blakebeck Farm is set amidst the wildflower meadows of Mungrisdale. On the C2C cycle route & the Cumbrian Way. Perfect as a weekend break for walkers. The large upstairs room has bunk beds for 8 people (BYO sleeping bags) & a large farmhouse table. The kitchen has all you need to cook a simple meal. Cooked English breakfasts are available for groups, when ordered prior to arrival. One dog by prior arrangement. Not suitable for parties or children under 11.

DETAILS
- **Open** - All year. All day
- **Beds** - 8: 1x8 + holiday cottages
- **Price/night** - £15pp. No children < 11.

CONTACT: Judith
Tel: 017687 79957 or 07789 287121
j.egan001@btinternet.com
blakebeckfarm.co.uk
Blakebeck, Mungrisdale, Penrith,
CA11 0SZ

CALDBECK
GLAMPING BARNS
104b

Caldbeck Glamping accommodation is in the centre of Caldbeck Village close to Wainwright's Northern Fells. Opposite The Odd Fellows pub and close to the village store. The self contained barns sleep 8 and 5. Two people can sleep in the Bothy and there is space for a small tent or two. Caldbeck is a 25 minute drive from M6 and right on The Cumbria Way and The Reivers Cycle route. Sit back and enjoy everything this hidden Lake District village has to offer.

DETAILS
- **Open** - All year
- **Beds** - 15: Hayloft 8: 1x8, High Pike 5: 1x5, The Bothy 2:1x2. Plus 3 camping
- **Price/night** - From: Hayloft £255. High Pike £225. Bothy £155. All barns: £650.

CONTACT: John & Isabelle Nicoll
Tel: 07410 694305 or 07976 617276
johnnicoll10@gmail.com
www.caldbeckglamping.com
Caldbeck, Lake District, Cumbria,
CA7 8EA

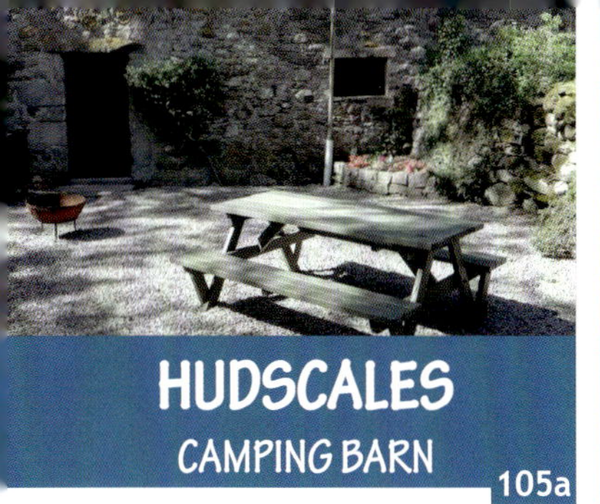

HUDSCALES
CAMPING BARN
105a

Hudscales Camping Barn perches at 1000ft on the northern-most flank of the Lakeland Fells. It overlooks the villages of Caldbeck and Hesket Newmarket and is on the Cumbria Way. BYO sleeping bags, mats, stove & utensils. There is a separate toilet and wash basin and a metered shower. A wood-burning stove provides added comfort (logs extra), there is electric lighting plus metered power points, (electric heaters are provided if required). There's also a games room with pool table/dart board.

DETAILS
- **Open** - All year. All day.
- **Beds** - 12: 1x12
- **Price/night** - £15 per person. £180 sole use.

CONTACT: Elizabeth
Tel: 016974 78637 or 07717 803744
hudscalescampingbarn@gmail.com
www.hudscalescampingbarn.co.uk
Hudscales, Hesket Newmarket, Wigton, Cumbria, CA7 8JZ

SKIDDAW HOUSE
HOSTEL
105b

The highest hostel in Britain! Escape the crowds at this remote mountain hostel. Hire the whole place for a small group of friends and family, or book a room or bed. No roads, no other buildings, no phone signal: just uninterrupted beautiful mountain views. An easy walk or mountain bike ride from Keswick or Threlkeld. Rustic but comfortable with a wood burning stove, hot showers, a well-stocked shop/bar and full bedding.

DETAILS
- **Open** - Open from April 2026. Check in from 5pm; please contact the hostel if you would prefer to arrive a little earlier.
- **Beds** - 20 : 1x8, 1x6,1x4, 1x2
- **Price/night** - Enquire for individuals. Sole use from £500 per night. Min of 2 nights in winter. (YHA discounts apply). School / Youth Groups £375 /night.

CONTACT: Sue Edwards
info@skiddawhouse.co.uk
www.skiddawhouse.co.uk
Bassenthwaite, Keswick, CA12 4QX

DENTON
HOUSE
106a

Denton House is a purpose built hostel in Keswick in the Lake District. Surrounded by stunning scenery, great cycling and wonderful walking. Derwentwater is just a short stroll away.

Recently refurbished, the hostel is warm, comfortable and well equipped.

Book by the bed, the room or book sole use of the whole place (sleeps 66).

DETAILS
- **Open** - All year. Office hours 9am - 5pm
- **Beds** - 66: 1x14, 1x12, 2x10, 1x8, 2x4, 2x2
- **Price/night** - £40pp. Mid-week sole use from £2,000. Breakfast £13.50. Pack lunch £9.50. Dinner £15

CONTACT: Christina Whipp
Tel: 01768 775351
keswickhostel@hotmail.co.uk
www.dentonhouse-keswick.co.uk
Penrith Road, Keswick, Cumbria, CA12 4JW

HAWSE END
CENTRE
106b

Hawse End Centre in the Lake District sits at the head of the magnificent Borrowdale Valley on the shores of Derwentwater. Guests enjoy easy access to Keswick and the mountains beyond via launch or lakeside walk.

The house is a large, comfortable, country mansion ideal for large groups, while the cottage is more suited to smaller groups or large families.

Outdoor activities can be arranged.

DETAILS
- **Open** - All year.
- **Beds** - 73: House 49: (10 rooms). Cottage 24: (7 rooms) + camping
- **Price/night** - Enquire for prices.

CONTACT:
Tel: 01768 812280
cumbriaoutdoors.enquiries@cumbria.gov.uk
cumbriaoutdoors.org
Portinscale, Keswick, Cumbria, CA12 5UE

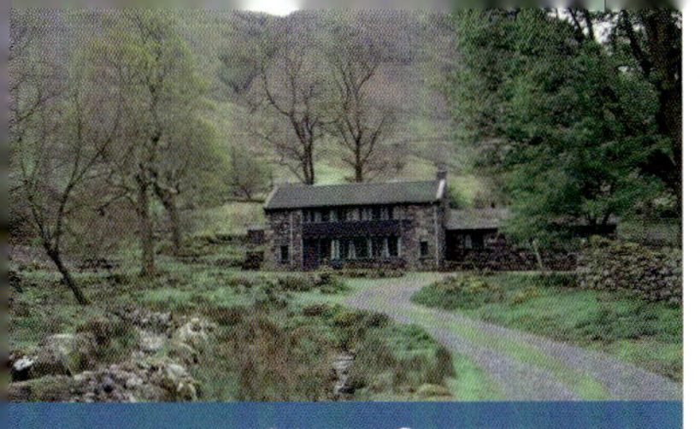

HIGH HOUSE

107a

High House in Seathwaite, at the head of the beautiful valley of Borrowdale, offers comfortable bunkhouse accommodation. Popular with walking/climbing clubs and educational groups, early booking is advised. Group bookings only. Large common room with stove (fuel provided). Fully equipped self-catering kitchen, 2 washrooms with shower and 2 toilets. Drying room. Large grounds with tables, benches and firepit. Accessible by car. Club members may occasionally use a 3rd dorm unless exclusive use is booked (midweek only).

DETAILS

- **Open** - All year. All day.
- **Beds** - 26: 1x18, 1x8
- **Price/night** - £250 (see website for more detail).

CONTACT: Maja While
bookings.kff@gmail.com
highhouseborrowdale.co.uk
Seathwaite, Borrowdale, Keswick,
CA12 5XJ

LOW GILLERTHWAITE
FIELD CENTRE

107b

In the untouched Ennerdale Valley of the Lake District, Low Gillerthwaite Field Centre beckons. At the base of Pillar and Red Pike, this eco-friendly centre offers spacious communal areas, a classroom, and a sprawling meadow for relaxation or activities. Ideally located for self-led adventures, with connections to outdoor providers, you are sure of a memorable stay for all ages, especially schools and universities.

DETAILS

- **Open** - All year (except Christmas and Boxing Day). 24 hours.
- **Beds** - 40: 2x4, 1x8, 1x10, 1x14.
- **Price/night** - Sole use: £540 (schools £480). Individuals: Adult £20.50. Child (under 17) & students £15. Under 5s Free. Bank Hol rates: +50%. N/Year: x2.

CONTACT: Ellen or Walter
Tel: 01946 861229 or 07736 803756
Warden@lgfc.org.uk
www.lowgillerthwaite.com
Ennerdale, Cleator, CA23 3AX

THE WILD WOOL
BARN
108a

The Wild Wool Barn nestles in the peace of the Ennerdale Valley, overlooking Ennerdale Water. It offers 3 overnight options + camping. The Byre sleeps 6 in bunks & a double bed & is sole use only. The Spinning Barn sleeps 4 & can be booked by the bed. The Bothy has a pull-out double bed. The Bothy & Spinning Barn share WC/shower with the campers. With no mobile signal/WiFi, you can escape & explore the rarely visited Western Lakes.

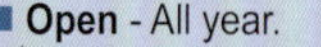

DETAILS

- **Open** - All year.
- **Beds** - 12: 1x6, 1x4,1x2 + 6 camping
- **Price/night** - Spinning Barn; £27pp. Bothy: £30pp. B/house: £160 to 7 nights £890. Camping £12pp. Enquire for sole use. Bank hols min 3 nights.

CONTACT: Susan Denham-Smith
Tel: 01946 861270
susan@wildwoolworkshop.co.uk
www.wildwoolbarn.co.uk
Routen Cottage, Ennerdale, CA23 3AU

REAGILL
VILLAGE HALL
108b

Reagill Village Hall offers simple budget accommodation to C2C walkers, cyclists, families & outdoor enthusiasts. Situated in a tiny hamlet of just 20 houses, there are no street lights, little traffic and wonderful dark skies for star gazing. There are plenty of lovely walks from the doorstep, while Shap is 3 miles away, Appleby 10 miles and Penrith 12 miles. Facilities include a kitchen with a new cooker, fridge & microwave, 2 new multi stove heaters and a new power shower. Blow up mattresses are provided (1 dbl, 2 twin, 2 kid's). BYO bedding.

DETAILS

- **Open** - All year. Closed Mondays during term time.
- **Beds** - 6+: 1xdbl, 2xtwin, 2xchilds (all blow up beds) + floor space
- **Price/night** - £12pp. Min charge £25.

CONTACT: Margaret Wilcox
Tel: 07804 291972
margaret.wilcox69@gmail.com
Fern Bank, Reagill, Cumbria. CA10 3ER

HAGGS BANK
BUNKHOUSE & CAMPING
109a

Set in the stunning North Pennines AONB, England's last wilderness. This modern conversion of a historic mine building provides warm accommodation with excellent hot showers for lovers of the great outdoors. Isaac's Tea Trail and the C2C pass right by. There are self catering facilities and meals can be provided for groups. The campsite has tiered pitches and views across the Nent valley. Electric hook-ups, secure cycle storage and plenty of parking.

DETAILS
- **Open** - All year. All day access.
- **Beds** - 25: 1x4/5, 1x9, 1x11
- **Price/night** - £20pp. Sole use £400, £1080 (3 nights). Camping: £12, U15, £7. Motorhomes/caravans £25 up to 2.

CONTACT: Danny Taylor
Tel: 07919 092403 or 01434 382486
info@haggsbank.com
haggsbank.com
Haggs Bank Bunkhouse, Nentsbury,
Alston, Cumbria, CA9 3LH

NINEBANKS
HOSTEL
109b

Book a chalet room, or the whole hostel. Ninebanks 4* Hostel, in stunning rural Northumberland, has en suite bedrooms, a sitting room with log-burner and a spacious dining room. In the chalet are two high quality studio rooms, fully self-contained and separate from the hostel. Dogs welcome with prior notice for sole use or in the chalet. In the North Pennines close to Hadrian's Wall and on Isaac's Tea Trail.

DETAILS
- **Open** - All year. All day.
- **Beds** - Hostel capacity 24, 28 beds in 6 rooms: 2x2/3, 2x4, 1x6, 1x8.   Chalet: 1 x dbl. 1 x dbl/twin
- **Price/night** - Whole hostel from £480. Chalet from £65. Fee for dogs.

CONTACT: Pauline or Ian
Tel: 01434 345288 or 07510 219834
contact@ninebanks.org.uk
www.ninebanks.org.uk
Orchard House, Mohope, Hexham,
Northumberland NE47 8DQ

ALSTON
YOUTH HOSTEL
110a

Alston Youth Hostel is within the historic town of Alston nestled in the North Pennines on the eastern side of Cumbria. Situated directly on the Pennine Way and Isaac's Tea Trail and also about halfway on the very popular Coast to Coast (C2C) cycle route with great indoor cycle storage.

The perfect stop-over for walkers and cyclists. You'll receive a warm welcome. Exclusive hire also available!

DETAILS

■ **Open** - All year: (Groups only from 1st Nov-1st Mar). 8am-10am, 5pm-9pm
■ **Beds** - 28: 1x1 (or twin), 2x4 (or twin), 3x6
■ **Price/night** - Private rooms from £30. Sole use from £800.

CONTACT: Mat Austin
Tel: 01434 381509
info@alstonhostel.co.uk
alstonhostel.co.uk
The Firs, Alston, Cumbria, CA9 3RW

CARRSHIELD
CAMPING BARN
110b

Surrounded by the stunning North Pennines, Carrshield Camping Barn offers basic accommodation for 18 across 3 rooms, each with a wood-burner & a wooden sleeping platform. There's a separate cooking area & a composting WC. BYO stove, utensils & sleeping bag/mat. On the Isaac Tea Trail, C2C cycle route & close to mountain bike routes. Camping may be available.

DETAILS

■ **Open** - All year. Check in 3pm, check out 10am
■ **Beds** - 18: 1x8, 1x6, 1x4
■ **Price/night** - 8 bed room £65, 6 bed £55, 4 bed £45. Includes a basket of logs. Whole barn £148.50 (use code THEWHOLEBARNPLEASE) to book

CONTACT: Paul Stafford
Tel: 07896 900956
carrshieldcampingbarn@gmail.com
www.carrshieldcampingbarn.co.uk
Near Blue Row Cottages, Carrshield, Hexham, NE47 8AF.

GARRIGILL
VILLAGE HALL

111a

Perfect for the Pennine Way or C2C cycle route. In the lovely village of Garrigill, the bunkroom above the village hall sleeps 8 with bedding hire available. Larger groups can BYO bedding and use the hall itself where 12 camp beds are available. There is free WiFi, a well equipped kitchen, showers and drying room. It makes the ideal long distance walk/C2C stop over.

DETAILS

■ **Open** - All year. All day
■ **Beds** - 35: Bunkroom: 8 bunks. Main Hall: 12 camp beds + floor space for 15.
■ **Price/night** - £18pp. Bunkroom bedding hire (if required) £5pp per stay. Camping £8pp (DofE or other youth activity groups half price).

CONTACT: Bookings Secretary
Tel: 01434 647516
bookings@garrigillvh.org
www.garrigillvh.org.uk
Garrigill Village Hall, Garrigill, Alston, Cumbria, CA9 3DS

BARRINGTON
BUNKHOUSE

111b

Situated in the peaceful village of Rookhope, in Weardale, Barrington Bunkhouse accommodates 15 people. There's room for 13 in the bunkhouse, whilst the adjacent caravan sleeps two. Camping space is also available. The kitchen is equipped with two toasters, a kettle, a microwave, electric hob and a fridge. Ideal for cyclists, walkers and family groups. Dogs by arrangement. A warm welcome awaits.

DETAILS

■ **Open** - All year. All day.
■ **Beds** - 15: Bunkhouse 13. Caravan 2 + camping
■ **Price/night** - £24pp incl. snack b/fast. Camping £14 with b/fast, £10 without. Sole use rates negotiable.

CONTACT: Valerie Livingston
Tel: 01388 517656
barrington_bunkhouse@hotmail.co.uk
www.barrington-bunkhouse-rookhope.com
Barrington Cottage, Rookhope, Weardale, Co. Durham, DL13 2BG

CARRS FARM
BUNKHOUSE

112a

EDMUNDBYERS YHA
AT LOW HOUSE HAVEN

112b

Carrs Farm Bunkhouse is a converted 17th century barn with stunning views over Weardale. It provides comfortable bunk bed accommodation for groups of up to 21 people in three rooms. There is a fully equipped self-catering kitchen, games/lounge area and outdoor seating with BBQ.

Situated on a working farm at the heart of the North Pennines. Guided walks and outdoor activities are available for groups and schools.

Edmunbyers hostel lies in moorland, close to the Northumberland/County Durham boundary, with fine views. It's just two miles from Derwent Reservoir, for sailing & fishing. Ideal for walking holidays, it's also on the C2C cycle route & is close to Hadrian's Wall & Beamish outdoor museum. Cosy & comfortable with optional home cooked evening meals & breakfasts.

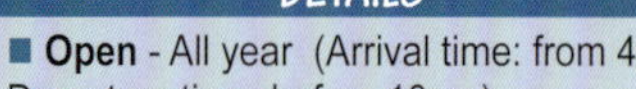

DETAILS

■ **Open** - All year (Arrival time: from 4pm. Departure time: before 10am)
■ **Beds** - 21: 2x6, 1x9
■ **Price/night** - £30 per person. Enquire about sole use.

DETAILS

■ **Open** - All year (camping Apr-Oct). Check in 5-10pm. Check out 8-10am.
■ **Beds** - 31: 1x8, 1x6, 2x5, 1x4, 1x3 plus 14 camping pitches (6 with electric)
■ **Price/night** - From £25pp (adult). Room for 3: £70, 4: £90, 5: £90. Discounts for YHA members

CONTACT: Patrick Leigh Pemberton
Tel: 07756 268722
patrick@carrsfarm.co.uk
carrsfarm.co.uk
Wolsingham, County Durham, DL13 3BQ

CONTACT: Debbie Clarke
Tel: 01207 255651
debbie.clarke1@hotmail.co.uk
www.lowhousehaven.co.uk
Low House, Edmundbyers, Consett, Durham, DH8 9NL

HILLSIDE FARM
BUNKBARN

113a

A Georgian working farm, right on Hadrian's Wall National Trail & Cycleway near the Solway Coast AONB. Stunning views over the Solway Firth marshes towards Scotland.

The bunkbarn has cooking facilities & hot showers and is heated with a bio mass boiler. Breakfast or bacon sandwiches available with notice. The barn is available to walkers, cyclists, traverlers and peaceful family groups.

DETAILS

- **Open** - March to November
- **Beds** - 12
- **Price/night** - £20pp inc shower. £5.00 for duvets (pre-booked) £5.00 full English, £2.50 hot sandwiches.

CONTACT: Mrs Sandra Rudd
Tel: 07498 921746
sandrahillsidefarm@gmail.com
www.hadrianswalkbnb.co.uk
Hillside Farm, Boustead Hill, Burgh-by-Sands, Carlisle, Cumbria, CA5 6AA

FLORRIE'S
BUNKHOUSE

113b

Located right on the Hadrian's Wall National Trail this friendly bunkhouse is aimed at walkers and cyclists. With a drying room and cycle storage this is the perfect stop-over on the trail.

Open from April to October. Florrie's provides a comfortable bed, breakfast and evening meals plus the opportunity to socialise with other guests at the bar. In the winter season the bunkhouse is open to groups with self-catering.

DETAILS

- **Open** - April to October (self-catering groups in the winter season).
- **Beds** - 16 (17) : 3x4, 1x4 (or 5 if family)
- **Price/night** - B&B from £32 pp. Private Rooms available.

CONTACT: Rebecca & Joss
Tel: 01697 741704
hello@florriesonthewall.co.uk
florriesonthewall.co.uk
Florrie's on the Wall, Kingbank, Walton, Cumbria, CA8 2DH

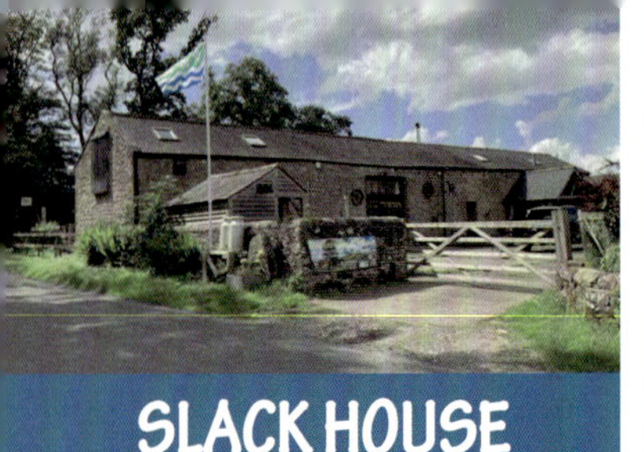

SLACK HOUSE
FARM

114a

Slack House Farm is an organic dairy farm overlooking Birdoswald Roman Fort on Hadrian's Wall. It is on the NCN 72 cycle trail and close to Hadrian's Wall National Trail. The bunk barn has 3 ensuite bedrooms of 3, 5 and 8 beds.

A wood pellet-fired stove gives a warm heart to the kitchen/lounge and provides under-floor heating throughout the barn.

Book a bed, a private room or sole use of the whole bunkhouse.

DETAILS

■ **Open** - March to October
■ **Beds** - 16: 1x3,1x5, 1x8
■ **Price/night** - £35pp including continental breakfast, bedding and towels. Private rooms from £70 (2 person).

CONTACT: Denise Canning
Tel: 07818 002074
cycleroute72@yahoo.com
slackhousefarm.co.uk
Gilsland, Brampton, Cumbria, CA8 7DB

GREENHEAD
HOSTEL

114b

Situated in the village of Greenhead on the Pennine Way & Hadrian's Wall, this bunkhouse is ideal for walkers or for exploring Roman sites. It has a self-catering kitchen big enough for large groups. Run by Greenhead Hotel just over the road with award winning food. Dorms & private rooms. Book by the bed, the room or for sole use.

DETAILS

■ **Open** - All year (sole use only in Winter). April-May (closed Sun-Mon).
■ **Beds** - 48: Hostel: 4x6, 2x8. Flat: 2xdbl, 1xtriple.
■ **Price/night** - £24pp (dorm). Private rooms: double £60, family quad £80, 6 bed room £140, 8 bed room £185. Whole hostel £850 (Discount for 3+ nights).

CONTACT: Greenhead Hotel & Hostel
Tel: 01697 747411
bookings@greenheadbrampton.co.uk
www.greenheadhostel.co.uk
Greenhead Hotel, Greenhead,
Brampton, Cumbria, CA8 7HG

GIBBS HILL
FARM HOSTEL
115a

Gibbs Hill Farm Hostel is on a working hill farm in Northumberland National Park on Hadrian's Wall near Oncebrewed and close to the Pennine Way. Designed to reduce energy consumption it is centrally heated throughout. Comprising 3 bunkrooms, 2 shower rooms, 2 toilets, a well equipped kitchen, a comfortable communal area and a large deck where you can enjoy the evening sun. Ideal for families who can book a whole room with private facilities. Study groups welcome. Self catering only.

DETAILS
- **Open** - All year
- **Beds** - 18: 3x6
- **Price/night** - £25 adult, £20 child (under 12), minimum of 8 people.

CONTACT: Valerie Gibson
Tel: 01434 344030 or 07904 027513
val@gibbshillfarm.co.uk
www.gibbshillfarm.co.uk
Gibbs Hill Farm, Bardon Mill, Nr Hexham, Northumberland, NE47 7AP

WINSHIELDS
BUNKBARN & CAMPSITE
115b

A small comfortable walkers/cyclists bunkbarn & campsite on Hadrian's Wall, the Pennine Way, Hadrian's Cycleway & The Pennine Journey.

The bunkhouse sleeps 8 in 2 rooms of single beds. Bedding & towels are provided, A simple breakfast is included in the price and there's a kitchenette with microwave, kettle & fridge. 5 mins walk to a pub serving meals 7 days a week.

No arrivals by car.

DETAILS
- **Open** - March to end of October - some flexibility
- **Beds** - 8: 1x3, 1x5 (all single beds).
- **Price/night** - £30pp.

CONTACT: Malcolm
Tel: 07968 102780
malcolm@winshieldscampsite.co.uk
www.winshieldscampsite.co.uk
Windshields Farm, Bardon MIll, Hexham, Northumberland. NE47 7AN

NEWBROUGH
BUNKHOUSE
116a

GREENCARTS
BUNKHOUSES & CAMPING
116b

In the centre of the village of Newbrough, this community run bunkhouse sleeps 22 across 3 dorms. Facilities include 2 shower/WC rooms, 2 sink areas & a small equipped kitchen. A large communal area is available to groups by arrangement. With footpaths leading directly to Hadrian's Wall, approx 3 km away, it is popular with walkers. While for cyclists the Sandstone Way & Hadrian's Cycleway pass right by.

DETAILS

- **Open** - All year. Check in 3pm. Check out before 10am.
- **Beds** - 22: 2x8, 1x6
- **Price/night** - £24pp (incl bedding). 6 bed room £90, 8 bed room £118. Whole bunkhouse £292 (bedding £6pp per stay).

CONTACT: Nick Springham
Tel: 07596 081642 or 07767 802868
newbrough2018@gmail.com
www.newbroughbunkhouse.co.uk
The Stanegate, Newbrough, Hexham, Northumberland, NE47 5AR

Greencarts Bunkhouses & Camping are on a working farm in Northumberland National Park. Right next to Hadrian's Wall, they are perfect for walkers or cyclists. There are two accommodation units: The Bunkhouse sleeps 10 in two rooms, while the Barn sleeps 13 in one open plan room. All bedding is provided and continental breakfast is available. There is also a large campsite.

DETAILS

- **Open** - B/house: 1 Mar - 31 Oct. Barn: mid May - 31 Aug. All year for groups.
- **Beds** - 23: Bunkhouse: 2x5. Barn 1x13
- **Price/night** - Bunkhouse: £30pp or £40 single occ. Continental b/fast extra. Barn: £20pp + £7 continental b/fast. Enquire for sole use.

CONTACT: Jean Newton
Tel: 01434 681320
sandra@greencarts.co.uk
greencarts.co.uk
Greencarts Farm, Humshaugh, Northumberland. NE46 4BW

HOUGHTON NORTH
FARM ACCOMMODATION

117a

TARSET TOR
BUNKHOUSE & BOTHIES

117b

Houghton North Farm, partly built with stones from Hadrian's Wall, is in the Northumberland countryside, right on the Hadrian's Wall trail, 15 miles from the start. This spacious new build is perfect for groups, individuals or families. Every group or individual gets a private room. There's a self-catering kitchen (continental b/fast included). The TV lounge has a log fire & WiFi. Long-term parking, baggage transfer & packed lunches are available on request.

In the heart of the Northumberland International Dark Sky Park and close to the Pennine Way. These striking timber eco-buildings integrate into their natural surroundings making the most of this remarkable location and providing the perfect base for outdoor adventures.

The bunkhouse and bothies provide stylish, versatile & comfortable self-catering accommodation which can be used for events, conferences & parties.

DETAILS

- **Open** - All year. Arrive after 3.30pm depart by 10am.
- **Beds** - 22: 1x5, 3x4, 1x3, 1x2.
- **Price/night** - B&B from £40-£55 (adult) Group discounts.

DETAILS

- **Open** - Mid January - December.
- **Beds** - 52: Bunkhouse:16-20. Bothies: 4x8. 3 camper van bays.
- **Price/night** - Bunkhouse: £360 to £500. Bothies: £125 to £250.

CONTACT: Mrs Paula Laws
Tel: 01661 954364 or 07708 419911
wjlaws@btconnect.com
www.houghtonnorthfarm.co.uk
Heddon-on-the-Wall, Northumberland,
NE15 0EZ

CONTACT: Robert and Claire Cocker
Tel: 01434 240980 or 07891 252801
info@tarset-tor.co.uk
www.tarset-tor.co.uk
Greystones, Lanehead, Tarset, Hexham,
NE48 1NT

CHARTNERS FARM

118a

Deep within Harwood Forest, near the Simonside Hills, Chartners Farm is a 5 mile drive along forest tracks. It's off grid; electricity from a wind turbine & solar panels, spring water supply (tested) heating by log stove & radiators. With no TV and limited phone signal, it's perfect spot to relax, walking or biking. Fully equipped with LPG cooker, shower, microwave, fridge/freezer, radio, CD and board games etc. Basket of logs, sheet & pillowcases provided; bring your own sleeping bag and towels.

DETAILS

■ **Open** - Mid Feb-Nov (subject to weather warnings). Arrival 4pm departure 11am.
■ **Beds** - 12: 2x5,1x2 (bunks and singles)
■ **Price/night** - £130 for up to 6 guests; £160 for 7 to 12 guests. Min stay 2 nights.

CONTACT: Nick Davies
chartnersfarm@gmail.com
Chartners, Harwood Forest, Ewesley, Morpeth NE61 4LJ

RADCLIFFES
LODGE

118b

Radcliffes Lodge is a purpose-built hostel overlooking the Marina in the vibrant harbour town of Amble on the Northumberland Coast. It sleeps 48 across 9 en suite rooms, has a large open-plan communal area & oozes quality & style. With the Coast & Castles cycle route & the Northumberland Coastal Path on the doorstep, the Lodge is perfect for walkers, cyclists, & groups of friends & families.

DETAILS

■ **Open** - All year
■ **Beds** - 48: 1x8, 4x6, 4x4 (all private rooms with en suite)
■ **Price/night** - Family suites from £140 for 4 people. Bunkbed rooms from £70 for 2 people.

CONTACT: Reception
Tel: 01665 252122 or 07943 682727
info@radcliffeslodge.co.uk
www.radcliffeslodge.co.uk
Coble Quay, Amble, Northumberland.
NE65 0FB

ALNWICK
YOUTH HOSTEL
119a

The family friendly hostel has private en suite rooms, dorms, lounge, games room & a spacious dining room. Located in town centre, so ideal for Alnwick Castle, Alnwick Garden, Lilidorei and Barter Books. Ideal for cyclists, bike storage in dedicated cycle hub. The coast, with glorious sandy beaches is just 15 mins drive, whilst inland the Cheviot Hills & Hadrian's Wall await.

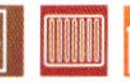

DETAILS
- **Open** - All year. 8-10am, 4-7pm
- **Beds** - 55:1x sgl, 2x dbl, 2x2, 1x3, 5x4, 1x5, 3x6.
- **Price/night** - Peak: Dorm £34. Private rooms 1 person £59, 2 £70, 3 £96, 4 £116, 5 £128, 6 £139. Off-peak reductions eg dorm £29, private rooms from £44.

CONTACT: Reception
Tel: 01665 660800
info@alnwickyouthhostel.co.uk
www.alnwickyouthhostel.co.uk
34 - 38 Green Batt, Alnwick,
Northumberland, NE66 1TU

MOUNTHOOLY
BUNKHOUSE
119b

Nestled in the beautiful College Valley, North Northumberland, Mounthooly Bunkhouse is a perfect stop-off on the Pennine Way and St Cuthbert's Way. Dogs are welcome by arrangement. There is a well equipped kitchen and living area with log burner. Bedding, WiFi and car permit (to access this private valley) are provided. A haven for wildlife with birds, red squirrels, and a thriving population of feral goats in the valley. The perfect wild get away from it all.

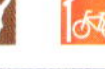

DETAILS
- **Open** - All year. All day.
- **Beds** - 24: 2x9 1x2 1x4(family)
- **Price/night** - £22pp, £15pp under 18 & concessions. Family room for 4 £75. Sole use £300, £370 (weekends & holidays).

CONTACT: Charlene Drysdale
Tel: 01668 216210
mounthooly@college-valley.co.uk
www.college-valley.co.uk
Mount Hooly, College Valley, Wooler,
Northumberland, NE71 6TU

ILDERTON
DOD BARNS
120a

WOOLER
HOSTEL
120b

Ilderton Dod Barns, in Northumberland National Park, include The Barn (6 permanent beds plus sofa bed & space for cot & Z beds) & Cuckoo Cottage (king-sized bed plus sofa bed & space for a cot/Z bed). On a working hill farm down a 1.5 mile track. Close to The Pennine Way & The Sandstone Way with many other footpaths & bridleways on the doorstep. The perfect base for walkers, mountain bikers & horse riders.

Wooler Hostel & Shepherd's Huts are on the edge of the town and offer an ideal base for exploring the Northumberland National Park, the Cheviot Hills, local castles and fine sandy beaches. For walkers there's St Cuthbert's Way and for cyclists, Wooler cycle hub routes, Pennine Cycleway and the Sandstone Way. There are bridleways perfect for mountain biking and lots of bouldering and climbing.

DETAILS

- **Open** - All year.
- **Beds** - 8: The Barn 6: Cottage 2.
- **Price/night** - The Barn: £451 - £764 (up to 3 nights), £588 - £987 (7 nights). 10% reduction for 3 or less people. Cottage: £308 - £506 / £402 - £655.

DETAILS

- **Open** - January to December. 9am - 6pm
- **Beds** - 53: 1 x 3 3 x 2, 5x4, 1x6, 1x8. Shepherd's Huts 3x2, 1x3 (family).
- **Price/night** - From £27 per person. Group discounts available.

CONTACT: Pam Brown
Tel: 07786 253793 or 0793 2782611
ildertondodbarns@hotmail.com
www.ildertondodbarns.co.uk
The Dod, Powburn, Alnwick,
Northumberland NE66 4JL

CONTACT: Hostel Manager
Tel: 07492 018545
info@woolerhostel.com
woolerhostel.com
30 Cheviot Street, Wooler,
Northumberland, NE71 6LW

JOINERS SHOP
BUNKHOUSE

121a

Nestled in the hamlet of Preston, The Joiners Shop Bunkhouse is just 5 miles from the Northumberland coastline & 7 miles from Alnwick famed for its Castle & Gardens. The charming 19th century building takes groups of up to 18 with one double bed and 16 single pine bunks arranged in sections of 3's & 5's.

Fully equipped kitchen, spacious dining area, lounge with fire & hot showers. Close to NCN Route 1, Seahouses, Beadnell and the famous coastal castles.

DETAILS
- **Open** - All year. All day.
- **Beds** - 18
- **Price/night** - Sole use: from £200 to £350, dependant on number of guests.

CONTACT: Kirsten Sutherland
Tel: 07955 230328
hello@bunkhousenorthumberland.co.uk
www.bunkhousenorthumberland.co.uk
Joiners Cottage, Preston, Chathill,
Northumberland. NE67 5ES

THE HIDES

121b

Located in Seahouses with an easy walk to St Aidan's beach. The Hides provide affordable accommodation on the magnificent Northumbrian Coast.

Perfect for groups, families or independent travellers. Each Hide is an ensuite room sleeping 4 in beds & bunks. The rooms open onto a communal courtyard with access to the well equipped self-catering kitchen, bike storage, drying room & laundry.

DETAILS
- **Open** - All year.
- **Beds** - 20: 5x4
- **Price/night** - £28. Children £25. Minimum 2 night stay. Duvet & towel hire £5. Dogs £6

CONTACT: Kerry
Tel: 07762 997599 or 01665 720645
info@the-hides.co.uk
www.the-hides.co.uk
146 Main Street, Seahouses
Northumberland NE68 7UA

SEAHOUSES
HOSTEL
122a

Within easy walking distance of Seahouses, this recently refurbished hostel offers affordable, spacious & comfortable accommodation. A perfect base for visiting the beaches and castles of the Northumbrian Coast. Particularly popular with divers, families, cyclists, walkers, school, church and youth groups. Groups of all sizes welcome. Sole use available. Booking essential.

DETAILS

- **Open** - All year. Arrive after 4pm, depart by 10am unless otherwise agreed.
- **Beds** - 42: 1x10, 1x8 (ensuite), 1x6, 1x6 (ensuite wet room), 2x4, 2x2 (ensuite)
- **Price/night** - Recognised youth groups £22pp. Other groups £27 to £32pp. Children under 5's free. Min 2 nights.

CONTACT: Julie Torkington
Tel: 07531 305206
seahouseshostel@outlook.com
www.seahouseshostel.org.uk
157 Main Street, Seahouses,
Northumberland NE68 7TU

BLUEBELL
FARM BUNKBARN
122b

Bluebell Farm Bunkbarn is within walking distance of shops and pubs. It is ideally located for exploring Nothumberland's Heritage Coast, the Cheviot Hills and the Scottish Borders. The Bunkbarn has a shared modern toilet block and sleeps 12 in bunks, plus a fold down small double sofa bed. BYO sleeping bags/towels or hire a linen set. There are also 2 studio apartments and 5 self-catering cottages.

DETAILS

- **Open** - All year. Check in by 9 pm, departure by 10 am.
- **Beds** - 18: Bunkbarn 14: 1x8, 1x6. Studio 4: 1x4. Plus apartments & cottages
- **Price/night** - Bunkbarn: £20 (under 16s £10). Studio: £25 (under 16s £12.50). Linen & towel set hire £10/stay. Swan Suite & West View from £80 per night.

CONTACT: Phyl
Tel: 01668 213362 or 0770335430
corillas@icloud.com
Bluebell Farm Caravan Park, Belford,
Northumberland, NE70 7QE

EAT SLEEP
LINDISFARNE

123a

Perfectly located for visiting Lindisfarne and the castles and beaches of the North Northumberland coast, Eat & Sleep Lindisfarne sleeps 28 across 5 rooms, one of which is accessible. Eat at the on-site bistro or self-cater in the bunkhouse kitchen. Situated close to St Cuthberts & St Oswalds Way and directly on the Sandstone Way and the Coast and Castles route. There's secure cycle storage, a drying room & laundry facilities, comfy beds & piping hot showers for the weary adventurers.

DETAILS

■ **Open** - All year. All day.
■ **Beds** - 28: 4x6, 1x4(accessible) + 3 shepherd huts
■ **Price/night** - £25pp. Enquire for huts.

CONTACT: Shaun Dixon
Tel: 07966 206671
shaunhush99@yahoo.co.uk
eatandsleeplindisfarne.co.uk
West Mains House, Beal, Berwick upon Tweed, TD15 2PD

KING WILLIAMS
COLLEGE

123b

King William's College, the only independent school in the Isle of Man, is located on Castletown Bay in the south of the island. The College lets its 3 boarding houses during the school holidays to individuals & groups of any size up to 130. Each house has a large lounge & a small kitchen. Catering can be provided for groups of 20+. Guests have access to the College's impressive grounds. Sports facilities, classrooms, theatre & swimming pool can be hired.

DETAILS

■ **Open** - School Holidays
■ **Beds** - 130: Colbourne House 50, School House 50, Jackson House 30
■ **Price/night** - £35pp. Enquire for whole house or whole site bookings.

CONTACT: Hannah Howland
Tel: 01624 820474 or 01624 820400
lets@kwc.im
kwc.im/community/venue-hire
King William's College, Castletown, Isle of Man, IM9 1TP

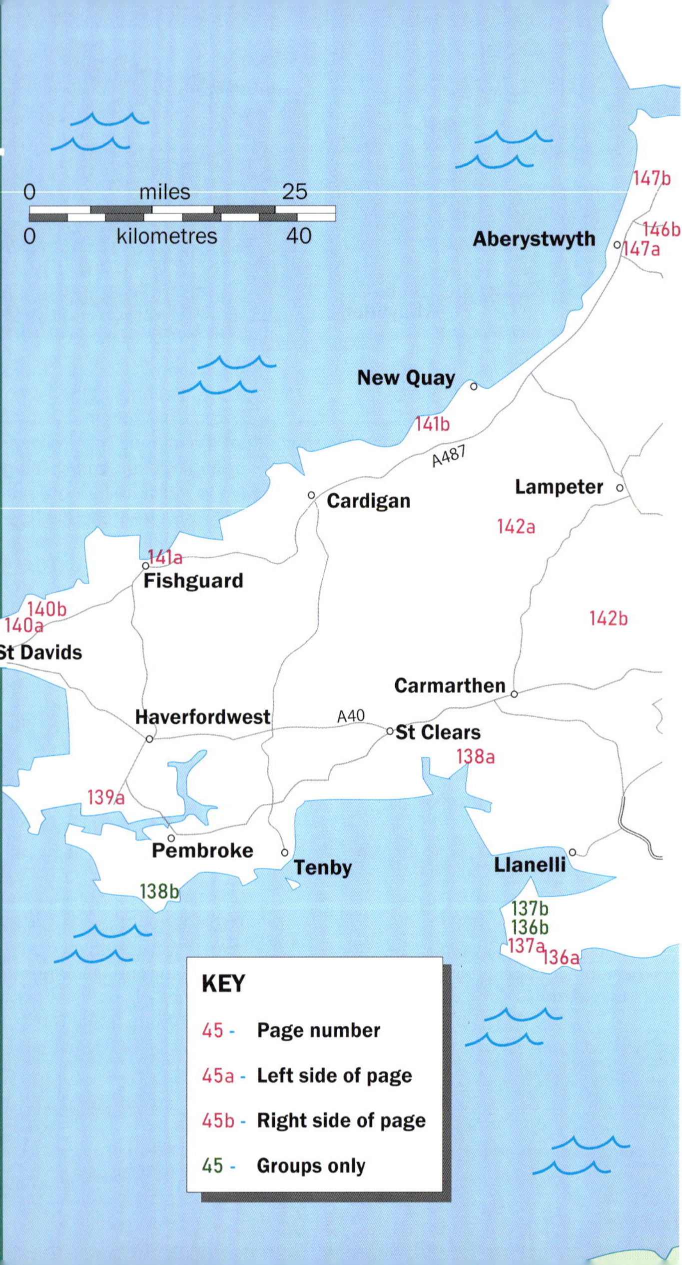

South Wales

0 miles 25
0 kilometres 40

Aberystwyth
147b
146b
147a

New Quay
141b
A487
Lampeter
Cardigan
142a
141a
Fishguard
140b
140a
142b
St Davids
Carmarthen
Haverfordwest
A40
St Clears
138a
139b
139a
Pembroke
Tenby
Llanelli
138b
137b
136b
137a 136a

KEY
45 - Page number
45a - Left side of page
45b - Right side of page
45 - Groups only

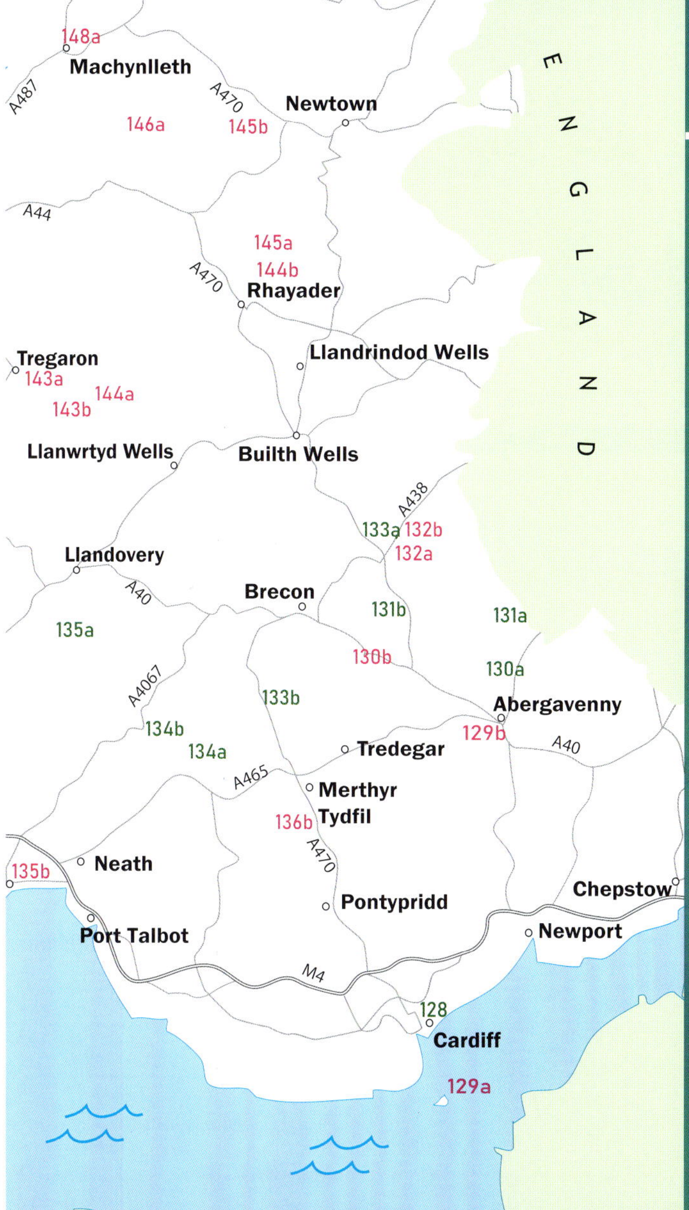
148a
Machynlleth
A487
A470
Newtown
146a
145b
A44
145a
A470
144b
Rhayader
Tregaron
143a
144a
143b
Llandrindod Wells
Llanwrtyd Wells
Builth Wells
A438
133a 132b
132a
Llandovery
A40
Brecon
131b
131a
135a
130b
130a
A4067
133b
Abergavenny
134b
129b
A40
134a
A465
Tredegar
Merthyr
Tydfil
136b
A470
135b
Neath
Pontypridd
Chepstow
Port Talbot
Newport
M4
128
Cardiff
129a
E
N
G
L
A
N
D

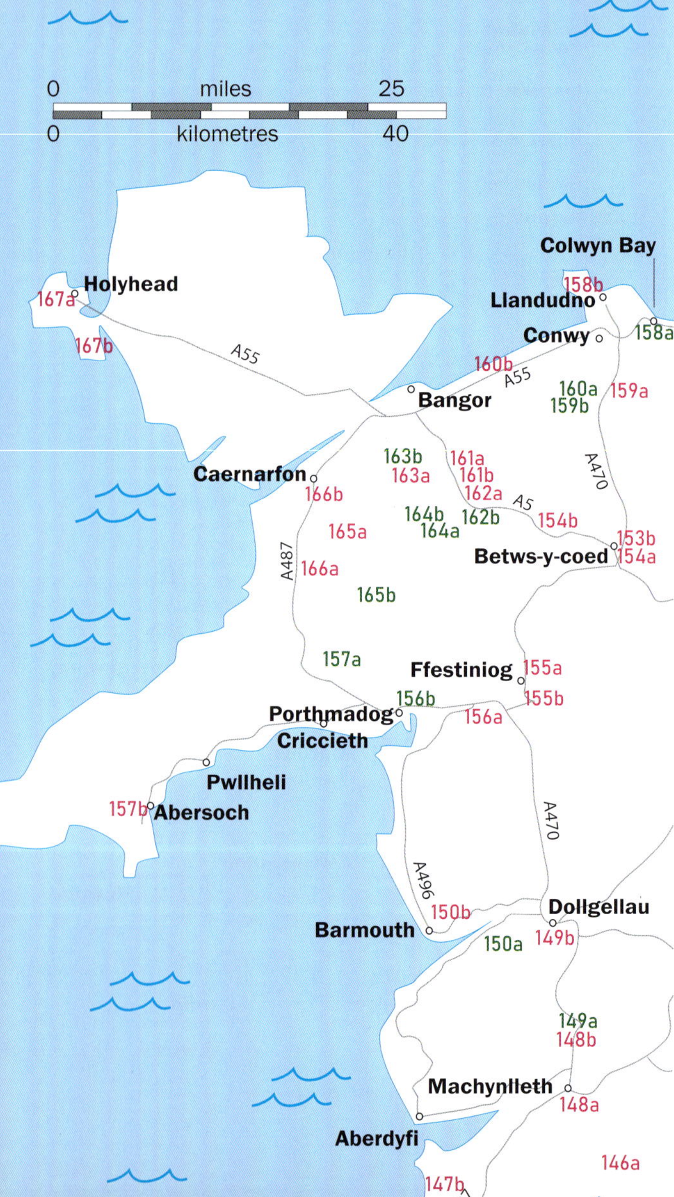
North Wales
0 miles 25
0 kilometres 40
Holyhead
167a
167b
A55
Colwyn Bay
158b
Llandudno
Conwy
158a
160b
A55
Bangor
160a
159b
159a
A470
Caernarfon
163b
163a
161a
161b
166b
162a
A5
164b
162b
154b
165a
164a
153b
166a
Betws-y-coed
154a
A487
165b
157a
Ffestiniog
155a
156b
155b
Porthmadog
156a
Criccieth
Pwllheli
157b
Abersoch
A470
A496
150b
Dollgellau
Barmouth
149b
150a
149a
148b
Machynlleth
148a
Aberdyfi
146a
147b

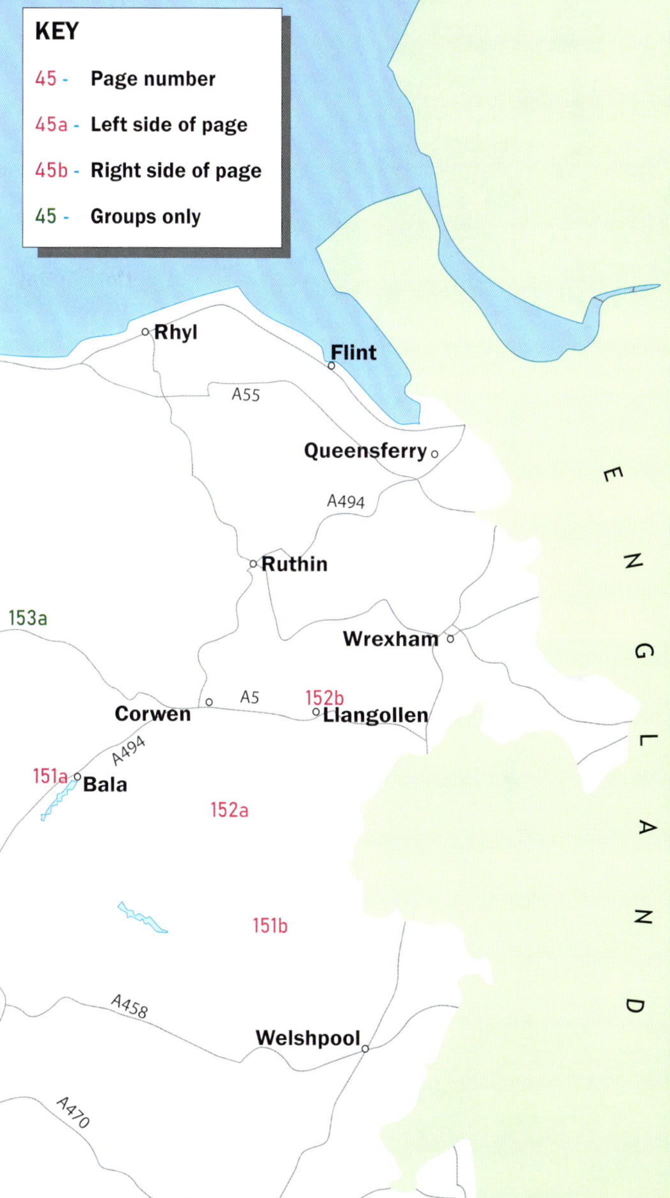
KEY
45 - Page number
45a - Left side of page
45b - Right side of page
45 - Groups only
Rhyl
Flint
A55
Queensferry
A494
Ruthin
153a
Wrexham
A5
152b
Corwen
Llangollen
A494
151a
Bala
152a
151b
A458
Welshpool
A470
145b
Newtown
ENGLAND
North Wales

CARDIFF
RESIDENTIAL CENTRE
128a

GWERSYLL YR URDD
CAERDYDD
128b

This 4-star hostel in Cardiff Bay is part of a striking modern development, sharing a roof with the world-renowned Wales Millennium Centre.

It's ideal for all kinds of groups.

With 29 ensuite bedrooms, a hall/theatre, lounges, dining hall, and classrooms.

Mae'r hostel 4-seren hwn wedi cael ei leoli ym Mae Caerdydd ac yn rannu tô gyda Chanolfan Mileniwm Cymru, ac groesffordd â Senedd Cymru
Mae'n ddelfrydol ar gyfer pob math o grwpiau.
Gyda 29 ystafell wely ensuite, neuadd/theatr, lolfa, neuadd fwyta a dosbarthiadau.

DETAILS

- **Open** - All year (occasionally available to individuals and families)
- **Beds** - 153: 3x2, 1x3, 3x4, 22x6 (all en suite)
- **Price/night** - Cardiff Residential Centre is located opposite the Senedd building in Bute Place.

CONTACT: Reception
Tel: 02920 635678
caerdydd@urdd.org
www.urdd.cymru/en/residential-centres/cardiff/
6b Bute Place, Cardiff, CF10 5AL

MANYLION

- **Ar agor** - Trwy gydol y flwyddyn ar gyfer grwpiau (ar gael i unigolion a theuluoedd ar adegau).
- **Gwlâu** - 153: 3x2, 1x3, 3x4, 22x6 (i gyd ag ensuite)
- **Pris/y noson** - Prisoedd amrywiol, cysylltwch â Gwersyll Caerdydd.

CYSYLLTU: Derbynfa
Ffôn: 02920 635678
caerdydd@urdd.org
www.urdd.cymru/cy/ein-gwersylloedd/gwersyll-caerdydd
6b Plas Bute, Caerdydd, CF10 5AL

FLAT HOLM
ISLAND ACCOMMODATION

129a

Flat Holm accommodation is located on the small island just five miles from the capital city of Cardiff, so why not visit and discover the magic of island life? Experience the wealth of history and wildlife on a guided tour, take a short walk and watch the sunset, or just sit back and relax in the cosy island pub. Mixed dormitories with bunkbeds, self-catering cottage, camping site, four individual pods, and a Yurt.

DETAILS

- **Open** - March to October.
- **Beds** - Farmhouse 24: 1x10, 1x12, 1x2 . Cottage 6: 1x dbl, 1x twin, 1x dbl sofabed. Pods 4: 4x1, Yurt 4: 1x4, Camping 20 pitches
- **Price/night** - Please enquire for prices..

CONTACT: Flat Holm booking office
Tel: 029 2087 7900
flatholmproject@cardiff.gov.uk
www.flatholmisland.com
Flat Holm Island, Seven Estuary, Cardiff

MIDDLE NINFA
BUNKHOUSE

129b

Middle Ninfa Farm, on the edge of Blaenavon World Heritage Site in the Brecon Beacons, offers bunkhouse/ cottage accommodation & camping on eleven 'remote' pitches with fine views over the Vale of Usk. Sympathetically renovated to retain its rustic charm, the 400-year-old bunkhouse provides self-catering accommodation for 6 people. BYO food, sleeping bags, towels & pillowcases. The electric heating may be cool for some in winter.

DETAILS

- **Open** - All year.
- **Beds** - 6: 1x4, 1x2 (dbl) plus camping.
- **Price/night** - From £13pp. Weekly rate for 6 persons £430-480. Camping (inc hammocks) £6 pp + pitch fee of £6/£12.

CONTACT: Richard and Rohan Lewis
Tel: 01873 854662 or 07497 818354
bookings@middleninfa.co.uk
www.middleninfa.co.uk
Middle Ninfa Farm, Llanellen, Abergavenny, NP7 9LE

SMITHYS
BUNKHOUSE

130a

Smithy's Bunkhouse accommodates groups of up to 24 in two dormitories of 12 bunks.

Located on a working farm just outside Abergavenny in the Brecon Beacons, there are great walking/running and cycling routes from the doorstep.

A range of outdoor activities can be organised if required. There's a traditional pub serving bar snacks and meals at the end of the drive for the times you don't want to self-cater.

DETAILS

- **Open** - All year
- **Beds** - 24 : 2x12 + camping
- **Price/night** - From £20pp

CONTACT: Tracey
Tel: 07482 226103 or 07885 257788
tracey@smithysbunkhouse.net
www.smithysbunkhouse.net
Lower House Farm, Pantygelli,
Abergavenny, Monmouthshire, NP7 7HR

THE STAR
BUNKHOUSE

130b

Perfect for exploring Bannau Brycheiniog (Brecon Beacons) National Park. In the village of Bwlch alongside the Beacons Way. Expect a warm & comfortable stay in a dog friendly bunkhouse. Spacious bedrooms, lounge/dining areas, fully equipped self-catering kitchen, BBQ, hot showers, drying room & off-road parking. Accommodation for up to 20 people over 6 bedrooms. Private bedrooms or sole use for individuals, couples & groups.

DETAILS

- **Open** - All year. All day.
- **Beds** - 20 beds over 6 bedrooms: 1 or 2 bunkbeds in each bedroom (including some single-over double bunkbeds)
- **Price/night** - Private bedrooms from £27 per room. Sole use from £280.

CONTACT: Emma & Peter Harrison
Tel: 01874 730080 or 07341 906937
info@starbunkhouse.com
www.starbunkhouse.com
Brecon Road (A40), Bwlch, Brecon,
Powys, LD3 7RQ

THE WAIN HOUSE

131a

BRECON
BUNKHOUSE

131b

This old stone barn continues the tradition of 900 years when Llanthony Priory next door provided accommodation. Surrounded by the Black Mountains in the Brecon Beacons National Park, it is your ideal base for all mountain activities. There is a fully equipped kitchen, hot showers, heating throughout and a wood burning stove. Small or large groups are welcome with sole use and a minimum charge. Two pubs nearby offer real ale and bar food.

Brecon Bunkhouse is a spacious, comfortable bunkhouse in the Brecon Beacons. Offering fantastic value for money with a large self-catering kitchen, big dining room and a separate sitting room with a cosy wood-burner. Situated in a small valley in the Black Mountains, the eastern part of the Brecon Beacons National Park, with mountain walks from the door. Area is ideal for horse riding, mountain bikes & white water canoeing. Nice pub 15 min walk (bring a torch!)

DETAILS

- **Open** - All year. All day. No restrictions.
- **Beds** - 16: 1x8, 1x4, 1x6.
- **Price/night** - £45 per person for a two-night weekend, with a minimum charge of £450. Mid-week reductions.

CONTACT: Cordelia Passmore
Tel: 01873 890359
courtfarm@llanthony.co.uk
www.llanthonybunkbarn.co.uk
Court Farm, Llanthony, Abergavenny, Monmouthshire, NP7 7NN

DETAILS

- **Open** - All year. All day.
- **Beds** - 28: 1x10, 1x8, 1x6, 2x2,
- **Price/night** - £280 per weeknight. £700 for a whole weekend, usually with no Sunday checkout time.

CONTACT: Paul and Emily Turner
Tel: 01874 711500 or 07855 967399
breconbunkhouse@gmail.com
www.brecon-bunkhouse.co.uk
Cwmfforest Farm, Pengenfford, Talgarth, Brecon, LD3 0EU

THE LIVING ENERGY
BARNS

132a

The Living Energy B and B is located in the Brecon Beacons National Park with 360 degree panoramic views from the Black Mountains to Wye Valley.

There is direct access to the Black Mountains and 6 acres of gardens.

A remote & peaceful location but only 15 mins from Hay-on-Wye & Talgarth.

DETAILS

- **Open** - April to October
- **Beds** - 27/31: Living Energy Barn 16 /20 4x4/5. Spring Barn 7: 2x2, 1x3. Cottage 4: 2x2
- **Price/night** - Price guide from £30 per person per night. Pricing depends on booking size and length of stay.

CONTACT: David Avis
Tel: 07831 755187 or 01497 847103
lcfholidays@yahoo.com
www.thelivingenergyholidays.co.uk
The Living Energy, Lower Cwmcadarn Farm, Velindre, LD30TB

RIVER WYE
HOSTEL AND CAMPSITE

132b

Nestled in 7 acres of parkland on the banks of the river Wye in the pretty village of Glasbury-on-Wye. Perfect for individuals & groups of up to 150, it is an ideal base exploring this beautiful part of the world. Canoeists, paddle boarders & wild swimmers have direct access to the river Wye. Situated on the Wye Valley Walk and close to the Offa's Dyke. National cycle route 8 and 42 are on the doorstep. Brecon Beacons nearby.

DETAILS

- **Open** - All year
- **Beds** - 150: Hostel 26: 1x12, 1x6, 1x4, 2x2. Main House 124: dorms and dbl/twin.
- **Price/night** - Dorm from £25. Private rooms from: £50 (2 beds), £150 (6 beds), £300 (12 beds). Enquire for sole use.

CONTACT: Rob Finley
Tel: 01432 264 807 or 07980 126 562
bookings@riverwyehostel.co.uk
www.riverwyehostel.co.uk
Glasbury House, Glasbury-on-Wye, Powys HR3 5NW

WOODLANDS
BUNKHOUSE

133a

Woodlands Bunkhouse is a converted stable block set in the 10 acre grounds of Woodlands Centre. It overlooks the River Wye & has wonderful views of the Black Mountains. The historic town of Hay-on-Wye is nearby. The Bunkhouse provides comfortable, accommodation for families and groups, with availability at weekends and during school holidays. There's a well equipped kitchen and dining room and 25 beds in 9 rooms, including some accessible rooms. Outdoor activities available. Group or family bookings only.

DETAILS

- **Open** - All year. 24 hours.
- **Beds** - 22 in 9 rooms of 1 to 6 plus camping in the grounds.
- **Price/night** - £20pp + VAT. Group or family bookings only.

CONTACT: Chris Pierce
Tel: 01497 847272
chris.pierce@oxfordshireoutdoors.co.uk
www.oxfordshireoutdoorlearningservice.co.uk
Glasbury on Wye, Powys, HR3 5LP

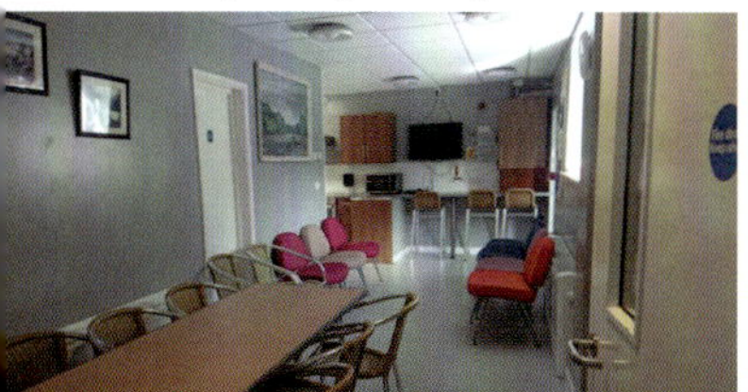

COED OWEN
BUNKHOUSE

133b

Set on a hill farm in the heart of the Brecon Beacons, 2 hours' walk from Pen Y Fan. This Bunkhouse provides well appointed self-catering accommodation; ideal for stag, hen and family parties. Outdoor activities can be organised or there's direct access onto the mountains and waterfalls close by. Bike Park Wales, Merthyr Tydfil, Penderyn Whisky and Brecon are all within easy reach. The pub at the bottom of the drive serves great food and fine ales.

DETAILS

- **Open** - All year. All day.
- **Beds** - 26: 2x6, 1x10, 1 dbl, 1 twin.
- **Price/night** - From £25pp with bed linen. Min of two nights at weekends. Min of 18 people.

CONTACT: Molly Rees
Tel: 07508 544044
info@breconbeaconsbunkhouse.co.uk
www.breconbeaconsbunkhouse.co.uk
Coed Owen Farm, Cwmtaff, Merthyr Tydfil, CF48 2HY

CLYNGWYN
BUNKHOUSE
134a

Groups of 4-19 can book sole use of Clyngwyn Bunkhouse. Mins away from waterfalls & great walking. It has a fully equipped kitchen, big lounge, central heating & 3 bedrooms with 14 single beds & two sets of bunks. Outside fire pit & covered BBQ area. Catering & organised outdoor activities if required. Also available: exclusive use of large campsite and use of a 90' polytunnel can be arranged for a range of activities.

DETAILS

- **Open** - All year
- **Beds** - 27: B/house 19. Farmhouse: 8. Camping: up to 200
- **Price/night** - B/house £570. Farmhouse Camping £10pp. Camper Vans £25.

CONTACT: Linda Williams
Tel: 01639 722930 or 07828 878996
stay@clyngwyn.co.uk
www.bunkhouse-south-wales.co.uk
Clyngwyn Farm, Ystradfellte Rd,
Pontneddfechan, Powys, SA11 5US

SLEEPING GIANT
BUNKHOUSE
134b

Large bunkhouse in the Brecon Beacons provides great value, comfortable & flexible accommodation for groups of up to 47. In a quiet location with direct access to great walking, water falls & wild swimming. Instructor lead outdoor activities can be provided if required. Sitting in 8 acres of private grounds with a BBQ, large outdoor fire pit & plenty of off-road parking. Also there's a 2 person apartment & a campsite.

DETAILS

- **Open** - All year
- **Beds** - 47: 2x2 (twin), 2x4, 1x5, 5x6. Plus apartment: 1x2. Plus camping
- **Price/night** - Sole use for 25 people £600. £15 for each additional person

CONTACT: Steve Rose
Tel: 01639 730518 or 07564 823180
enquiries@absoluteadventure.co.uk
absoluteadventure.co.uk
Absolute Adventure, Rhongyr Isaf Centre
Pen-Y-Cae, Upper Swansea Valley,
Powys. SA9 1GB

ALMOND LODGE
BRECON BEACONS

135a

Formerly YHA Llanddeusant, Almond Lodge Brecon Beacons (Bannau Brycheiniog) has been tastefully refurbished. It offers bunkhouse accommodation to groups of up to 26, let as exclusive hire of the whole building. It's ideal for clubs, universities, corporate team building and friends & family get-togethers. It is the perfect place for a retreat, for walking, hiking, running, cycling or mountain biking, kayaking or hiking to wild swim spots and exploring this stunningly wild part of the country.

DETAILS

- **Open** - All year.
- **Beds** - 26 (exclusive use only)
- **Price/night** - Sole use only: Weekdays £350. Weekends & Band Hols £450.

CONTACT: Jon Dodd
Tel: 07799 440557
jon@almondlodgeBB.com
almondlodgeBB.com
The Old Red Lion, Llanddeusant,
Llangadog, Carmarthenshire, SA19 9UL

CWTSH
HOSTEL

135b

Cwtsh hostel is new, exciting and trend-setting. Situated in the heart of Swansea City Centre, overlooking Castle Gardens, Cwtsh Hostel provides a modern and unique base to explore the city and surrounding areas.

Choose from pod-bunk or private accommodation. Electric bike hire and introductory Welsh classes - bendigedig available. Backpackers, explorers, families, party-goers, schools and freelancers are all welcomed.

DETAILS

- **Open** - All year
- **Beds** - 54
- **Price/night** -   Pod-bunk beds from £20. Private rooms from £50.

CONTACT: Llyr Roberts
Tel: 01792 986556
hello@cwtsh-hostel.co.uk
www.cwtsh-hostel.co.uk
10-14 Castle St, Swansea SA1 1JF

EASTERN SLADE
BARN
136a

RHOSSILI
BUNKHOUSE
136b

Eastern Slade Barn is a luxury farmhouse conversion on a working farm on the Gower Peninsula. The Gower has glorious beaches, castles and traffic free lanes. The coast path passes through the farm. Port Eynon seaside village is a 30 min walk, while Oxwich Bay with its castle, beach & hotel serving tasty meals is just 20 mins walk. Camping available and weddings/birthdays welcome.

Rhossili 4* Bunkhouse is situated at the end of the Gower Peninsula, in the first Area of Outstanding Natural Beauty.

Within easy walking distance of three glorious beaches, (including Rhossili Bay which has been voted the best beach in Europe & in the top ten in the World).

Ideal for families & groups, it is perfectly located for a wide range of outdoor activities including walking, surfing, paddle boarding, cycling & climbing.

    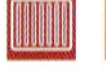    

DETAILS

- **Open** - All year. 24 hours.
- **Beds** - 15: 1x5, 2x2/3 (double with bunk above), 1x2, 2 in lounge
- **Price/night** - Low season: £20pp, £200 sole use, 2 nights min. High season: £25pp, £260 sole use, 3 nights min. £30 cleaning charge .

DETAILS

- **Open** - All year except January. Check in 4-9pm. Check out by 10:30am.
- **Beds** - 22: 1x4, 2x3, 4x2. + 4 sofa-beds in lounge.
- **Price/night** - Sole use £525.

CONTACT: Kate
Tel: 07970 969814
tynrheol@hotmail.com
easternsladebarngower.co.uk
Eastern Slade Farm, Oxwich, Gower,
Swansea, SA3 1NA

CONTACT: Josephine Higgins
Tel: 01792 391509
manager@rhossilibunkhouse.com
www.rhossilibunkhouse.com
Rhossili, Swansea, SA3 1PL

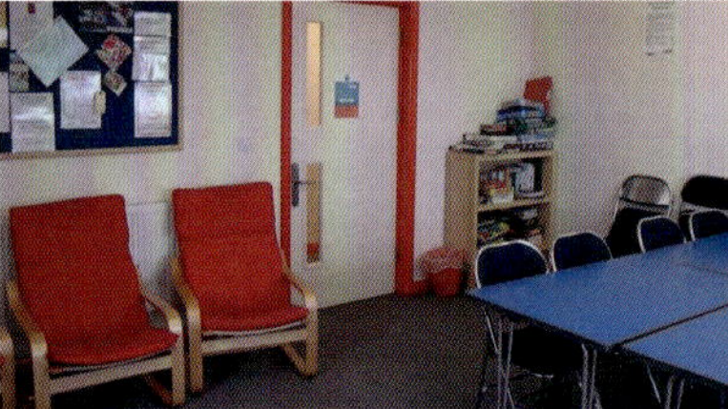

HARDINGSDOWN
BUNKHOUSE

137a

Hardingsdown Bunkhouse and The Chaffhouse both provide accommodation for families or groups.
Comfortable and well appointed they are perfect for exploring Gower and all it has to offer. The properties can be hired individually or together. Rates vary with numbers.

DETAILS

■ **Open** - All year. All day.
■ **Beds** - 22: Bunkhouse 12: 1x5, 1x3, 2x2. Chaffhouse: 10: 1x4 3x2
■ **Price/night** - Hardingsdown Bunkhouse: (12 people max) £220. The Chaffhouse: (10 people max) £220. Midweek. £200. Enquire for rates for both units together. Weekly rates available. INDIVIDUALS mid week only, £35pp.

CONTACT: Allison Tyrrell
Tel: 01792 386222
bunkhousegower@btconnect.com
www.hardingsdowncottages.co.uk
Lower Hardingsdown Farm, Llangennith, Gower, Swansea, SA3 1HT

ST MADOC
CENTRE

137b

Superb facilities for groups of 30-81 on The Gower Peninsular. With 76 acres of fields, woodland, headland & coastline, tennis & volleyball courts, playing fields & a campfire area, St Madoc Centre is ideally suited to schools, youth & church groups, corporate events, weddings & friends & family get-togethers. Optional outdoor activities & catered packages available for school groups.

DETAILS

■ **Open** - All year
■ **Beds** - 81: 2x2, 2x4, 1x5, 4x10, 2x12. Mostly en suite.
■ **Price/night** - From £23.10pp. Youth groups from £19.25pp. Min group size varies: from 30 (winter) to 60 (summer hols). Discounts for groups over 50.

CONTACT: Heather Lyne
Tel: 01792 386291
info@stmadoc.co.uk
www.stmadoc.co.uk/
LLanmadoc, Gower, Swansea, SA3 1DE.

PANTYRATHRO
INTERNATIONAL HOSTEL
138a

STACKPOLE
CENTRE
138b

Llansteffan is a beautiful village at the tip of the Towi River & Carmarthen Bay. The sandy beaches below the castle offer sun bathing and relaxation. The virtually traffic free country lanes are ideal for cycling. The Wales Coastal Path is on the doorstep and the city of Carmarthen is close by. The hostel provides private rooms, family rooms and en suite rooms.

The Stackpole Centre is the perfect venue for large families/groups, universities, schools & outdoor activities. Close to wild woodlands & stunning beaches. It comprises four large group houses, two of which are dog friendly, as well as three holiday cottages. Book by the house or book the whole centre for your sole use.

  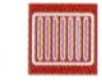           

DETAILS

- **Open** - February to January. 24 hours.
- **Beds** - 43: 1x10, 1x8, 1x6, 3x4, 1x3, 2x2
- **Price/night** - Private rooms: Twin/double £49 each. 4 bed rooms available privately for 1,2,3, or 4 people. Priced from £20 per person enquire for details. Groups welcome.

CONTACT: Ken Knuckles
Tel: 01267 241721 or 01267 241014
kenknuckles@hotmail.com
www.backpackershostelwales.com
Pantyrathro International Hostel,
Llansteffan, Carmarthen, SA33 5AJ

DETAILS

- **Open** - All year. All day. Reception 9-5.
- **Beds** - 139: Kingfisher 44:10 rooms. Kestrel: 38:13 rooms. Swan 24:13 rooms. Shearwater 15:7 rooms. Rosemary, Lavender & Thyme each 6: 3 rooms.
- **Price/night** - Kingfisher £834, Kestrel £684, Swan £714, Shearwater £440. Check website for cottage prices.

CONTACT: Stackpole Reception
Tel: 01646 623110
stackpole.bookings@nationaltrust.org.uk
www.nationaltrust.org.uk
The Old Home Farm Yard, Stackpole, nr Pembroke, Pembrokeshire, SA71 5DQ

UPPER NEESTON
LODGES

139a

Environmentally sensitive barn conversions close to the Milford Haven Waterway in the Pembrokeshire Coast National Park. Ideal for divers, climbers, walkers or family get-togethers. The four independent 4 star lodges are all independent and self catering. There is access to garden/patio, laundry/drying room, secure storage and ample parking.

DETAILS

■ **Open** - All year. Check in from 4pm. Check out before 10.30am.
■ **Beds** - 23: Cowshed 10: 1x6,1x4. Barn 8: 1x6,1x2, Granary 1x3. Dairy 1x2
■ **Price/night** - From £20 (inc linen). Min 2 nights at w/ends (3 nights b/h). Sole use: min 6 in Barn, 8 in Cowshed. Smaller groups/individuals by agreement.

CONTACT: Sean or Mandy Tilling
Tel: 01646 690750
mail@upperneeston.co.uk
www.upperneeston.co.uk
Upper Neeston Farm, Dale Road,
Herbrandston, Milford Haven, SA73 3RY

SKOMER
ISLAND HOSTEL

139b

Staying overnight on Skomer Island provides the perfect chance to get away from the hustle and bustle of everyday.

You'll be one of a maximum of 16-overnight guests staying in the 3-star hostel accommodation, nestled at the very heart of the island. With so few people, there's always a quiet place with amazing wildlife to encounter just around the corner. Beautiful, peaceful, and entirely unforgettable.

DETAILS

■ **Open** - 1st April - 30th September
■ **Beds** - 16: 1x5, 1x4, 1x3, 2x2
■ **Price/night** - From: April: £65pp. May/June/July: £90pp. August/September: £55pp. Children 12 & under: half price.

CONTACT: Booking office
Tel: 01656 724100
islands@welshwildlife.org
www.welshwildlife.org
Skomer Island, Martins Haven,
Haverfordwest, SA62 3BJ.

CAERHAFOD
LODGE
140a

OLD SCHOOL
HOSTEL
140b

Situated between the famous cathedral city of St Davids and the Irish ferry port of Fishguard, the 4* Lodge overlooks the spectacular Pembrokeshire coastline. Within walking distance of the Sloop Inn at Porthgain and the internationally renowned Coastal Path. An ideal stopover for cyclists with the Celtic Trail cycle route passing the bottom of the drive. The lodge sleeps 23 in 5 separate rooms, all en suite with great showers. Dogs welcome by arrangement.

Escape to this wonderful rugged corner of the Pembrokeshire Coast National Park. Old School Hostel is in Trefin, a pretty village which has a pub and a café, just a quarter of a mile from the world famous coast path. Circular walks from the door take you to stunning wild beaches & harbours. The cathedral city of St. Davids and the popular Whitesands Bay are 20 minutes by car.

DETAILS

DETAILS

- **Open** - All year. Check in from 5pm, check out 10.30 am. All day access.
- **Beds** - 23: 3x4, 1x5, 1x6.
- **Price/night** - Adult: £25. Under 16: £20. Sole use (min 2-nights) from £425.

- **Open** - All year, but we strongly advise you check availability first.
- **Beds** - 22: 1x6, 3x2, 2x2/3 (bunk with dbl lower bed), 1x4 (1 dbl + 1 bunk). Single occupancy available.
- **Price/night** - From £32. Single occ from £45. Sole use from £400.

CONTACT: Carolyn Rees
Tel: 01348 837859
Caerhafod@aol.com
www.caerhafod.co.uk
Llanrhian, St Davids, Haverfordwest,
Pembrokeshire, SA62 5BD

CONTACT: Paul
Tel: 07845 625005
paul.moger@gmail.com
oldschoolhostel.com
Ffordd-yr-Afon, Trefin, Haverfordwest,
Pembrokeshire, SA62 5AU

THE
HAMILTONS

141a

James John Hamilton House and Hamilton Lodge are TWO SEPARATE HOSTELS but sit side by side in the coastal town of Fishguard close to the Pembrokeshire Coastal Path. They provide B&B rooms, a holiday cottage and quality self-catering accommodation for groups of up to 18/20 people. Fishguard is a natural harbour surrounded by the sweeping sands of Cardigan Bay, regularly visited by communities of grey seals and dolphins.

DETAILS

- **Open** - All year
- **Beds** - 20:   James John 12: 2x twin, 2xdbl, 1x4 (family). Hamilton Lodge 8: 1x4, 1xtwin, 1xdbl.
- **Price/night** - Please enquire for prices.

CONTACT: Quentin or Steve
Tel: 07505 562939 or 07813 687570
hamiltonlodgefishguard@gmail.com
www.hamiltonlodgefishguard.co.uk
19a and 23 Hamilton Street, Fishguard, Pembrokeshire SA65 9HL

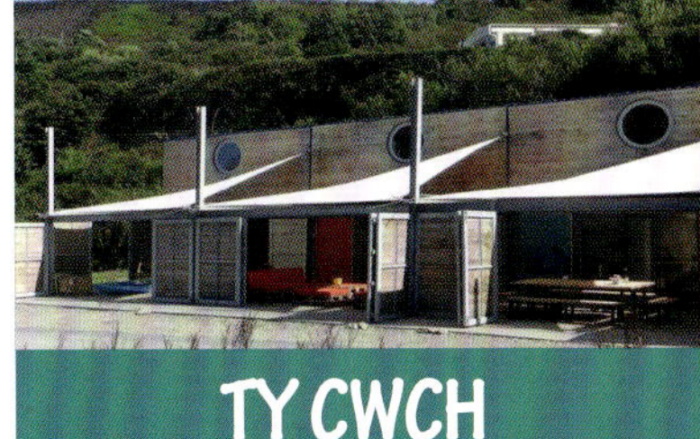

TY CWCH
BOATHOUSE

141b

Contemporary, quirky, award-winning, bunkhouse just metres from the sea on the Cardigan Heritage Coast. Built from mainly recycled materials the Boathouse sleeps 12 in 3 insulated first floor pods. Downstairs three further pods house a full kitchen, dining room, sitting area and utility room. These open out onto a covered deck with seating/dining. Right on the Wales Coast Path, easy access for launching boats, great fishing and swimming.

DETAILS

- **Open** - All year
- **Beds** - 12: 3x4
- **Price/night** - Sole use: From £136. Discounts for stays of 3+ night. Please book by phone to secure discounts.

CONTACT: Nigel Humphrey
Tel: 07753 700712 or 07919 891434
enquiries@tycwch.wales
tycwch.wales
Cwmtydu, Llwyndafydd, Llandysul, SA44 6LQ

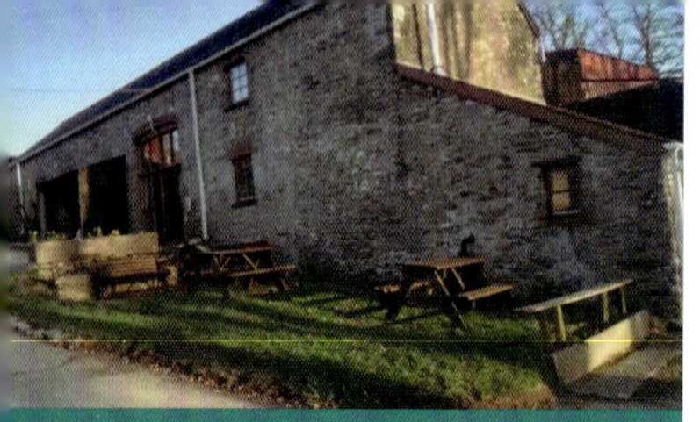

THE LONG BARN

142a

Penrhiw is an organic farm with views over the Teifi Valley. The stunning Ceredigion Coast and the Cambrian Mountains are an easy drive away and the busy small town of Llandysul (1.5 miles) has all essential supplies. The farm's location is ideal for exploring, studying or simply admiring the Welsh countryside. Local activities include swimming, climbing, abseiling, canoeing, farm walks and cycling.

DETAILS

- **Open** - All year. All day.
- **Beds** - 43: Long Barn 31: 1x15, 1x14, 1x2. Cowshed: 6: 1x6. Annex 3: 1x3 (dbl+sgl). Cwtch 3: 1x3 (dbl+sofa bed)
- **Price/night** - £20pp. Discount for groups and mid-week bookings.

CONTACT: Tom or Eva
Tel: 01559 363200 or 07733 026874
cowcher@thelongbarn.co.uk
www.thelongbarn.co.uk
Penrhiw, Capel Dewi, Llandysul,
Ceredigion, SA44 4PG

GILFACH WEN
BARN

142b

A homely, high quality, bunkhouse for individuals, extended families or groups on a working farm. The large social area is ideal for reunions or celebrations. There are 7 family bedrooms including one downstairs for disabled.
Perfect for exploring Carmarthenshire, Pembrokeshire, Brecon Beacons, Cambrian Mountains and the Gower. Walker, cyclist, dog & equestrian friendly. Viillage pub close by.

DETAILS

- **Open** - All year. All day.
- **Beds** - 32: 3x6,1x5,1x4,1x3,1x2. Total of 10 double beds & 12 single beds in 7 bedrooms.
- **Price/night** - From £19.00pp. Rooms from £50. Sole use from £450.

CONTACT: Jillie
Tel: 07780 476737 or 01267 240077
info@gilfachwenbarn.co.uk
www.gilfachwenbarn.co.uk
Gilfach Wen, Brechfa, Carmarthenshire,
SA32 7QL

CABAN CARON
HOSTEL

143a

Newly renovated to a high standard, this first floor hostel sleeps 8/10 across 2 en suite rooms. The hostel is situated in the vibrant town of Tregaron in the Cambrian Mountains. The area is a haven for walkers & cyclists who want to get away from the crowds, with access to the mountains from the doorstep. For mountain bikers Brechfa Forest & Bwlch Nant yr Arian MTB trails are a short drive away.

DETAILS

- **Open** - All year
- **Beds** - 8/10: 2x4 + 2 x camp beds
- **Price/night** - £25 a bed, £90 a room, £170 sole use for 8 people. £200 sole use for 10 people. Duvets £7.50 per stay.

CONTACT: Rhydian Wilson
Tel: 07813 702 982
rhydian@icyuk.co.uk
icyuk.co.uk
Yr Hen Popty – The Old Bakery, Pentre Uchaf, Tregaron, Ceredigionymru SY25 6NF

TYNCORNEL
HOSTEL

143b

Tyncornel Hostel is a former farmhouse and self-contained Shepherd's Hut in stunning Cambrian Mountain scenery at the head of the beautiful Doethie Valley. It is one of the most remote hostels in Wales, favoured by walkers, cyclists, and birdwatchers. Beds for 16 (hostel) + 4 (shepherd's hut). There is a cosy common room with wood-burning stove, two dormitories and a kitchen.

DETAILS

- **Open** - All year. Reception 5pm -11pm, 7am -10am.
- **Beds** - 20: Hostel 2x8. Shepherds Hut 1x4 (family)
- **Price/night** - £18,£9(under18s) Private rooms available. Whole hostel £250. Campers £10. Shepherd's Hut £100.

CONTACT: Janet or Richard
Tel: 01980 629259 or 07943 091941
Tyncornel.bookings@btinternet.com
www.elenydd-hostels.co.uk
Llanddewi Brefi, Tregaron, Ceredigion, SY25 6PH

DOLGOCH
HOSTEL
144a

Experience the peace of the remote Tywi Valley at this 17th century farmhouse. A traditional simple hostel owned by Elenydd Wilderness Trust. It has hot showers, log burner, kitchen, dormitories, private rooms & camping. You can also book the whole hostel. The Lôn Las Cymru and the Cambrian Way pass nearby and there are mountain tracks to explore. Ideal for bird-watchers, walkers, cyclists, wild swimmers and lovers of the solitude of the Cambrian Mountains

■ **Open** - All year. 24 hours. Reception 5pm -10pm, 8am -10am.
■ **Beds** - 20: 3 rooms inc private rooms.
■ **Price/night** - £15 per adult, £7.50 (under 18). 4 bed room £55. 6 bed room £80. Whole hostel £250. Campers £10.

CONTACT: Gillian Keen
Tel: 01440 730226
dolgoch.bookings@elenydd-hostels.co.uk
www.elenydd-hostels.co.uk
Tregaron, Ceredigion, SY25 6NR

BEILI NEUADD
BUNKHOUSE
144b

A converted 18th century stone barn in stunning countryside just 2 miles from the small market town of Rhayader.

Gateway to Elan Valley and the Cambrian Mountains. On three National Cycle routes and Trans Cambrian Route.

Beili Neuadd offers a centrally heated barn. It sleeps 16 in 3 en suite rooms and includes a fully equipped kitchen/ dining room, drying room and a lovely outside space with a fire-pit. There is also a self contained annex sleeping 4.

■ **Open** - All year.
■ **Beds** - Barn 16: 2x6,1x4. Annex: 4 1x4
■ **Price/night** - From £25pp. Sole use from £295.

CONTACT: Ruth Ward
Tel: 07961 210612
info@beilineuadd.co.uk
www.beilineuaddaccommodation.co.uk
St Harmon, Rhayader, LD6 5NS

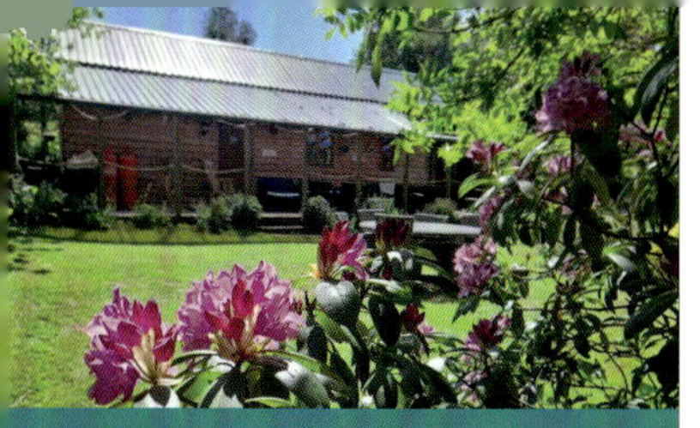

MID WALES
BUNKHOUSE
145a

Mid Wales Bunkhouse has a superb unspoilt rural location, close to the Elan Valley, with a stunning natural garden.

There's walking and biking from the door, and room for your horse. Fully equipped for self-catering. Meals are available on request. Bell tent and camping.

Welcomes groups or individuals.

DETAILS
■ **Open** - All year. 24 hours. Arrive after 4pm (advise if after 7pm), leave by 11am.
■ **Beds** - 25: Bunkhouse 19, plus bell tent & camping
■ **Price/night** - £25pp, 6-bed room £125. 14-bed room £260. Sole use of bunkhouse (21 people) £310.

CONTACT: Norma Leadbetter
Tel: 07926 781394 or 07585 998499
enquiries@woodhousefarmholidays.co.uk
www.woodhousefarmholidays.co.uk
Woodhouse Farm, St Harmon,
Rhayader, LD6 5LY

BWTHYN BACH
BUNKHOUSE
145b

Bwthyn Bach Bunkhouse, in Trefeglwys village in rural Mid Wales, is run by a small trust. It sleeps 17 across 5 rooms. Facilities are simple & add to the quirky feel of the 300 year old Grade II building. There's a kitchen/diner with hot water, kettle, electric cooker, microwave, fridge, freezer & the basic crockery/cutlery you'll need. A wood-burning stove for warmth and separate dining room has space for big groups. BYO bedding.

DETAILS
■ **Open** - All year.
■ **Beds** - 17: 1x6/7, 1x3/4, 1x2/3, 1xdbl, 1xsgl + camping
■ **Price/night** - From £25pp (+ £50 cleaning fee for sole use groups). Children & Concessions £12/ 15pp. Group rates available on request.

CONTACT: Amy
Tel: 07975 994164
hello@bwthynbach.com
www.bwthynbach.com
Trefeglwys, Caersws, Powys. SY17 5QE

HAFREN FOREST
HIDEAWAY

146a

Welcome to the edge of Hafren Forest. Choose from catered, self-catered exclusive group accommodation, or B&B with optional dinners.

The bedrooms offer simplicity and comfort, for a peaceful sleep. When booking B&B you have exclusive hire of your bedroom.

Unwind in the spacious lounge or enjoy breathtaking views in the dining room, you won't be disappointed. Perfect for outdoor enthusiasts or for those who just want to sit back and relax.

DETAILS

- **Open** - All year.
- **Beds** - 13: 2x2, 1x4, 1x5
- **Price/night** - Please enquire for prices.

CONTACT: Sarah Hackshall
Tel: 07871 740514
info@hafrenforesthideaway.com
hafrenforesthideaway.com
Staylittle, Llanbrynmair, SY19 7DB

PLAS DOLAU
COUNTRY HOUSE HOSTEL

146b

Plas Dolau is set in 25 acres just 3 miles from Aberystwyth. Ideal for exploring West Wales, walking, cycling, riding, fishing & golf. The mansion has mainly dormitory style accommodation for up to 45. An adjoining Swedish style farmhouse sleeps another 15. Plas Dolau includes meeting rooms, dining rooms, games room & outdoor areas. Suited to youth groups, field courses, retreats, house parties or individuals.

DETAILS

- **Open** - All year. 24 hours.
- **Beds** - 49: Main house: 45 (+cots). Farmhouse: 4
- **Price/night** - From £30 (inc b/fast) to £90 (private, en suite, full b/fast). From £700 whole mansion. From £450 half mansion.

CONTACT: Sam Bennett
Tel: 01970 617834
sam@plasdolau.co.uk
www.plasdolau.co.uk
Lovesgrove, Aberystwyth, SY23 3HP

ABERYSTWYTH
UNI BUNKHOUSE
147a

Aberystwyth University Bunkhouse is on the Wales Coast Path, close to beaches, dramatic walking and white knuckle mountain biking. Aberystwyth has all the attractions of a Victorian seaside town with the added adventure of an ancient castle and thriving nightlife. Accommodation is in single rooms with shared self-catering kitchens and bathrooms. Meals available. Ideal for education trips, conferences or those looking for a base for an outdoors group.

DETAILS

- **Open** - All year. Reception 9am-5pm.
- **Beds** - 90 Individual bedrooms
- **Price/night** - £42.00 (2+nights) or £48.00. Reduced rates for educational groups.

CONTACT: Conference Office
Tel: 01970 621960
constaff@aber.ac.uk
www.aber.ac.uk/en/visitors/bunkhouse
Penbryn Reception, Aberystwyth
University, Penbryn, Penglais, SY23 3BY

BORTH
YOUTH HOSTEL
147b

With 4 miles of stunning beach just 20 metres from the front door, Borth Youth Hostel is perfect for a beach holiday. This Edwardian house has 11 bedrooms and is a great base for visits to the Centre for Alternative Technology, Aberystwyth or the beautiful Dyfi Biosphere. Snowdonia National Park is just a short drive away making Borth perfect for mountain biking, golfing & surfing. The Ceredigion Coast Path passes the door. With two classrooms Borth YH is ideal for school trips. There's free WiFi, a games & TV room, bike storage & drying room. Breakfast, packed lunch & licensed bar.

DETAILS

- **Open** - All year. Check in 5pm-10.00pm. Check out 8am-10am
- **Beds** - 60
- **Price/night** - From £18 pp

CONTACT: John Taylor
Tel: 01970 871498
john@borthyouthhostel.co.uk
Borth, Ceredigion, Wales, SY24 5JS

TOAD HALL

148a

Toad Hall sits beside the River Dovey, close to Snowdonia National Park in the market town of Machynlleth. NCN Cycle Route 8 & Glyndwrs Way pass nearby. The accommodation sleeps 8 in 4 private bedrooms with small shared self-catering kitchen & single shower room. There are no bunks & no shared dormitories. Toad Hall is above the owner's family home. There is a small shed / garage available for bike storage.

DETAILS

■ **Open** - Not always open, please phone to find out and always pre-book. Please vacate rooms between 12-1pm for cleaning. No arrivals after 11pm please.
■ **Beds** - 8: 1x triple, 1xdbl, 1xtwin,1x sgl
■ **Price/night** - £27 pp. Reductions (e.g. for groups) negotiable.

CONTACT: Will
Tel: 07866 362507 or 01654 700597
Toadhallhostel@outlook.com
Railway Terrace, Doll St, Machynlleth,
Powys, SY20 8BH

BRAICH GOCH
BUNKHOUSE AND INN

148b

Braich Goch Bunkhouse is a 16th century coaching inn just 3 miles from Cadair Idris in Snowdonia National Park. The location is ideal for outdoor enthusiasts with walking, mountain biking, cycling, climbing and canoeing at all levels on the doorstep. Run by a charity, the bunkhouse sleeps 23 in 6 or more rooms (mostly en suite). A large workshop/event space can also be hired. Re-opening in June after renovations.

DETAILS

■ **Open** - Re-opening June 2026.
■ **Beds** - 23: 1x6, 4x4 1x1 (dbl). All ensuite except the dbl and a 4 bed room.
■ **Price/night** - Dorm bed: £35pp. Private double room: £50. Sole use: £830. Discounts possible for charities or groups of migrants or refugees.

CONTACT: Javier or Maria
Tel: 01654 701632
info@theannematthewstrust.org
theannematthewstrust.org
Corris, Machynlleth, Powys, SY20 9RD

CORRIS
HOSTEL
149a

Perfect for schools, education groups, family celebrations and groups of all kinds, The homely self catering hostel is a haven from the stresses of the outside world with its caring staff & cosy wood fires. Enjoy the gardens with BBQ & campfire areas. Situated in Snowdonia National Park close to Cadair Idris, Machynlleth, the CAT centre and the Dyfi Bike Park, a mecca for trail bikers. CAMRA pub, Corris Railway and Craft Centre in village.

DETAILS

- **Open** - Most of year by arrangement
- **Beds** - 38:1x18, 1x10, 1x6, 1x4. Occasionally: 1x double+2, 1x double+1
- **Price/night** - From £500 (for up to 20 people). Exclusive use only. Minimum stay: 2 nights (3 nights on Bank Holidays).

CONTACT: Michael
Tel: 01654 761686 or 07429 344132
mail@corrishostel.co.uk
Old School, Corris, Machynlleth, Powys, SY20 9TQ

PLAS ISA
149b

In the centre of Dolgellau, Eryri (Snowdonia), Plas Isa welcomes outdoor adventurers. This Grade II listed building has 5 spacious private bedrooms with 3-5 beds per room. All bathrooms are shared. The self-catering kitchen, lounge & dining room are great for socialising. The perfect base for active holidays in South Snowdonia for walkers (Cader Idris, Snowdonia Way), mountain bikers (Traws Eryri, Coed y Brenin and Dyfi Bike Park) and cyclists (Mawddach Trail, Lon Las Cymru).

DETAILS

- **Open** - All year. Check in after 4pm, check out by 10am.
- **Beds** - 19: 2x3, 2x4, 1x5 (no dorms)
- **Price/night** - Twin occ. £80. Single occ. £50. 3-10 sharing £35pp.

CONTACT: Ian and Hanneke
Tel: 07984 737066
info@plasisaguesthouse.co.uk
www.plasisaguesthouse.co.uk
Lion Street, Dolgellau, LL40 1DG

KINGS
HOSTEL

150a

Kings Hostel offers groups a uniquely private and affordable place to stay amidst the mountains of Snowdonia. With fabulous walking and cycle routes on the doorstep, a short drive to the coast and all the attractions of the National Park close by, there is something for everyone. Sleeping groups of up to 42 on a sole use basis, this historic hostel is ever popular with schools, clubs and family and friend get-togethers

DETAILS

■ **Open** - All year. Check in from 4pm. Check out by 10am
■ **Beds** - 42: Main building 18: 3x6. Annex 24: 4x6 (all en suite)
■ **Price/night** - Sole use £350 to £650 depending on season & length of stay.

CONTACT: Dave Dimmer
Tel: 01341 422392
kings@kingsofsnowdonia.com
www.kingsofsnowdonia.com
Islawrdref, Dolgellau, LL40 1TB

BUNKORAMA

150b

Whether cycling or walking you will love this cosy, clean and comfortable accommodation with breathtaking views of Cader Idris and Cardigan Bay. Handy for Cycle Route 8, Cambrian Way & Mawddach Trail. Bunkorama is an ideal place to stopover for a few days exploring the mountains, rivers and beaches of the Cambrian Coast. There is also a camping pod and campsite.

DETAILS

■ **Open** - All year.
■ **Beds** - 8 bunkbeds in 2 dorms (+ 2 sofa beds in lounge if sole booking)
■ **Price/night** - 1 bed £25 (£27 in winter). If required bedding and towel are £5 and £2 per stay. Discounts available for 2 + and 5 + nights.

CONTACT: Graham
Tel: 07738 467196 or 01341 281134
thebunkorama@gmail.com
www.bunkorama.co.uk
Gwastad Agnes Off Panorama Road, Barmouth, Gwynedd, LL42 1DX

BALA
BACKPACKERS

151a

For outdoor adventures in Snowdonia National Park, Bala Backpackers offers great value 'hostel-style' accommodation, including; 30 comfy SINGLE BEDS in 4 x 4's, 2 x 3's and 1 x 9-bedded room. A twin room is sometimes available in a silent-overnight building. Located in a quiet, sunny, chapel square, in the bustling market town of Bala with its 5 mile lake & white-water river for rafting.

DETAILS

- **Open** - All year by arrangement. 8.00-20.00. House Rules apply
- **Beds** - 30: 2x3, 4x4, 1x9 SINGLE BEDS
- **Price/night** - 1 night £25, 2 nights £49, 3 nights £69, weekly £149. Plus Linen Sheet hire £3/week. Twin room: £60. En suite from £70

CONTACT: Stella Shaw
Tel: 01678 521700
info@Bala-Backpackers.co.uk
www.Bala-Backpackers.co.uk
32 Tegid Street, BALA, LL23 7EL

LLANFYLLIN
WORKHOUSE BUNKHOUSE

151b

The well equipped, community run bunkhouse at Y Dolydd Llanfyllin Workhouse is handy for Welshpool & Shrewsbury and close to the Berwyn Mountains. With access to a wide range of adventurous activities including Lake Vyrnwy, Pistyll Rhaeadr waterfall (the tallest in the UK) and Revolution Bike Park. Visit the on-site cafe and the free History Centre to learn more about the building and the people who lived and worked in it.

DETAILS

- **Open** - All year
- **Beds** - 20: 1x4, 2x8
- **Price/night** - Per person Mar-Oct £22 - £25, Nov-Feb £30 - £34 including bedding. Groups of 15+ are guaranteed sole use of the bunkhouse.

CONTACT: Martyn Greenwood
Tel: 07711 025761
llanfyllinbunkhouse@gmail.com
www.llanfyllinworkhouse.org.uk
Y Dolydd, Llanfyllin, SY22 5LD

WILD VALLEY
BUNKHOUSE
152a

Nestling in the beautiful Maengwynedd Valley with the backdrop of the Berwyn Mountains, Wild Valley Bunkhouse & rustic shepherd huts offer the perfect base for adventurers or a rural retreat. The bijou, quality bunkhouse sleeps 4, while the 2 shepherd huts each sleep two. One in a double bed & the other in a king bed. Book the bunkhouse or huts separately or book the whole site for a larger group or a special occasion.

DETAILS
- **Open** - March 1st - October 31st.
- **Beds** - 8: Bunkhouse: 1x4. Huts 2x2
- **Price/night** - £82.50 midweek, £115 weekend (Fri or Sat). £575 per week. Use Code IHG26 to get £30 off a 2 night weekend stay.

CONTACT: Heather 07956 793 791 or Graeme 07949 606 331
hello@wildvalleyhuts.co.uk
www.wildvalleyhuts.co.uk
Pwllpridd, Maengwynedd, Llanrhaeadr Ym Mochnant, Oswestry, SY10 0DE

LLANGOLLEN
HOSTEL
152b

Llangollen Hostel, in the Dee Valley, is perfect for walking, cycling, canoeing & white water rafting. Families will love visiting the steam railway, horse drawn canal boats & Pontcysyllte Aqueduct - a World Heritage Site. The town has a great choice of restaurants/pubs and is home to the Fringe music & arts festival, plus the International Eisteddfod. Llandegla, Chester, Wrexham & Offa's Dyke Path are all nearby. A warm welcome awaits!

DETAILS
- **Open** - All year. All day.
- **Beds** - 31: 4x4, 1x4(en suite), 1x5, 1x6
- **Price/night** - From: Private room £45. Double private room for 2 people £59. Private room for 4 £76. Private room for 6 £104. Sole use from £600.

CONTACT: Jamie or Sion Dennis
Tel: 01978 861773 or 07384 344622
info@llangollenhostel.co.uk
www.llangollenhostel.co.uk
Berwyn Street, Llangollen, LL20 8NB

TYDDYN BYCHAN

153a

Tyddyn Bychan is an 18th century small holding surrounded by farmland. It is an excellent self-catering base for all outdoor activities.

The main bunkhouse sleeps 18 in two en suite rooms. The smaller bunkhouse sleeps 9 in two en suite rooms. There is also a Shepherd's Hut with a double bed. All bedding included. Delicious homemade food available if booked in advance. Ample off road parking.

DETAILS

- **Open** - All year. All day.
- **Beds** - 27: Main b/house 1x10,1x8. Small b/h 1x6, 1x3. Shepherd's hut 1xdbl
- **Price/night** - B/house from £25 pp including bedding. Shepherd's hut £90.

CONTACT: Hayley Parker
Tel: 07920795448
Hayley@tyddynbychan.co.uk
www.tyddynbychan.co.uk
Cefn Brith, Cerrigydrudion, Corwen,
LL21 9TS

WOODLANDS
CENTRE

153b

This large Victorian property has been specially adapted to provide self-catering accommodation for groups of up to 33. The 8 dormitories vary in size from 1 to 10 beds, complete with duvets & linen. The Centre is central heated and has a common room, large kitchen, drying room, hot showers and outdoor seating. Located in Betws-y-Coed, the Woodlands Centre is an ideal base for outdoor activities in Snowdonia.

DETAILS

- **Open** - All year. All day
- **Beds** - 33: 1x10,1x8,1x4,2x3,2x2,1x1
- **Price/night** - From £22.50pp. Exclusive use: Youth groups £260. Adult groups £650. Further reductions for members, midweek bookings & for uniformed organisations.

CONTACT: Fiona Witton
bookings@woodlandscentre.com
www.woodlandscentre.com
Vicarage Road, Betws-y-Coed, Conwy,
LL24 0AD

BASE CAMP
SNOWDONIA
154a

154b
THE ROCKS
AT PLAS CURIG

This modern hostel makes your perfect base for exploring Snowdonia. Situated in Betws-y-Coed, you'll have a choice of walking and cycling routes from the doorstep. While the mountains and many attractions of Snowdonia are just a short drive away. If you worry about parking there are hourly buses that will take you direct to Snowdon.

The hostel sleeps up to 38. Book a bed in a dorm, a private room (some are en suite) or the whole hostel for your group.

Set in the heart of Eryri (Snowdonia) National Park, this friendly hostel is minutes from Betws-y-Coed, the Ogwen Valley and the Snowdon Horseshoe, offering unbeatable access to mountain walks, beaches, and miles of spectacular scenery. Enjoy the welcoming lounge with log fire, spacious dining areas, a large self-catering kitchen, and gardens with unrivalled views. Choose a private room, a dorm bed, or hire the whole hostel.

DETAILS

- **Open** - All year.
- **Beds** - 38: 3x4, 2x4 en suite, 2x6, 1x6 en suite
- **Price/night** - £35-£55 per bed.

DETAILS

- **Open** - All year. Check in 5-10pm.
- **Beds** -   59: 1x8, 2x6, 4x4, 1x4/5, 2x 3/4, 2x2/3,1xdouble, 1xtwin
- **Price/night** -   From £35 per person. Exclusive hire from £2460.

CONTACT: Reception
Tel: 07562 954604
snowdonia@basecamphostels.com
basecamphostels.com
Holyhead Road, Betws-y-Coed, Conwy, LL24 0BN

CONTACT:
Tel: 01690 720 225
info@therockshostel.com
www.therockshostel.com
Capel Curig, Betws-y-Coed, North Wales, LL24 0EL

CELLB

155a

Conveniently located in the centre of Blaenau Ffestiniog. CellB sleeps up to 7 with 2 rooms (sleeping 2 & 3) and a sofa bed in the lounge. Book by the room or book the whole hostel.

It's an ideal location for adventures such as Zip World, Go Below, mountain and beach walks or mountain biking.

CellB is the perfect place to recover, recuperate, and soak up the vibrant landscape.

DETAILS

- **Open** - All year. All day
- **Beds** - 7:1x2,1x3 (bunk style beds), sofa bed sleeping 2
- **Price/night** - From £120. Min 2 nights.

CONTACT: Rhys
Tel: 07867 650703
prisoner@cellb.org
cellb.org
Park Square, Blaenau Ffestiniog
LL41 3AD

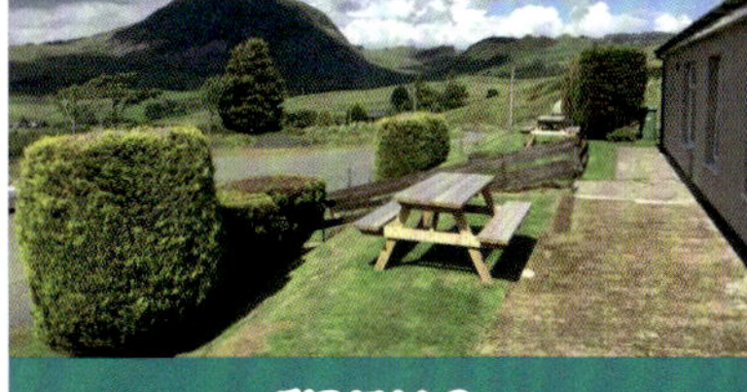

TREKS
BUNKHOUSE

155b

Treks 4* Bunkhouse is in the mountains on the edge of the village of Blaenau Ffestiniog. Ideal for enjoying the rugged beauty of Snowdonia. It is a former golf club converted to provide self-catering accommodation for groups. Sometimes available to individuals midweek. Attractions nearby include Llechwedd Slate Caverns, Bounce Below, Zip World, Antur Stiniog, steam railways, Go Below Adventures, Coed y Brenin Mountain Bike Centre, Harlech Castle and Black Rock Sands.

DETAILS

- **Open** - All year. Exclusive hire only at weekends. Check in 3pm-8pm.
- **Beds** - 13
- **Price/night** - Sole use: £312. Min 2 nights. Enquire for indidivuals midweek.

CONTACT: Dyfed
Tel: 07796 172318
treksbunkhouse@gmail.com
www.treksbunkhouse.co.uk
Y Cefn, Ffestiniog, Gwynedd, LL41 4PS

MAENTWROG
BUNKHOUSE

156a

Maentwrog bunkhouse is a newly converted cowshed on a working farm. It has a fully equipped kitchen, underfloor heating, TV/DVD, BBQ area, laundry facilities, power washer and bike lockup. Local activities include hill walking (Moelwyn and Cnicht 10 mins away), white water rafting, Coed y Brenin cycling centre, Blaenau Ffestiniog down hill cycle track, RopeWorks & canyoning. Ffestiniog railway and beautiful beaches are within 15-20 mins' drive. The Welsh Coastal Path passes the end of the lane.

DETAILS

- **Open** - All year.
- **Beds** - 4
- **Price/night** - £25pp. Bring sleeping bags or hire bed linen @£5/person/stay

CONTACT: Mrs Eurliw M Jones
Tel: 01766 590231
emj2@hotmail.co.uk
www.bunkhousesnowdonia.com
Felen Rhyd Fach, Maentwrog, Blaenau Ffestiniog, Gwynedd, LL41 4HY

SNOWDON LODGE
GROUP HOSTEL

156b

Snowdon Lodge, the birthplace of Lawrence of Arabia, is ideal for get-togethers with friends & family, school, university & religious groups. This self-catering group base in Snowdonia is a large Victorian property set in 4-acre grounds in a pretty village. Well-equipped kitchen. Spacious dining room. Modern lounge. BBQ area. Private parking. Games room. Lecture/seminar/prayer room for hire. En suite bedrooms including accessible room. Pet friendly.

DETAILS

- **Open** - January - December. All day.
- **Beds** - 35: doubles, twins and dorms.
- **Price/night** - Packages for 2-7 nights for groups of 15-35. From £565-£1095pn.

CONTACT: Carl or Anja
Tel: 01766 515354
info@snowdonlodge.com
www.snowdonlodge.com
Lawrence House, Church Street, Tremadog, Nr Porthmadog, Gwynedd, Snowdonia, LL49 9PS

BRYNKIR
COACH HOUSE

157a

Formerly Cwm Pennant Hostel, Brynkir Coach House offers welcoming & relaxed accommodation for groups of 10-66 across dorms, en suite family/private rooms & a self contained flat. Set within stunning grounds in the Snowdonia National Park with fantastic views of the Cwm Pennant valley & Moel Hebog. Local caterers are available. The area is ideal for hill walking, rock climbing, canoeing. For cyclists Lon Las Cymru is on the door step!

DETAILS

- **Open** - All year
- **Beds** - 66: 1x15, 1x14, 1x9, 1x8, 1x6/8 (family en suite), 2x2/3 (family en suite). Flat for 6.
- **Price/night** - From £25pp, under 2's free. Min of 6 people.

CONTACT: Dawn Harding
Tel: 07866 631538 or 07787 501780
dawnharding14@icloud.com
Golan, Garndolbenmaen, Gwynedd, LL51 9AQ

ABERSOCH
SGUBOR UNNOS

157b

Bunkhouse accommodation on a family farm in the village of Llangian. Just one mile from Abersoch which is famed for watersports, the bunkhouse is an ideal base for walking the Llyn Coast Path, surfing, cycling, golf, fishing, running & sailing. Spinning & knitting courses using the farm's own wool are available. The three modern bunkrooms are ideal for individuals or groups with a fully equipped kitchen/lounge, disabled facilities, secure storage & parking.

DETAILS

- **Open** - All year. All day.
- **Beds** - 14: 2x4, 1x6
- **Price/night** - £23 (adults & children over 10), £11 any other children. Hire bed linen for £2 per bed per visit.

CONTACT: Phil or Meinir
Tel: 01758 713527
enquiries@tanrallt.com
www.tanrallt.com
Fferm Tanrallt Farm, Llangian, Abersoch, Gwynedd, LL53 7LN

GLAN ABER
RYDAL PENRHOS SCHOOL
158a

Glan Aber, a charming boarding house at Rydal Penrhos School, accommodates up to 41 guests at any time of year.

Just a five-minute walk from Rhos-on-Sea's sandy beaches and a short drive to Snowdonia, Glan Aber offers access to the school's first-in-class sports and meeting facilities. Fully or partly catered packages are available, with optional on-site and off-site activities.

DETAILS

■ **Open** - All year except Xmas and the New Year
■ **Beds** - 41: 1x2, 3x3, 5x4, 2x5
■ **Price/night** - Whole hostel: Oct-Mar £900, April-May £1050, June-Sept £1200

CONTACT: Maria McLean or Helen Thomas
Tel: 01492 530155
events@rydalpenrhos.com
rydalpenrhos.turtl.co
Pwllycrochan Avenue, Colwyn Bay, Conwy, LL29 7BT

LLANDUDNO
HOSTEL
158b

Llandudno Hostel is a Victorian 4* boutique, award-winning hostel where individuals, families & groups (including schools) are welcome all year. Set in the heart of the Victorian seaside town of Llandudno, it's your perfect base for shopping & exploring many local attractions, including blue flag beaches, dry slope skiing, Zip World, Surf Snowdonia, bronze age copper mine, traditional pier, museums & fishing trips.

DETAILS

■ **Open** - All year (telephone in winter prior to arrival). All day.
■ **Beds** - 46: 2x8,2x6,4x2,1x4,1xfamily(6)
■ **Price/night** - From £21 per person, £55 per private twin room, £60 per private twin en suite. Group and family rates on request. Special offers autumn/winter.

CONTACT: James or Melissa
Tel: 01492 877430
info@llandudnohostel.co.uk
www.llandudnohostel.co.uk
14 Charlton Street, Llandudno, LL30 2AA

CONWY VALLEY
BACKPACKERS BARN
159a

Conwy Valley Backpackers Barn is situated on a peaceful organic farm in the heart of the beautiful Conwy Valley, with excellent access to Snowdonia.

Centrally heated with a fully equipped self-catering kitchen, log fires and hot showers. Bike/canoe storage and tourist information are available. Local activities include fishing, hiking, white water rafting and mountain biking. Surf Snowdonia is within walking distance and Zip World is a short drive.

DETAILS

- **Open** - All year
- **Beds** - 16: 1x4, 2x6 + camping
- **Price/night** - From £25pp. Sole use from £350. Camping £10pp

CONTACT: Claudia
Tel: 01492 660504 or 07956 851425
info@conwyvalleybarn.com
www.conwyvalleybarn.com
Pyllau Gloewon Farm, Tal-y-Bont, Conwy, Gwynedd, LL32 8YX

BRON-Y-GADER
BUNKHOUSE
159b

Perched at 290m (950ft) in the foothills of Eyri (Snowdonia) with direct access to the Carneddau mountains and close to the end of the Welsh 3000s Challenge route, Bron-y-Gader Bunkhouse offers comfortable & great value accommodation for up to 37.

Remote and isolated but just 8 miles to Conwy and 2 miles to the nearest pub. The many attractions and high adrenaline activities in Snowdonia are just a short drive away.

DETAILS

- **Open** - March to November
- **Beds** - 37: 4x8, 1x3, 1x2
- **Price/night** - £17pp. Minimum charge of 12 people, min stay of 2 nights. DofE, school & youth orgs: £12pp.

CONTACT:
info@bron-y-gader.org
www.bron-y-gader.org
Bron-y-Gader Centre, Llanbedr-y-Cennin, Conwy, LL32 8UT

ROWEN
BUNKHOUSE
160a

Once Rowen Youth Hostel, this traditional Welsh farmhouse has breathtaking views over the Conwy Valley & Eryri (Snowdonia). Downstairs is a modern kitchen, dining room with fire & a cosy lounge with smart TV & WiFi. 4 toilets & 3 shower rooms. Boot room & laundry room. Upstairs are 4 bedrooms sleeping up to 16 people. In the old granary there is a heated games room with pool table, darts, football table, TV & separate WC. The garden has picnic tables & a campfire.

DETAILS
- **Open** - All year
- **Beds** - 16: 1x2, 1x4, 2x5
- **Price/night** - Bunkhouse: £250 - £600 (2 night min). Please enquire for flat.

CONTACT: Gwenan Jones
Tel: 01492 650011
gwenancefncae@gmail.com
www.rowenbunkhouse.co.uk
Rhiw Farmhouse, Rowen, Conwy, LL32 8YW

PLATTS FARM
BUNKHOUSE
160b

Platt's Farm Campsite and 3* Bunkhouse is situated in a range of Victorian farm buildings, in the charming village of Llanfairfechan. Close to the A55, the Bunkhouse lies at the start of the walks to 14 of the Welsh 3000 Peaks. It is in Snowdonia National Park, within a 10 min walk of the Wales Coastal Path and on the NCN 5 Cycle Route. Shops, pubs and cafés are within 5 mins' walk. Just 15 mins from Zipworld, Bethesda & 20 mins from Surf Snowdonia.

DETAILS
- **Open** - All year. Check out by 10am, check in after 2pm.
- **Beds** - 10
- **Price/night** - £20pp. Sole use £200 per night.

CONTACT: Sam Davies
Tel: 01248 680105
sam@plattsfarm.com
www.plattsfarm.com
Platts Farm Bunkhouse, Aber Road, Llanfairfechan, Conwy, LL33 0HL

CABAN CYSGU
GERLAN BUNKHOUSE
161a

Caban Cysgu, run by Gerlan community, offers purpose-built accommodation at the foot of the Carneddau. Perfect for walking in Eryri (Snowdonia), Tryfan 10 mins away and Yr Wyddfa (Snowdon) 25 mins' drive. A great base for the 'Welsh 3,000'. Convenient for Snowdonia & Cambrian Ways & Slate Trail. Just 5 mins from Zip World; the longest & fastest zip line in Europe. Mountain bike trails on the doorstep & for road cyclists the Sustrans Lôn Las Ogwen route is a mile away. For climbers, Idwal is nearby, for canoeists Afon Ogwen is popular.

DETAILS
- **Open** - All year. All day.
- **Beds** - 16 : 1x5, 1x2, 1x1, 1x8.
- **Price/night** - From £20 - £24

CONTACT: Dewi Emyln, Manager
Tel: 01248 605573 or 07464 676753
cabancysgu@hotmail.com
www.cabancysgu-gerlan.co.uk
Ffordd Gerlan, Gerlan, Bethesda,
Bangor, LL57 3ST

SNOWDONIA
MOUNTAIN HOSTEL
161b

In the heart of the Ogwen Valley and surrounded by the Welsh 3000s, this hostel is the perfect base for walkers, climbers and cyclists with the best routes straight from the door. Snowdon/Yr Wyddfa is a 30 minute drive away. For adventure seekers Zip World is within walking distance and the Anglesey/Ynys Môn beaches are a short drive. Newly refurbished, Snowdonia Mountain Hostel has comfy beds with bedding provided & a superb kitchen diner. Sorry no stag or hen parties.

DETAILS
- **Open** - All year.
- **Beds** - 24: 2x6, 2x4, 1x4 (self contained flat)
- **Price/night** - Check website

CONTACT: Hannah Hughes
Tel: 07756 167342 or 07703 546711
info@snowdoniamountainhostel.com
www.snowdoniamountainhostel.com
Tai Newyddion, Nant Ffrancon, Bangor
LL57 3DQ

OGWEN VALLEY
BUNKHOUSE

162a

In Snowdonia National Park, just over a mile from the small town of Bethesda, Ogwen Valley Bunkhouse provides spacious, eco friendly accommodation for individuals, families and groups.

The large open plan communal area has a well equipped kitchen, a large dining table and plenty of comfy chairs. With comfortable beds and a drying room guests invariably return. On Snowdonia Slate Trail & Lon Las Cymru.

DETAILS

- **Open** - All year. Check out 10.30am.
- **Beds** - 16: 2x4, 1x6, 1x camp bed, 1x bed settee
- **Price/night** - £19pp. Please enquire for exclusive use prices.

CONTACT: Gwyn Morgan
Tel: 01248 601958 or 07775 978405
bookings@ogwenvalleybunkhouse.co.uk
www.ogwenvalleybunkhouse.co.uk
Capel Saron, Tyn Y Maes, Bethesda, Gwynedd LL57 3LX

YR HAFOD
HOSTEL

162b

Surrounded by the stunning peaks of Eryri National Park, Yr Hafod Hostel is nestled at the foot of Y Garn in the Ogwen Valley. The hostel is only available for exclusive hire.

Yr Hafod Hostel sleeps up to 32 across four bunk rooms and offers a lounge, dining room, fully equipped kitchen, two washrooms, free WiFi, gas heating, a drying room, and secure storage for wet gear, with private parking for up to 10 vehicles.

 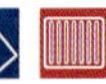     **GROUPS ONLY**

DETAILS

- **Open** - All year
- **Beds** - 32: 1x4, 2x8, 1x12
- **Price/night** - £475. Dscounts for Scout and Girl Guiding groups available.

CONTACT:
Tel: 0845 519 6113
hostel@yr-hafod.org.uk
yr-hafod.org.uk
Nant Ffrancon, Bethesda, Gwynedd, LL57 3LZ

LODGE DINORWIG

163a

Nestled in the heart of North Wales, Lodge Dinorwig is your ultimate basecamp for mountain adventures.

Located near Yr Wyddfa (Snowdon), the 14-bed bunkroom caters to groups but also provides privacy for solo travellers with bespoke beds and curtains. With comfortable accommodation, delicious homemade meals and insider tips on the best trails, it's the ideal base for your hiking, running and mountain biking adventures.

DETAILS

- **Open** - March - November
- **Beds** - 14: 1x14
- **Price/night** - £35-45pp. Sole use £410-460. FREE breakfast and parking

CONTACT: Sonni
Tel: 07593 818230
info@lodge-dinorwig.co.uk
www.lodge-dinorwig.co.uk
Dinorwig, Caernarfon, Gwynedd, LL55 3EY

LON DRYLL
OUTDOORS

163b

Ideally situated on the edge of Snowdonia National Park yet just a 15 minute drive to the seaside town of Caernarfon, Lon Dryll is your perfect base for exploring North Wales. Under new ownership & completely refurbished, Lon Dryll offers groups of between 10-30 exclusive use of all its facilities. Guests will enjoy privacy, space & breath-taking panoramic views. Dogs are welcome.

DETAILS

- **Open** - All year. Check in from 5pm. Check out by 11am
- **Beds** - 30: Bunkhouse 17: 1x6, 1x5, 1x4, 1x2. Main House 13: 2x5 1x3
- **Price/night** - Main House: £400 for up to 13. Main House & Bunkhouse: £600 for up to 30. Please contact us for school & youth group prices.

CONTACT: Eve Williamson
Tel: 07921610696
info@londrylloutdoors.com
www.londrylloutdoors.com
Strata House, Dryll, LL55 3NF

SNOWDON HOUSE
BUNKHOUSE

164a

Ideal group accommodation for up to 10 people, Snowdon House Bunkhouse lies in the iconic Llanberis Pass at the foot of Snowdon. It has a 7 person hot tub with amazing views. Surrounded by stunning Snowdonia landscape, it is the perfect base for walkers, climbers, cyclists & families wanting to explore Snowdonia. With walks, scrambling & climbing on the doorstep & a short drive to beaches, castles, steam trains and the famous Zip Wire, there is something for everybody.

DETAILS

- **Open** - All year. All day
- **Beds** - 10: 1x10 (two alpine sleeping platforms) with duvets, pillows & towels.
- **Price/night** - Enquire for prices. Midweek 3 night stays can be as little as £15pppn based on full occupancy.

CONTACT: Jim & Anne Cumberton
Tel: 01286 512503
info@snowdonhouse.co.uk
www.snowdonhouse.co.ukNant Peris,
Caernarfon,LL55 4UL

CEUNANT ISAF
BUNKHOUSE

164b

Nestling at the foot of Snowdon, just north of Nant Peris and at the end of a dead end track, Ceunant Isaf bunkhouse is the perfect base for your next Snowdonia advenutre.

Be it climbing, hiking, mountain biking, cylcing or exploring the attractions of Snowdonia, you'd be hard pushed to find a better location. Ceunant Isaf Bunkhouse is available on an exclusive use basis for groups of up to 18.

DETAILS

- **Open** - All year.
- **Beds** - 18: 1x13, 1x5, 2x2(double beds), 1x1.
- **Price/night** - Exclusive Use: £400 per night. Minimum of 2 nights. Showers take 50p coins - we leave enough 50p for one shower per person per night.

CONTACT: Kate
ceunantisafbunkhouse@outlook.com
Ty Isaf Farm, Nant Peris, Caernarfon,
Gwynedd, LL55 4UN, Wales

PENTRE BACH
BUNKHOUSE
165a

Situated between Waunfawr and Betws Garmon, Pentre Bach Bunkhouse provides alpine style, dog friendly accommodation and a campsite. The ground floor of the bunkhouse has a dining/cooking area while upstairs there are alpine sleeping platforms with mattresses for 16. Showers, toilets and washing/drying facilities, shared with the campsite, are just across the yard.

DETAILS

- **Open** - All year. All day. Enquires 9am - 9pm. Arrive from 4pm, leave by 11am.
- **Beds** - 16: 1x16.
- **Price/night** - £22pp (inc gas, electric & showers). Sole use bookings negotiable according to group size. Dogs £2 per night, max 2 if sharing.

CONTACT: Karen Neil
Tel: 07798 733939 (9am-9pm)
info@pentrebachbunkhouse.co.uk
www.pentrebachbunkhouse.co.uk
Pentre Bach, Waunfawr, Caernarfon, Gwynedd, LL54 7AJ

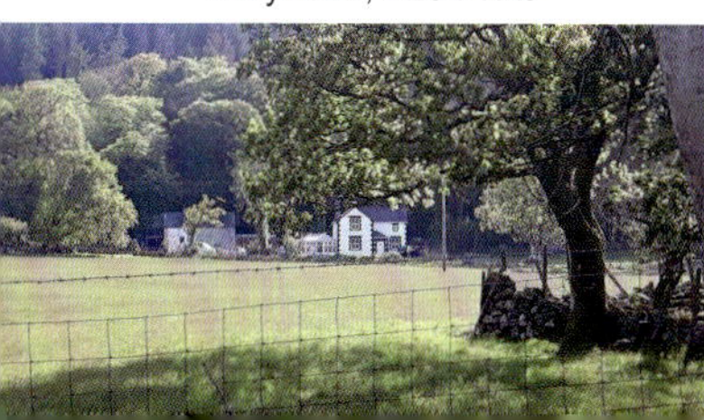

RHYD DDU
OUTDOOR CENTRE
165b

The Rhyd Ddu Bunkhouse provides group accommodation at the foot of Yr Wyddfa (Snowdon) & the Nantlle Ridge. Sleeping 30 in 6 bedrooms, it has a fully equipped kitchen & a large communal dining room with a big screen. Glorious views, central heating, fast WiFi, parking, secure bike storage, drying room & garden. Bring your own sleeping bag, pillow case & towel. Pub, café, & steam train station all within 2 minutes' walk.

DETAILS

- **Open** - All year. All day. Check in from 4pm, check out by 11am.
- **Beds** - 30: 1x12, 4x4, 1x2
- **Price/night** - Exclusive hire from £490. Great weekend group rates. 4 nights for 3 on a range of midweek dates.

CONTACT: Rob
Tel: 01286 882688
stay@canolfan-rhyd-ddu.cymru
www.snowdonia-bunkhouse.wales
The Old School, Rhyd Ddu, Snowdonia, Gwynedd, North Wales LL54 6TL

CAPEL TANRALLT
SELF CATERING

166a

TOTTERS

166b

Located in a tiny hamlet in the picturesque and historic Nantlle valley, Capel Tanrallt is the perfect base for exploring Eryri/ Snowdonia and the Llyn Peninsular. With stunning mountains and beaches on the doorstep, as well as two UNESCO World Heritage sites (the slate quarries and Caernarfon Castle), cafes and numerous other visitor attractions, you are sure to find your ideal activities.

Totters sits in the heart of the historic castle town of Caernarfon just 30m from the Menai Straits. Close to many pubs and restaurants but with good public transport to the Snowdonia National Park. The hostel is a 200 year old, five floored town house with five bedrooms sleeping either 4 or 6 and a huge double/ family en suite. Opposite there is a self-catering town house sleeping 6.

DETAILS

- **Open** - All year. Check in 4-10pm. Check out 10am (unless otherwise agreed).
- **Beds** - 17: Chapel: 3x2, 2x3. Hideaway: 2x2 + extra bed in either room.
- **Price/night** - Chapel: £300-£320. Hideaway: From £120. Min 2 nights.

CONTACT: Louise Tully or Jon Byrne
Tel: 07771 161671 or 07976 016039
capeltanrallt@gmail.com
www.capeltanrallt.co.uk
Tanrallt Terrace, Llanllyfni, Caearnarfon, Gwynedd, LL54 6RR

DETAILS

- **Open** - All year. All day. Check in by 10 pm.
- **Beds** - 28: 3x6, 2x4, 1x2 (en suite), 1x2 (twin)
- **Price/night** - £19.50pp in a dorm. £55 for a double/twin en suite. £47.50 for a twin. Discounts for groups.

CONTACT: Bob/Henryette
Tel: 01286 672963 or 07979 830470
totters.hostel@gmail.com
www.totters.co.uk
Plas Porth Yr Aur, 2 High Street, Caernarfon, Gwynedd, LL55 1RN

ANGLESEY
OUTDOOR CENTRE

167a

Anglesey Outdoors is an ideal base for groups, individuals or families. Just a mile from Porthdafarch Beach & the coastal path & only 2km from Sustrans Cycle Route 8. It has 4 self-contained areas each with their own self-catering & bathroom facilities. These can be hired individually or together. Optional full catering. There's an on-site bar/bistro & a drying room. Glamping also available.

DETAILS

■ **Open** - All year. 24 hour access.
■ **Beds** - 68: Main Centre 33: 1x7,4x5,1x4,1x2. Maris Annexe 10: 5x2. Ty Pen Annexe 8: 1x4,2x2. Gogarth Dorms 16: 1x7,1x7,1x2.
■ **Price/night** - From £16pp (dorms) to £45pp (en suite twin). Ask for sole use.

CONTACT: The Team
Tel: 01407 769351
info@angleseyoutdoors.com
www.angleseyoutdoors.com
Porthdafarch Road, Holyhead, Anglesey, LL65 2LP

OUTDOOR
ALTERNATIVE

167b

Located in Rhoscolyn, a great base for adventure, education & exploring. Escape the busy world, enjoy the outdoors with low environmental impact. A family run 4* bunkhouse in Rhoscolyn, AONB on Anglesey Coast. 5 mins' walk to beach at Borthwen, close to Anglesey Coastal Path. Perfect for family groups, clubs, schools, universities. Ideal for kayaking, climbing, sailing, walking, bird watching, beaches.

DETAILS

■ **Open** - All year. 24 hour access
■ **Beds** - 41:19:(1x2,2x4,1x5) + 22:(1x4, 4x4/5)
■ **Price/night** - From £30pp. £1118.25 for weekend/bunkhouse. Discount for youth/school/uni groups & for 7 nights.

CONTACT: Jacqui Short
Tel: 01407 860469
enquiries@outdooralternative.co.uk
www.outdooralternative.co.uk
Cerrig-yr-Adar, Rhoscolyn, Holyhead, Anglesey, LL65 2NQ

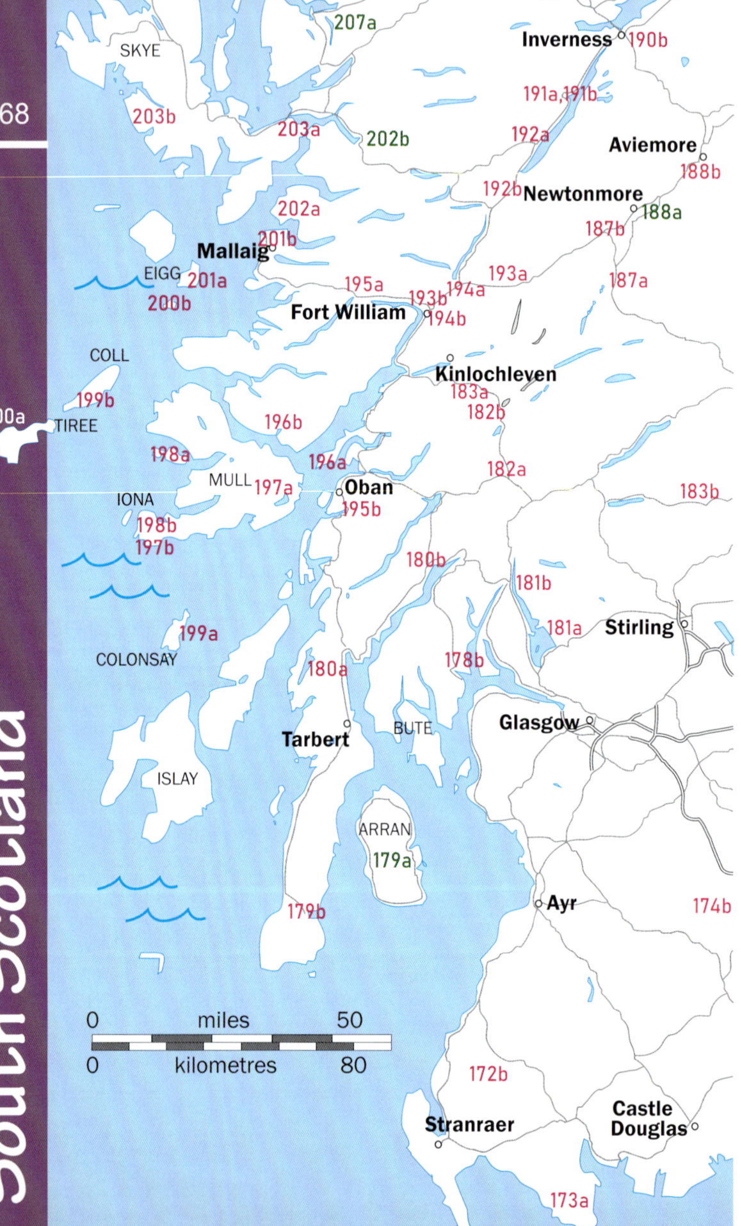
SKYE
207a
Inverness 190b
203b
191a,191b
203a 202b
192a
Aviemore
188b
202a
192b Newtonmore
201b
187b 188a
Mallaig
EIGG 201a
195a 193a 187a
200b 193b 194a
Fort William 194b
COLL
Kinlochleven
199b
183a
200a
TIREE 182b
196b
198a 196a
182a
MULL 197a
Oban 183b
IONA 195b
198b
197b
180b
181b
199a
181a Stirling
COLONSAY
180a 178b
Glasgow
Tarbert BUTE
ISLAY
ARRAN
179a
179b
Ayr 174b
0 miles 50
0 kilometres 80
172b
Stranraer Castle
Douglas
173a

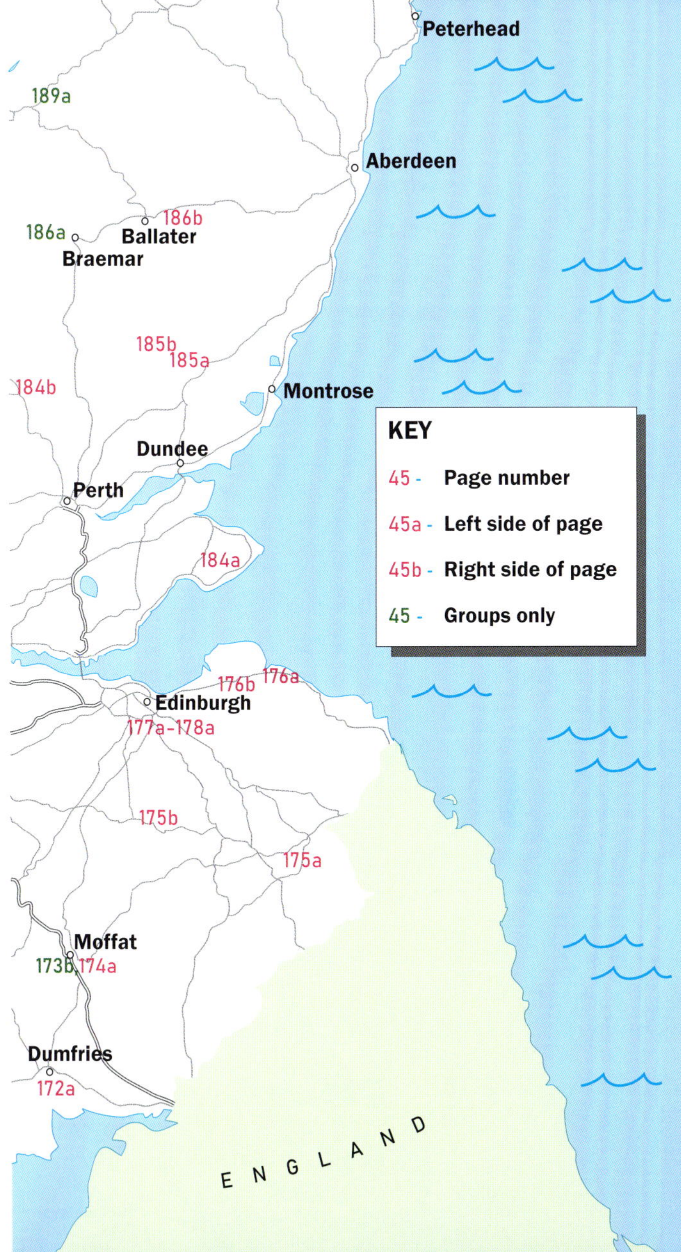
169
South Scotland
Peterhead
Aberdeen
189a
186b
186a
Ballater
Braemar
185b
185a
184b
Montrose
Dundee
Perth
184a
KEY
45 - Page number
45a - Left side of page
45b - Right side of page
45 - Groups only
176b 176a
Edinburgh
177a-178a
175b
175a
Moffat
173b 174a
Dumfries
172a
ENGLAND

North Scotland

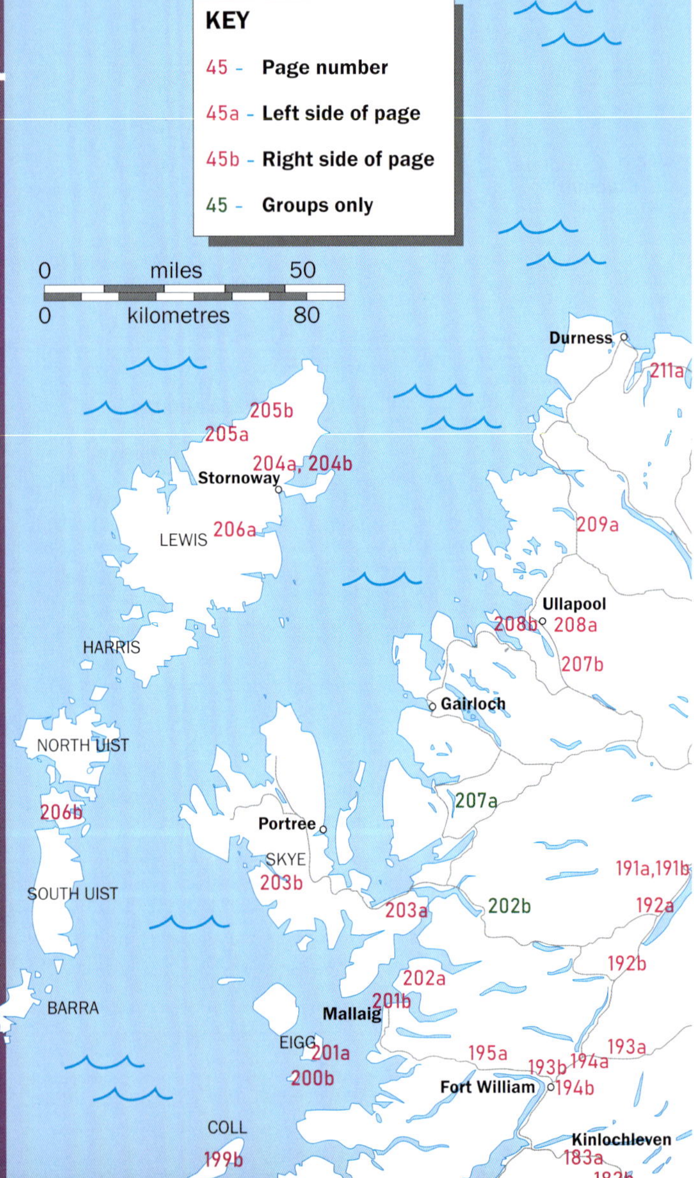

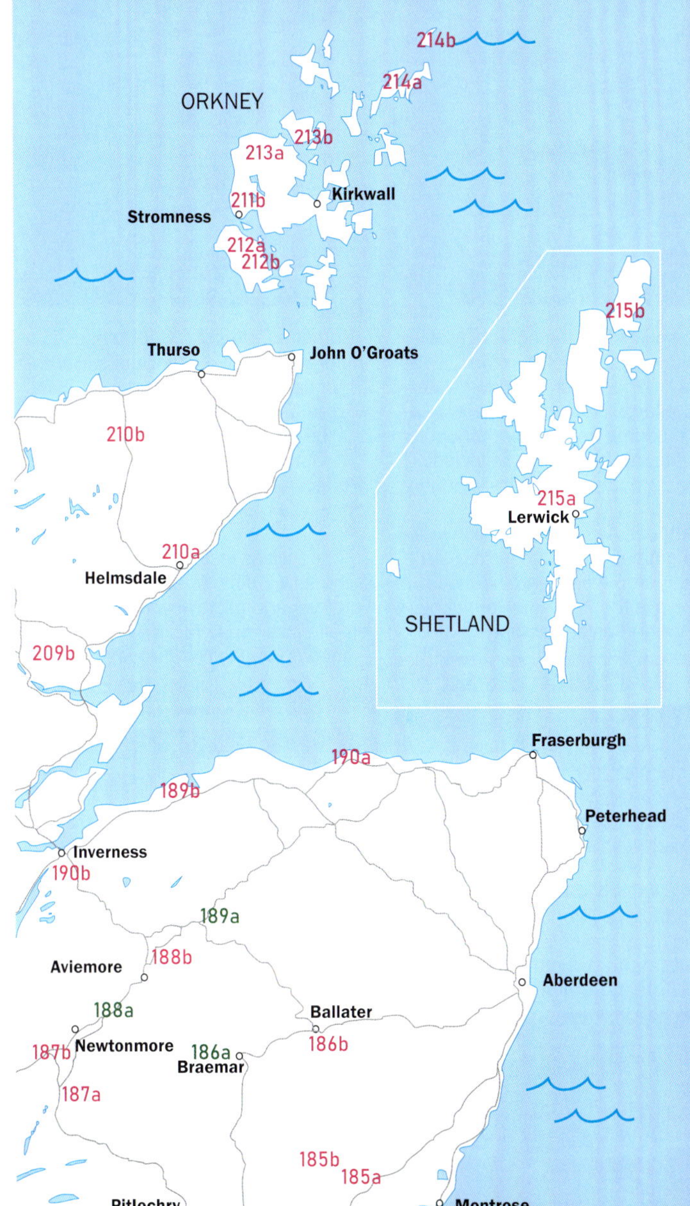

ORKNEY
214b
214a
213b
213a
211b
Stromness
Kirkwall
212a
212b
Thurso
John O'Groats
215b
210b
215a
Lerwick
210a
Helmsdale
SHETLAND
209b
Fraserburgh
190a
189b
Peterhead
Inverness
190b
189a
188b
Aviemore
Aberdeen
188a
Ballater
Newtonmore
186b
187b
186a
Braemar
187a
185b
185a
Pitlochry
Montrose
184b

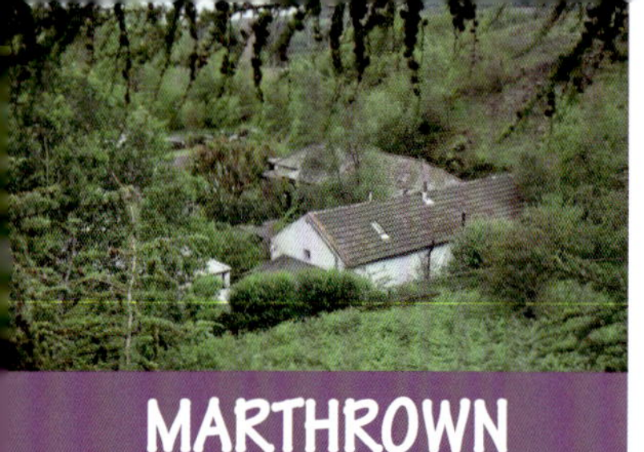

MARTHROWN
OF MABIE

172a

Marthrown is set in the heart of Mabie Forest, 6 miles south of Dumfries. It has a sauna, a wood burning spring water hot tub, a large BBQ, garden areas, a challenge course and plenty of room for groups. Mountain bike routes including the 7Stanes mountain bike trails nearby.

The bunkhouse has now been converted to self-contained units, there are also Mongolian yurts, a bell tent and the jewel in the crown is the Iron Age Roundhouse for parties or weddings

DETAILS

- **Open** - All year. 10am-8pm - late arrival by arrangement.
- **Beds** - 18: 1x6, 1x8 + Roundhouse. 3 Yurts. Bell tent + Camping.
- **Price/night** - Please enquire

CONTACT: Scott
Tel: 01387 247900 or 07786 628456
info@marthrownofmabie.co.uk
www.marthrownofmabie.com
Mabie Forest, Dumfries, DG2 8HB

BARHOLM
ACCOMMODATION

172b

Barholm Enterprise Centre houses a variety of businesses including Barholm Accommodation which has en suite shared and private rooms. Up to 28 can be accommodated in 9 rooms.

Perfect for cyclists, walkers, anglers or those who generally enjoy the outdoors.

Facilities include a communal kitchenette (fridge/freezer, kettle, toaster, air fryer and microwave), sitting room, on-site bike repair facilities, secure bike shed & electric car charging station.

DETAILS

- **Open** - All year. All day
- **Beds** - 28
- **Price/night** - From £25

CONTACT: Andrew Watson
Tel: 01671 820810
Panny.barholm@gmail.com
barholm-centre.co.uk
St Johns Street, Creetown, Dumfries and Galloway, DG8 7JE

NEW TOWN HALL
BUNKHOUSE

173a

The New Town Hall Bunkhouse offers modern, eco-friendly accommodation for up to eighteen guests in ensuite rooms, including a fully accessible option.

With free Wi-Fi, a well-equipped kitchen, and facilities for cyclists, it's a cosy, sustainable base on the Whithorn Way.

Close to the 7stanes trails and the coast. Perfect for families, adventurers, and travellers alike.

DETAILS

- **Open** - All Year. Checkin 3-9 pm, checkout by 10 am.
- **Beds** - 18: 2x2, 2x4, 1x6
- **Price/night** - From £45pp, with all linens and towels provided.

CONTACT: Hazel
Tel: 01988 401296 or 07876 032485
allroadswhithorn@gmail.com
allroadsleadtowhithorn.com
53 St John Street, Whithorn, Newton Stewart, DG8 8PD

WELL ROAD
CENTRE

173b

The Well Road Centre sits in its own grounds in the charming town of Moffat. It is ideal for family get-togethers, conferences, residential workshops, sports and outdoor activity clubs. The Centre has two spacious meeting rooms, a large, bright self-catering kitchen, dining room fully equipped for 65, games hall and table tennis room. Bring your own sleeping bags/linens, or order our linen packs. Ample parking and storage.

DETAILS

- **Open** - All year. All day.
- **Beds** - 70: in 13 rooms (2 en suite).
- **Price/night** - From £1700 for two night weekend for up to 40 people, plus £25 pp for each extra person. Linen packs for single beds £7.50. Mid week stays always on offer. Just ask for a quote.

CONTACT: Ben Larmour
Tel: 01683 221040
ben8363@aol.com
www.wellroadcentre.com
Well Rd, Moffat, DG109BT

MOFFAT
INDEPENDENT HOSTEL 174a

This friendly family run hostel has been designed with comfort and the outdoor enthusiast in mind. Situated on the edge of the pretty town of Moffat, the hostel sleeps up to 18 in a selection of en suite quad, twin & double rooms. It has bike/kayak storage, bike wash area, drying room and all bedding is provided. A perfect stopover on the Lejog cycle route & the Southern Upland Way. Book a bed, a room or the whole place.

DETAILS

- **Open** - All year: Check in after 4pm. Check out by 10.30am. 24-hr access.
- **Beds** - 18: 3x4, 2xtwin, 1xdbl.
- **Price/night** - From: dorm £30pp. Twin £64.50. King double £75. Quad £110. Sole use (18 guests) from £600.

CONTACT: Tom Wellings
Tel: 07920 460105
booking@moffathostel.com
moffathostel.com
Bridge House, Well Road, Moffat, Dumfries and Galloway, DG10 9JT

HOPETOUN
BOTHY
174b

Hopetoun Bothy is a fully modernised traditional bunkhouse sleeping up to eight in hand-crafted bunks, with dorms, private ensuite rooms, and shared kitchen facilities - keeping it authentic, social, and affordable. Enjoy hearty breakfasts or fine evening meals at the Hopetoun Arms next door, or pick up essentials at the village store. Located right on the SWC300 and Southern Upland Way routes, close to Wanlockhead and visitor attractions.

DETAILS

- **Open** - All year
- **Beds** - 8: 4x2 (en suite)
- **Price/night** - £20pp, £60 en suite twin. Breakfast from £3.50, evening meals £15.75. Bedding & Towel hire £6 per stay..

CONTACT: Gordon Wishart
Tel: 07525 754697   or 0141 445 6228
admin@hopetounbothy.uk
hopetounbothy.uk
37b Main St, Leadhills, South Lanarkshire ML12 6XP

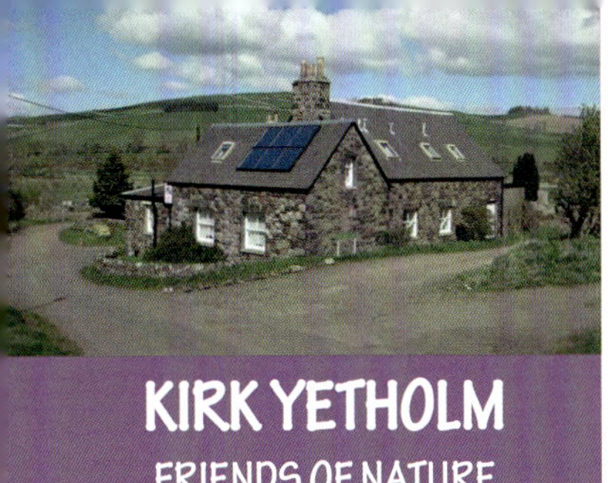

KIRK YETHOLM
FRIENDS OF NATURE

175a

THIS HOSTEL IS CLOSED FOR ALL OF 2026. IT MAY RE-OPEN IN 2027 - CHECK WEBSITE FOR UPDATES.

Kirk Yetholm Friends of Nature House is perfectly located at the start/end of the Pennine Way. It is also close to St. Cuthbert's Way, the Borderloop Cycle Route and Sustrans Route 84. It's a great base too for local day hikes, ideal for individuals, families and small groups. Recently upgraded, the house offers a comfortable, friendly and peaceful retreat. Evening meals and breakfast are available in the adjacent hotel.

DETAILS

- **Open** - Closed for all of 2026
- **Beds** - 22: 1x7, 1x5, 1x4, 2x2 (twin), 1x2 (bunk).
- **Price/night** - Closed for 2026

CONTACT: The Manager
Friends of Nature House, Waukford, Kirk Yetholm, Kelso, Roxburghshire, TD5 8PG

CLEIKUM MILL
LODGE

175b

Cleikum Mill Lodge, in the heart of the Tweed Valley, sleeps 10 in two apartments. Book a room, an apartment or the whole Mill. Innerleithen, a 7Stanes trail centre, is on NCR1, Southern Upland Way, Tweed Canoe Trail & the Capital Trail. Shops, pubs, cafés & restaurants a short stroll away. Dog friendly with sole use. B/fast by arrangement in nearby hotel.

DETAILS

- **Open** - All year. All day. Check in after 4pm, check out before 10am.
- **Beds** - 10: Lower: 6: 3x2. Upper 4: 2x2
- **Price/night** - Guide prices £60 single en suite, £80 twin en suite. Apartment for 4 £160. Apartment for 6 £296. Discounts for 3+ nights.

CONTACT: Graham
Tel: 07790 592747
hello@cleikum-mill-lodge.co.uk
www.cleikum-mill-lodge.co.uk
7 Cleikum Mill, High St, Innerleithen, Scottish Borders EH44 6QT

DOLPHIN DUNBAR
@THE DOLPHIN INN

176a

The Dolphin Inn is situated in the centre of the historic seaside town of Dunbar in East Lothian, 30 miles east of Edinburgh.

It is just a short walk to the beach, High Street and harbours and there are many adventure activities close by. The town is also located on a number of walking and cycle routes. The hostel sleeps 27 across 11 rooms, all on upper floors. Dogs are welcome by arrangement.

DETAILS

■ **Open** - Open all year with the exception of the first three weeks in January.
■ **Beds** - 27: 1x6, 1x3, 2xdbl (en suite) 4xdbl, 3xtwin
■ **Price/night** - Approx £40 for adults, £25 for children (12 and under).

CONTACT: Tom Page
Tel: 01368 868427 or 01414 270770
info@dolphindunbar.com
dolphindunbar.com
2 Queens Road, Dunbar, East Lothian
EH42 1JZ

BELLS BOTHY
BUNKHOUSE

176b

This small, cosy bunkhouse sits away from the crowds among the rolling hills of East Lothian. The shops and amenities of Haddington are just 3 miles away, while Edinburgh and the coast are both easily accessible.

The bunkhouse sleeps six in one room. Each booking gets sole use. With a log burning stove, a supply of logs & a fab little kitchen you are assured of a comfortable stay.

DETAILS

■ **Open** - All year.
■ **Beds** - 6: 1x6
■ **Price/night** - Sole use: From £55 (min stay 2 nights). If arriving by bike or foot £45 (no min stay).

CONTACT: Rupert
Tel: 07935 588819 or 01684 560253
bookings@bothies.com
bothies.com
Bell's Bothy Bunkhouse, Morham, Haddington, East Lothian. EH41 4LQ

ROYAL MILE
BACKPACKERS

177a

Royal Mile Backpackers is a small and cosy hostel with its own special character! Perfectly located on the Royal Mile, the most famous street in Edinburgh, Royal Mile Backpackers is the ideal place to stay for the independent traveller.

The comfortable beds and cosy common areas will make you feel at home and the friendly staff are always on hand to help you make the most of your time in Edinburgh.

DETAILS

- **Open** - All year. Reception 6.30am-11 am. 3pm -10pm.
- **Beds** - 46
- **Price/night** - From £21 per person. ID required for check in.

CONTACT: Receptionist
Tel: 0131 557 6120
royalmile@scotlandstophostels.com
www.royalmilebackpackers.com
105 High Street, Edinburgh, EH1 1SG

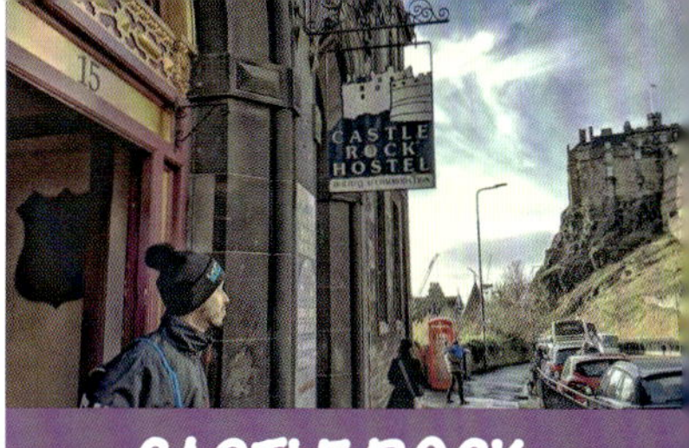

CASTLE ROCK
HOSTEL

177b

In a wonderful location, facing south with a sunny aspect and panoramic views over the city, Castle Rock Hostel is just steps away from the city centre. The historic Royal Mile, the busy pubs, the late-late nightlife of Grassmarket and Cowgate are all only a short walk away. Then, of course, there is the famous Edinburgh Castle.

Most of the rooms have no traffic noise and there are loads of great facilities, 24-hour reception and no curfew.

DETAILS

- **Open** - All year. Reception 24 hours.
- **Beds** - 302
- **Price/night** - From £22 per person. ID required for check in.

CONTACT: Receptionist
Tel: 0131 225 9666
castlerock@macbackpackers.com
www.castlerockedinburgh.com
15 Johnston Terrace, Edinburgh, EH1 2PW

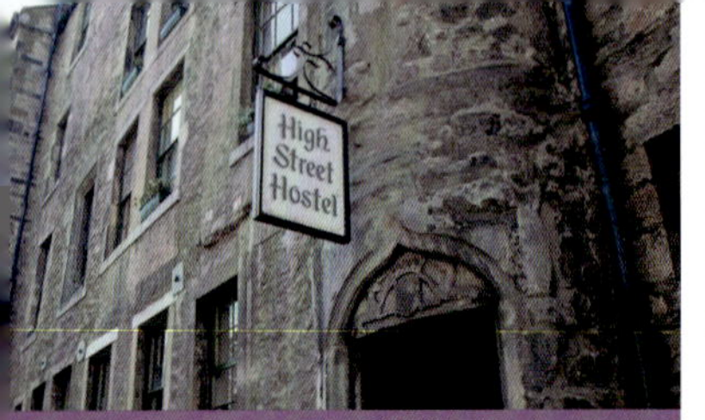

HIGH STREET
HOSTEL
178a

The High Street Hostel is one of Europe's best regarded and most atmospheric hostels. It is hugely popular with world travellers. Located just off the historic Royal Mile in a 470 year old building, it is your perfect base for exploring all the city's many attractions and of course its wonderful nightlife.

Providing excellence in location, ambience and facilities, the hostel is highly recommended by more than ten of the world's top backpacker travel guides. Come along and see for yourself!

DETAILS
- **Open** - All year. All day.
- **Beds** - 156.
- **Price/night** - From £21 per person. ID required for check in.

CONTACT: Reception
Tel: 0131 557 3984
highstreethostel@macbackpackers.com
www.highstreethostel.com
8 Blackfriars St., Edinburgh, EH1 1NE

ARDENTINNY
OUTDOOR CENTRE
178b

Ardentinny Outdoor Centre is a flexible accommodation venue set on the shores of Loch Long in the Trossachs National Park. Ideal for schools, clubs, families and activity groups, the centre can accommodate up to 120 guests in a mix of 1-6 bed dorm rooms, many of which are en suite. During the summer months, individual rooms may also be available for families, couples, and solo travellers. Catering and outdoor activities available on request.

DETAILS
- **Open** - All year
- **Beds** - 135: 12x6 3x5, 8x4, 5x twin en suite, 6x1 en suite
- **Price/night** - Schools and Groups please enquire. Summer Holidays: family/double from £60. Single Rooms from £45.

CONTACT: Peter Wilson
Tel: 01369 810271
info@ardentinnycentre.org.uk
ardentinnycentre.org.uk
Ardentinny, Dunoon, Argyll, PA23 8TR

SHORE LODGE
ARRAN

179a

Shore Lodge Bunkhouse, set in the grounds of Brodick Castle on the Isle of Arran, is designed with groups of explorers and families in mind. The bunkhouse sleeps up to 14 people in four bunkrooms. Guests can enjoy a cosy sitting room with a wood-burning stove, a self-catering kitchen, dining room, central heating, Wi-Fi, and hot showers. Arran offers a wide variety of landscapes – from rugged peaks to gentle rolling hills and scenic coastline.

DETAILS

- **Open** - All year
- **Beds** - 14: 2x2, 1x4, 1x6
- **Price/night** - £26 per person with a minimum of six people and two nights (£312).

CONTACT: Holidays Department
Tel: 0131 458 0305
holidays@nts.org.uk
www.nts.org.uk
Brodick Castle, Garden & Country Park,
Isle of Arran KA27 8HY

CAMPBELTOWN
BACKPACKERS

179b

Campbeltown Backpackers is housed in the Old Schoolhouse, a Grade B listed building.

The hostel offers easy access to the facilities of Campbeltown: swimming pool, gym, cinema and distillery tours. A good stop (for a shower) along the Kintyre Way which gives walkers great views of surrounding islands. The area offers very good windsurfing, surfing, mountain bike routes and is the start of Sustrans Route 76

DETAILS

- **Open** - All year. Be up by 10am for housekeeping. Dep by 11am on last day.
- **Beds** - 16: 1x6, 1x10
- **Price/night** - £33 per person

CONTACT: Alan
Tel: 01586 551188
info@campbeltownbackpackers.co.uk
campbeltownbackpackers.co.uk
Big Kiln, Campbeltown, Argyll, PA28 6JF
(next to Heritage Centre)

ARGYLL
BACKPACKERS

180a

Enjoy spectacular views & watching wildlife in modern comfortable self-catering accommodation? Then you'll love Argyll Backpackers! It's on the banks of Loch Fyne, just minutes from Cycle Route 78 in the hamlet of Inverneil. Perfect for island hopping to Arran & Islay. Shop at Tarbert or Ardrishaig/ Lochgilphead before arriving.

DETAILS

■ **Open** - All year (restrictions in winter).
■ **Beds** - 29: Hostel 24: 1xdbl, 1x3 (dbl+bunk above), 2x2, 2x4/5, 1x6. All en suite. Wee Snug: 4/5: 1xdbl; 1xtwin, (+z-bed if required).
■ **Price/night** - 1-2 nights: £35-£55pp. Ask about discounts for 3+ nights, sole use, weddings, Xmas & New Year.

CONTACT: Pam Richmond
Tel: 07786 157727
argyllbackpackers@sky.com
www.argyllbackpackers.com
Loch Fyne Lodge, Inverneil, Ardrishaig,
Argyll, PA30 8ES

INVERARAY
HOSTEL

180b

The historic town of Inveraray, on the western shore of Loch Fyne, is a superb location for exploring Scotland's Southern Highlands and Islands. Inverarary Hostel is perfect for independent holidaymakers who enjoy socialising.

The hostel offers simple, comfortable accommodation in private rooms, an excellent self-catering kitchen, communal dining area and a cosy wee lounge.

DETAILS

■ **Open** - March 29th - September 29th. Reception 8-10am - 4-9pm.
■ **Beds** - 22 in 10 rooms
■ **Price/night** - Private rooms from £26pp.

CONTACT: James
Tel: 01499 302562
info@inverarayhostel.co.uk
www.inverarayhostel.co.uk
Dalmally Road, Inveraray, Argyll
PA32 8XD

BALMAHA
BUNKHOUSE
181a

Set on the banks of Loch Lomond, this cosy self-catering bunkhouse offers excellent accommodation on the West Highland Way.

It can accommodate up to 10 people making an ideal base for families and small groups, as well as hikers. There are four bedrooms (two ensuite), a common room with kitchen, a drying room with laundry facilities and outdoor seating. Sorry no dogs (except Assistance Dogs).

DETAILS

- **Open** - 1 April - 31 October. Arrive 4pm-7pm (later by arrangement)
- **Beds** - 10: 1x3, 1x2, 1xdbl, 1x3(dbl + single).
- **Price/night** - From £39.50 pp including a self-service breakfast.

CONTACT: Ian Neale
Tel: 01360 870006 or 0785 301 0765
info@balmahabunkhouse.com
balmahabunkhouse.com
Balmaha, Loch Lomond, G63 0JQ

BEN LOMOND
BUNKHOUSE
181b

Ben Lomond Bunkhouse is on the West Highland Way at the foot of Ben Lomond. Run by the National Trust for Scotland, it's a great base for climbing Ben Lomond (4–6 hour round trip) or when walking the West Highland Way. All profits support conservation. Simple, comfortable accommodation with kitchen, lounge, drying room, Wi-Fi, and a wood-burning stove. Book a bed in shared bunkrooms or exclusive for a group. An honesty shop provides basics.

DETAILS

- **Open** - All Year. Groups only at Christmas and New Year
- **Beds** - 10: 1x4,1x6
- **Price/night** - Nov-Feb: £39 per person, exclusive use £300. Mar-Oct: £36 per person, exclusive use £360.

CONTACT: Ranger
Tel: 07837 784120 or 07825 204221
benlomond@nts.org.uk
www.nts.org.uk
Ardess Lodge, Rowardennan G63 0AR

BY THE WAY
HOSTEL AND CAMPSITE
182a

By The Way Hostel & Campsite is in Loch Lomond National Park. There's excellent walking, climbing & white water rafting in the area. The accommodation includes camping, various huts, (hobbit houses, posh pods, glamping, trekker huts & camping cabins) & a purpose built 4* hostel with twin, double & dormitory rooms & great self-catering facilities. For more comfort still there are 2 chalets; one 3-bed, the other 2-bed.

DETAILS

- **Open** - Hostel/huts open from April-end Oct. Camping open from April to end Sept. 8am - 10am & 2pm - 8pm.
- **Beds** - 52: 26 hostel, 36 huts. Plus 50 camping & 2 chalets.
- **Price/night** - Dorms £25pp. Twin/double £50. Huts vary. Camping £12pp.

CONTACT: Kirsty Burnett
Tel: 01838 400333
info@tyndrumbytheway.com
www.TyndrumByTheWay.com
Lower Station Rd, Tyndrum, FK20 8RY

KINGSHOUSE
BUNKHOUSE
182b

Within the grounds of the famous Kingshouse Hotel, this modern bunkhouse is right on the West Highland Way with spectacular Scottish mountain scenery. The Bunkhouse has 32 beds across 10 rooms. There is ample storage. Each bunk has a locker, reading light, power socket, linen & towels. Ideal as a stop-over for travellers or a base to explore Glencoe & beyond. There's skiing, walking & mountain biking on the doorstep. The Way Inn café offers all day dining & packed lunches. Open from 7.30am to 9pm daily (off-peak hours vary).

DETAILS

- **Open** - All year.
- **Beds** - 32: 1x6, 4x4, 5x2
- **Price/night** - From £35 per person.

CONTACT:
Tel: 01855 851259
contact@kingshousehotel.co.uk
www.kingshousehotel.co.uk
Glencoe, Argyll, PH49 4HY

HEART OF GLENCOE
HOLIDAYS

183a

Heart of Glencoe Holidays lies in woodland midway between Glencoe village & Clachaig Inn, with access to world-class cycling, walking, climbing & kayaking. Glencoe Ski Centre & West Highland Way are 20 mins away. The alpine bunkhouse sleeps up to 16 in 3 private rooms. There is also 1 cottage, 1 4-bedroom lodge, 3 luxury caravans & 3 luxury log cabins. Fantastic drying room, WiFi & epic mountain views

DETAILS

■ **Open** - All year. No reception, remote check-in, must book in advance.
■ **Beds** - 47: Bunkhouse:16. Cottage: 5. Lodge: 7 Caravans: 3x4. Eco Cabins: 2x2. Log Cabin: 1x3
■ **Price/night** - From £25 to £70pp

CONTACT: Cat,
Tel: 01855 811906
info@heartofglencoe.co.uk
heartofglencoe.co.uk
Glencoe, Near Ballachulish, Highland,
PH49 4HX

COMRIE
CROFT

183b

Comrie Croft is the Highland Edge retreat for hikers, families, friends & mountain bikers, just over an hour from Edinburgh & Glasgow. The eco-lodge offers beautiful en suite rooms with king-size beds, lots of wood & natural touches. Together with a barn, courtyard & wild places it is also available for sole use & weddings. On-site facilities include a field-to-fork café, bike shop & hire, lots of bike trails & farm shop. A footpath takes you to the village of Comrie & to stunning glens and mountains.

DETAILS

■ **Open** - All year. All day.
■ **Beds** - 60: 48 + 12
■ **Price/night** - Eco-lodge room: £52 per adult, £26 5-17 yrs. Under 5's Free.

CONTACT: Amanda
Tel: 01764 670140
info@comriecroft.com
www.comriecroft.com
Comrie Croft, By Crieff/Comrie,
Perthshire, PH7 4JZ

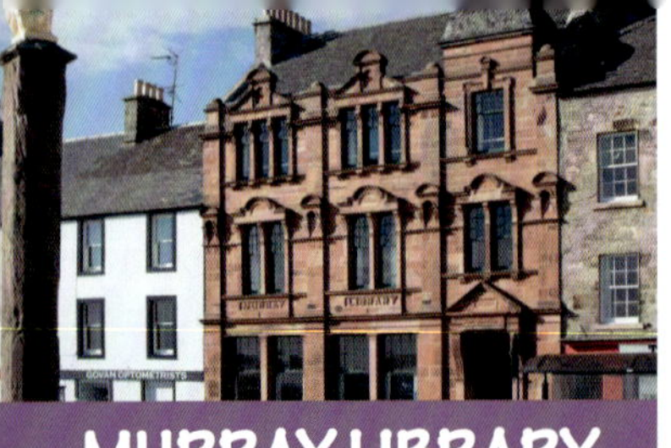

MURRAY LIBRARY
HOSTEL
184a

Murray Library Hostel offers cosy, welcoming accommodation in the quaint fishing village of Anstruther on the beautiful east coast of Scotland.

Located in a converted historic library with all bedrooms looking out over the beach, the hostel has a mix of private double, family and dorm rooms. Book a bed, a room or have sole use of the whole place for your group of 6-20.

DETAILS
■ **Open** - All year. Check-in: from 3pm. Early arrivals can leave luggage. Check-out 10am.
■ **Beds** - 20: 4x2 (dbl), 1x4 (dbl & bunks), 1x8
■ **Price/night** - Sole use from £499. For other prices check the online booking,

CONTACT: Darius
Tel: 01333 311123
murraylibraryhostel@gmail.com
murraylibraryhostel.com
7 Shore Street, Anstruther, Fife.

PITLOCHRY
BACKPACKERS HOTEL
184b

Located in the centre of beautiful Pitlochry, this friendly, cosy hostel is an old Victorian hotel literally bursting with character and provides dormitory and en suite private rooms. Comfy beds come with fitted sheets, duvets and 2 fluffy pillows and private rooms have fresh towels. The bright spacious lounge has comfy sofas and unlimited hot drinks. There's free WiFi, games, musical instruments and a free pool table. A great place to meet like minded people. You won't want to leave!

DETAILS
■ **Open** - March to Nov. 9-11am & 5-10pm (times may vary).
■ **Beds** - 79.
■ **Price/night** - From £27.50 for dorms. Private rooms from £65.00

CONTACT: Receptionist
Tel: 01796 470044
info@pitlochrybackpackershotel.com
scotlandstophostels.com
134 Atholl Road, Pitlochry, PH16 5AB

AUCHLISHIE
BUNKHOUSE

185a

Architect-designed bunkhouse on the outside Kirriemuir, at the gateway to the Angus Glens.Perfect for outdoor enthusiasts to enjoy the proximity to the Cairngorms National Park. This eco bunkhouse, with solar panels & air source heat pumps, provides top-quality accommodation for up to 22. It sleeps 18 in one large dorm plus a self-contained flat which sleeps 4 in 2 twin/king-sized double rooms. Individuals welcome.

DETAILS

- **Open** - All year
- **Beds** - 22: Bunkhouse 18: 1x18. Flat 4: 2 x twin/king-size
- **Price/night** - Bunkhouse: £38pp (subject to festive changes). Dogs £20 per stay. Flat from £240. Min 2 night stay.

CONTACT: Nicky Helyer
Tel: 07905 359648 or 01575 574458
events@auchlishie.co.uk
bunkhouse@auchlishie.co.uk
Auchlishie Farm, Kirriemuir, Angus
DD8 4LS

PROSEN
HOSTEL

185b

Glenprosen is the most intimate of the Angus Glens on the southernmost edge of the Cairngorms National Park. Two Munros; the Mayar and Driesh link Glenprosen to the Cairngorms plateau.

Prosen Hostel is close to the upgraded East Cairngorms footpath network. Converted to the latest and greenest specification, the 4* hostel offers cosy, quality accommodation for 18. With 4 rooms, sleeping 4, 4 and 6 in bunks and a family room sleeping 4. You can also hire the nearby village hall.

DETAILS

- **Open** - All year. All day.
- **Beds** - 18:1x6, 3x4
- **Price/night** - £27pp Sunday to Thursday, £35pp Friday & Saturday.

CONTACT: Michelle or Robert
Tel: 01575 540388 or 01575 540302
bookings@prosenhostel.co.uk
www.prosenhostel.co.uk
Glenprosen, Kirriemuir, Angus, DD8 4SA

MAR LODGE
BUNKHOUSE

186a

Mar Lodge Bunkhouse, near Braemar in the Cairngorms National Park, is on the National Trust for Scotland's Mar Lodge Estate. It offers comfortable accommodation for up to 12 guests in four bedrooms. There is a fully equipped kitchen, sitting and dining rooms, a drying room with washing machine, central heating, and hot showers. Ideal for walkers, mountaineering clubs, schools, or groups of family and friends. Exclusive-use with a minimum 2 night.

DETAILS

- **Open** - All year
- **Beds** - 12: 1x2, 1x2 (ensuite), 2x4
- **Price/night** - Minimum £192 for groups of up to six. Otherwise £32pp. Miniumum of 2 nights. £15 per dog (max 2 dogs).

CONTACT: Holidays Department
Tel: 0131 458 0305 or 01339 741276
holidays@nts.org.uk
www.nts.org.uk
Mar Lodge, Braemar, Royal Deeside,
Cairngorms National Park, AB35 5YJ

BALLATER
HOSTEL

186b

Ballater Hostel is in the centre of Ballater, near Balmoral, on the east side of Cairngorms National Park. Traditional dorms & private rooms, plus a large open plan kitchen/dining/communal area make great space to relax . Drying room, laundry & secure cycle storage available (+ outside tap, CCTV, electric points & bike racks). Book a room, a bed, or the whole hostel, with no minimum stay. Great facilities, comfy beds and a warm welcome - the kettle is always on!

DETAILS

- **Open** - All year. Reception 8-10am / 5-10pm.
- **Beds** - 29:1x8,1x6,1x4,1x2,3x3 (family)
- **Price/night** - Dorm beds £25. Private rooms from £41.

CONTACT: Dominique or Daniel
Tel: 01339 753752
info@ballater-hostel.com
www.ballater-hostel.com
Ballater Hostel, Bridge Square, Ballater,
AB35 5QJ

DALWHINNIE
OLD SCHOOL HOSTEL

187a

Dalwhinnie Old School Hostel is in the former village primary school, set in an acre of ground. Directly opposite the train station, it's a perfect base to climb the many Munros in the area, as a stop over on the N7 cycle route, for mountain biking at nearby Laggan Wolftrax, or simply as a beautiful overnight stop when visiting Skye or the NC 500.

Situated in the Cairngorms National Park it is across the field from the famous Dalwhinnie Distillery.

DETAILS

- **Open** - All year
- **Beds** - 27: 1x10, 2x6, 1xdbl+sgl, 1xdbl.
- **Price/night** - From £23pp. Private rooms from £65 per room.

CONTACT: Lee Cleghorn
Tel: 07960 174462
dalwhinniehostel@gmail.com
dalwhinniehostel.weebly.com
Ben Alder Road, Dalwhinnie, Highland,
PH19 1AB

LAGGAN
COMMUNITY HALL

187b

Well maintained community hall offers low cost accommodation for up to 25. BYO sleeping mat and bedding. Well equipped kitchen, showers/WCs, games rooms & free WiFi. Situated in the sleepy village of Laggan, en route for the East Highland Way. Ideal for mountain biking (Laggan Wolftrax mountain bike centre is down the road), walking, mountaineering, climbing (Creag Dubh an option) wildlife and much more. On the Scottish National Trail and close to the Great North Trail and the LEJOG cycle route.

DETAILS

- **Open** - All year
- **Beds** - 24
- **Price/night** - £20 per person. Groups of 10 or more - 10% discount on total cost

CONTACT: Jeanette Macpherson
Tel: 01528 544309 or 07890 114750
jeanettemmm@btinternet.com
www.laggan.com
Laggan Bridge by Newtonmore,
Inverness-shire, PH20 1AH

RAILWAY ROOMS
GROUP ACCOMMODATION

188a

Stay somewhere unforgettable. The Railway Rooms offer luxury group accommodation for up to 24 guests in beautifully restored Victorian railway buildings at Kingussie Station, right on the platform with stunning views of the Cairngorm Mountains. Easily accessible by train—no car needed—this stylish, self-catering retreat combines heritage charm with modern comfort. Ideal for group getaways, retreats, and outdoor adventures, with optional catering and activity packages available.

DETAILS

- **Open** - All year
- **Beds** - 24: 6 xtwin, 4 x double, 2 x king
- **Price/night** - W/end (2 nights) £1998, (3 nights) £2598. Mid week; (2 nights) £1740. Enquire for longer stays.

CONTACT: Jillian Robertson
Tel: 01540 661363 or 07891 374183
info@railwayrooms.co.uk
railwayrooms.co.uk
Ruthven Road, Kingussie. PH21 1EN

FRAOCH
LODGE

188b

Run by outdoor fans who have hosted walkers, cyclists and families for over 20 years, Froach Lodge is more then just a place to stay. Andy and Rebecca will help you or your group organise a fantastic activity each day. The Lodge is warm and welcoming. Accommodation is in private single, twin or triple rooms, there is log burner in the lounge and space for drying and storing outdoor gear. A self catering kitchen is available or you can treat yourself to Rebecca's delicious home cooking.

DETAILS

- **Open** - All year
- **Beds** - 12: 6 x 2 or 3
- **Price/night** - Rooms available from £60. Enquire for whole hostel rates.

CONTACT: Andy or Rebecca
Tel: 01479 831331
info.fraochlodge@gmail.com
fraochlodge.com
Deshar Road, Boat of Garten, Inverness-shire, PH24 3BN

GLENBEG
BUNKHOUSE & BOTHY
189a

Glenbeg Bunkhouse & Bothy are part of the award-winning Cairngorms Activities Centre, situated just outside Grantown-on-Spey in the Cairngorms National Park. The well-equipped bunkhouse sleeps 25 in 3 bedrooms, while the cosy bothy sleeps 6 in one bunkroom.

Outdoor activities are available. Aviemore, Speyside Way, Dava Way & the River Spey are all close by.

DETAILS
- **Open** - All year, 24 hour access.
- **Beds** - 31: Bunkhouse 25. Bothy 6.
- **Price/night** - Glenbeg Bunkhouse: £450 (Apr-Sep), £375 (Nov-Mar). Glenbeg Bothy: £100 (Apr-Sep), £85 (Nov-Mar).

CONTACT: Cairngorms Activities
Tel: 01479 873283
info@cairngormsactivities.co.uk
www.cairngormsactivities.co.uk
Glenbeg, Grantown-on-Spey, Moray, PH26 3NT

FINDHORN
VILLAGE HOSTEL
189b

Findhorn Village Hostel is right by the beautiful Moray Coast. Great wildlife sites & the Speyside distilleries are within reach. It provides self-catering accommodation for groups or individuals. It has shared bunkrooms, a two-person room & an en suite family room. Large communal kitchen/ dining/ living area. A self-contained studio (6 people) has a small kitchenette & en suite shower.

DETAILS
- **Open** - March-Oct. Studio & groups All Year. Office: 9am-12pm Mon-Fri.
- **Beds** - 32: 2x10, 1x4, 1x2, studio flat 6.
- **Price/night** - Dorms £25pp, Mates Cabin £50, Captains Suite £80, Lobster Pot £130. Discount for groups. Sole use from £475.

CONTACT: Sarah
Tel: 01309 692339
findhornvillagecentre@gmail.com
www.findhornvillagehostel.com
Church Place, Findhorn, Forres, Moray, IV36 3YR

THE SAIL LOFT
BUNKHOUSE

190a

Situated on the shore of the Moray Firth coast in Portsoy, The Sail Loft has a stunning location. Converted from a former sail making loft, The Sail Loft is modern and well equipped. It provides self-catering accommodation for 25 in a mixture of single accessible, twin, triple and bunk rooms, with secure cycle storage, cycle wash-down facilities and an outdoor hot tub.

The Sail Loft is a short easy walk from Portsoy town centre and its charming 17th century historic harbour. Groups welcome.

DETAILS

- **Open** - All year.
- **Beds** - 25: 1x6, 1x4, 2x3 (sgl), 4x2 (sgl), 1x1 (accessible)
- **Price/night** - From £31 per person.

CONTACT: Ian Tillett
Tel: 01261 842222 or 01261 842695
contact@portsoysailloft.org
www.portsoysailloft.org/
Back Green, Portsoy, AB45 2AF

INVERNESS
STUDENT HOTEL

190b

The cosy and friendly Student Hotel enjoys panoramic views of the town and the mountains beyond. Your perfect place to unwind, just yards from the city's varied night-life and a few mins' walk from bus and train stations. Relax in the fabulous lounge with real log fire and drink as much free tea, coffee & hot chocolate as you like. Visit the beautiful ancient pine forest of Glen Affric or the Culloden Battlefield. Famous Loch Ness lies just a few miles upstream and of course has its own special wild animal.

DETAILS

- **Open** - All year. All day. Reception 9-11am & 5-10pm
- **Beds** - 57
- **Price/night** - From £25

CONTACT: Receptionist
Tel: 01463 236556
info@invernessstudenthotel.com
scotlandstophostels.com
6 - 8 Culduthel Road, Inverness, IV2 4AB

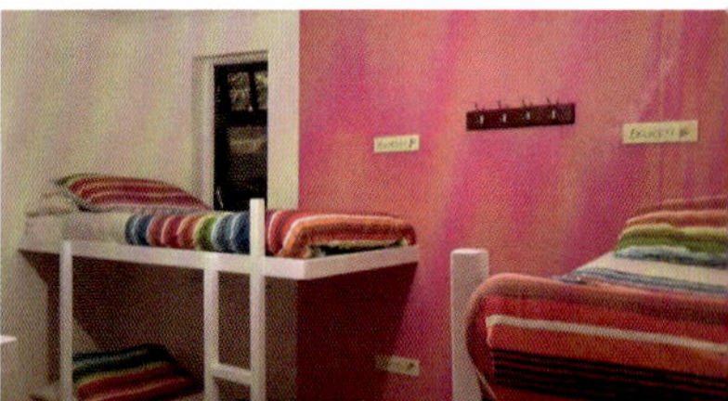

LOCH NESS
BACKPACKERS LODGE
191a

This Highland farmhouse provides warm & friendly hostel accommodation, within walking distance of Loch Ness, Urquhart Castle, the Great Glen Way, the Loch Ness 360'and the Affric-Kintail Way & with pubs, cafes, restaurants & a supermarket close by. Residents-only bar on site. Hiking tours, fishing, watersports & mountain biking can be arranged locally. Whisky & beer tasting by arrangement. Catering for groups of 10+. Pet-friendly by arrangement.

DETAILS

■ **Open** - April-Sept as a hostel. Oct-March as an exclusive-use venue.
■ **Beds** - 39: 4x6, 1x4, 1x5 (family), 1xtwin, 2xdouble
■ **Price/night** - From £25pp

CONTACT: Patrick & Nikki Kipfmiller
Tel: 01456 450807
info@lochness-backpackers.com
www.lochness-backpackers.com
Coiltie Farmhouse, East Lewiston,
Drumnadrochit, Inverness, IV63 6UJ

THE LOCHSIDE
HOSTEL
191b

Perched right on the banks of Loch Ness, the Lochside Hostel has fantastic views up and down the loch and can give you direct access to the water's edge. Why not go for a dip in Scotland's largest water body? Take a walk to watch for wildlife? Or even hunt the elusive Nessie?

The Great Glen walking route passes the front door, and the End to End cycle route is nearby. Drumnadrochit is just 12 miles away by boat.

DETAILS

■ **Open** - April-October. Check in 5pm to 11pm. Check out 10:30.
■ **Beds** - 47: 3x2 (twin), 2x4 (female), 5x4, 1x5, 1x8 all mixed dorms.
■ **Price/night** - From £23.

CONTACT: Reception
Tel: 01320 351274
lochside@macbackpackerstours.com
lochsidehostel.com
Alltsigh, Inverness. IV63 7YD

MORAGS LODGE
LOCH NESS

192a

A multi-award winning 4* hostel with a range of rooms to meet all needs and budgets in the bustling village of Fort Augustus on the banks of Loch Ness. Your perfect base to explore the Loch Ness area and an ideal stop off on the Great Glen Way. Surrounded by stunning mountain scenery and set in wooded grounds the hostel boasts 24 hour self-catering facilities, excellent home-made meal options, a rustic bar, free WiFi, and ample car parking.

DETAILS

■ **Open** - All year. Check in from 4pm (earlier by arrangement).
■ **Beds** - 75: 7x6, 6x4, 4x2/3
■ **Price/night** - From £27pp in dorm beds. Doubles/twins from £33pp. Family rooms from £86.

CONTACT: Claire
Tel: 01320 366289
info@moragslodge.com
www.moragslodge.com
Bunoich Brae, Fort Augustus, PH32 4DG

SADDLE MOUNTAIN
HOSTEL

192b

Saddle Mountain Hostel is a friendly 5* hostel in Invergarry, between Loch Ness & Fort William, at the junction with the road to Skye. The 20 bed hostel has 5 bedrooms (4 private & 1 dormitory), a large kitchen, dining room, lounge & drying room. Perfect for Munro bagging, long distance hiking, cycling, paddling & day trips. Available for individual bookings and exclusive use. Exclusive use bookings only during winter.

DETAILS

■ **Open** - Seasonal. Check website for availability. Check-in 4.30-10pm.
■ **Beds** - 20: 1x6, 1x5 (1 double, 3 singles), 2x4, 1x2 (1 double, 1 single)
■ **Price/night** - Dorm bed from £33pp, private rooms from £28pp. Exclusive use price on request.

CONTACT: Helen or Gregor
Tel: 01809 507240
info@saddlemountainhostel.scot
www.saddlemountainhostel.scot
Mandally Road, Invergarry, PH35 4HP

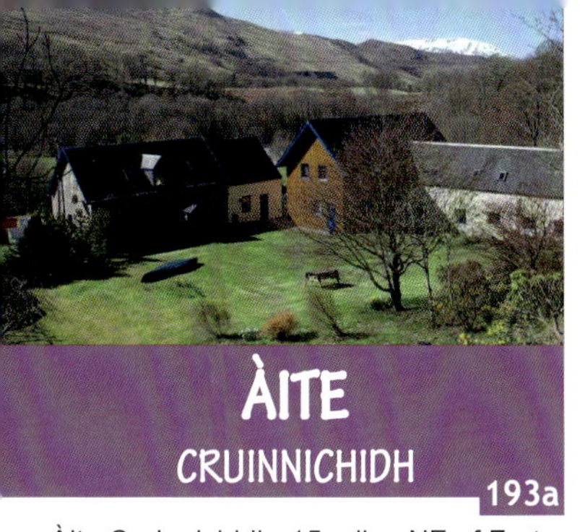

ÀITE
CRUINNICHIDH

193a

Àite Cruinnichidh, 15 miles NE of Fort William, occupies a sheltered spot next to Monessie Gorge where you can explore remote glens, mountain passes & lochs. There's a fully equipped kitchen/dining room, sitting room, excellent showers, sauna & garden. All bedding provided. Guests enjoy socialising & the natural environment around the hostel.

  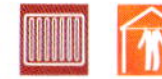      

DETAILS

■ **Open** - All year, except 23rd-28th Dec.
■ **Beds** - 28: 1x6, 4x4, 1x twin, 1x dbl, 1x family/dbl en suite. Twin also available.
■ **Price/night** - From £25pp. Twin/Double £30pp. En suite family room from £35pp reduced for children. Min of 4 people in winter. Exclusive use : up to 20 £550 a night ; 20-26 £600 a night.

CONTACT: Gavin or Nicola
Tel: 01397 712315
gavin@highland-hostel.co.uk
www.highland-hostel.co.uk
1 Achluachrach, By Roy Bridge, Near Fort William, PH31 4AW

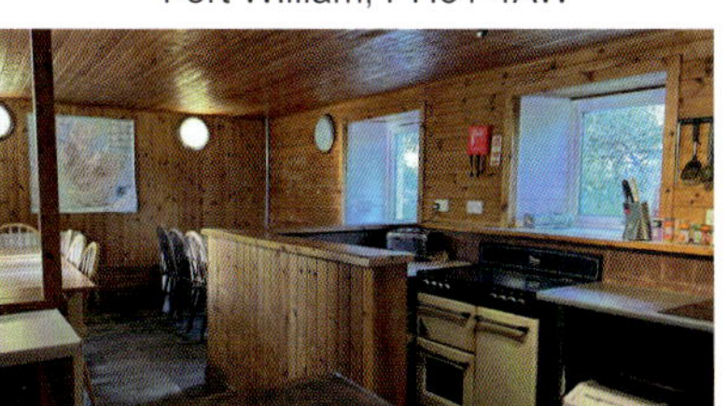

BLACKSMITHS
BUNKHOUSE

193b

Enjoy the loch-side location overlooking the Caledonian Canal, with Ben Nevis & Fort William just 4 miles away. Ideal for the outdoor enthusiast with advice & guiding available for walking/climbing, river, loch and sea kayaking, open canoeing & dinghy sailing. Outdoor equipment hire available.

After a day in the fresh air return to a hot shower and a comfy private bunkroom ideal for families, groups & clubs.

        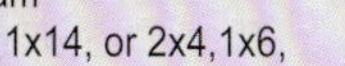

DETAILS

■ **Open** - All year. Check in 3pm-8pm. Check out 10am
■ **Beds** - 14: 1x14, or 2x4,1x6,
■ **Price/night** - 4 bed room from £96. 6 bed room from £144.

CONTACT: Tina Cuthbertson
Tel: 01397 772467
team@snowgoosecentre.co.uk
www.snowgoosecentre.co.uk
Snowgoose Mountain Centre, Station Road, Corpach, Fort William, PH33 7JH

CHASE THE WILD
GOOSE

194a

FORT WILLIAM
BACKPACKERS

194b

Chase The Wild Goose is on the Great Glen Way in the village of Banavie, near Fort William, at the end of the West Highland Way. You can be sure of a warm welcome, a comfortable bed and the company of like-minded travellers in a pleasant out-of-town environment. Whether you are on a relaxing holiday with family or friends, enjoying the adventure of a lifetime or travelling the world. Take time out in the Scottish Highlands. The scenery is breath-taking! The hospitality is second to none!

Surrounded by spectacular mountain scenery, Fort William is a mecca for those with a spirit of adventure. You can start (or end) the West Highland Way in Fort William, hike or bike along mountain trails, go for a boat trip on the sea loch or just take it easy amidst the wonderful scenery. Even in winter Fort William stays busy with skiing, snow-boarding, mountaineering and ice-climbing. Set on a hillside above the town, with wonderful views, this cosy hostel provides all you'll need after a day in the hills.

  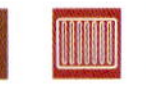           

DETAILS

- **Open** - April-September
- **Beds** - 38 : 3x4, 1x5, 1x6, 1x7, 1x8
- **Price/night** - From £33 per person. Exclusive use is available to groups.

CONTACT: Daniel & Jo
Tel: 07563 049068
bookings@chasethewildgoosehostel.co.uk
www.chasethewildgoosehostel.co.uk
Great Glen Way, Banavie, Fort William, Inverness-shire, PH33 7LY

DETAILS

- **Open** - All year. Reception: 7am-12 noon & 5-10pm
- **Beds** - 38
- **Price/night** - From £27.50 per person. ID required for check-in.

CONTACT: Receptionist
Tel: 01397 700711
info@fortwilliambackpackers.com
scotlandstophostels.com
Alma Road, Fort William, PH33 6HB

GLENFINNAN
BUNKHOUSE

195a

Glenfinnan Bunkhouse, situated between Fort William & Mallaig in the breathtaking Scottish Highlands is offered on an exclusive use basis to groups of up to 12. With climbing, walking, skiing and mountain biking on the doorstep, the bunkhouse is the perfect base for outdoor enthusiasts. For tourists and explorers, the Arisaig beaches, the Glenfinnan Viaduct, the bustling town of Fort William and the ferries to Skye and other Islands are a short drive away.

DETAILS

- **Open** - All year
- **Beds** - 12: 1x2, 1x4, 1x6
- **Price/night** - From £205 per night mid-week (2 night min stay). 2 night week end from £570. Week from £1500.

CONTACT: High Life Highland
Tel: 01349 781700
info@highlifehighland.com
highlifehighland.com
Kinlocheil, Fort William, Inverness-shire
PH33 7NP

OBAN
BACKPACKERS

195b

Perfectly situated in the heart of Oban, the gateway to the Isles, just 10 mins' walk from the bus, train & ferry terminals, this friendly hostel is a great place to stay and unwind. The fabulous sociable lounge has a real fire, pool table, free WiFi, comfy sofas and unlimited free hot drinks. The kitchen is fully equipped, perfect for cooking your favourite meals. Large dorm beds come complete with bedding including 2 comfy pillows. The hot powerful showers are legendary! Knowledgeable and friendly staff will help you make the most of your time in Oban.

DETAILS

- **Open** - April - Nov. 7-12pm & 5-10 pm
- **Beds** - 54: 1x12, 1x10, 1x8, 4x6
- **Price/night** - From £25. Whole hostel bookings please email for quote.

CONTACT: Reception
Tel: 01631 562107
info@obanbackpackers.com
scotlandstophostels.com
Breadalbane Street, Oban, PA34 5NZ

LISMORE
BUNKHOUSE
196a

This super warm and comfy eco bunkhouse on a traditional croft is the perfect base to explore the magical Isle of Lismore. The bunkhouse sleeps 12 in a mix of en suite dorms and private rooms and there is a campsite with 5 pitches and hook ups for 2 camper vans. The Isle of Lismore is just 7 miles by car ferry from Oban and is a tranquil, unspoilt island surrounded by stunning mountain scenery. Perfect for wildlife, walkers, cyclists and getting away from it all. Home grown veg and bike hire.

DETAILS

- **Open** - All year.
- **Beds** - 12: 1 x dbl, 1 x family (dbl + bunkbeds), 1x6. All en suite
- **Price/night** - From £25pp. Exclusive hire available. Camping £10pp.

CONTACT: Clare
Tel: 07720 975433
lismorebunkhouse@gmail.com
www.fb.com/thelismorebunkhouse
Isle of Lismore, PA34 5UG

HIGHLAND
BASECAMP
196b

Located in the small village of Lochaline on the remote Morvern Peninsula, Highland Basecamp is perfect for adventures on land or sea. It has 12 private en suite rooms (each with one set of single bunks) along with a spacious decking area, a well equipped self catering kitchen & cosy lounge. With underfloor heating, fluffy towels & hotel quality bed linen you are sure of a comfortable stay.

DETAILS

- **Open** - All year.
- **Beds** - 24: 12x2 single bunk beds (all en suite)
- **Price/night** - Please book directly and use discount code IHUK2026 to receive a 10% discount on stays of more than 1 night.

CONTACT: Highland Basecamp
Tel: 07824 541901
team@highlandbasecamp.com
www.highlandbasecamp.com
Lochaline, Morvern, PA80 5XT

CRAIGNURE
BUNKHOUSE

197a

CREICH HALL
BUNKHOUSE

197b

Craignure, a superior eco-sensitive bunkhouse, purpose built in 2014, is the perfect base for your Mull adventure.

Set on the water's edge close to the ferry port, there's the Craignure Inn next door for traditional island hospitality.

The 4 well-appointed bunkrooms have en suite showers & there's a spacious well-appointed communal area with kitchen, ample dining & relaxing space.

This village hall bunkhouse on the Isle of Mull is situated in a splendid rugged Moorland setting, just 1 mile outside the village of Fionnphort & the ferry to Iona, Staffa & Treshnish Isles. The bunkhouse sleep groups of up to 15 in two en suite rooms (6 & 8 single beds) plus an accessible ground floor single room. There's a self-catering kitchen and two halls which are available for use, they can be hired for exclusive use for an extra fee.

   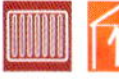       

DETAILS

- **Open** - 1st Dec-31st Oct. Closed 10am-4pm.
- **Beds** - 20: 2x4, 2x6
- **Price/night** - Please look on website.

DETAILS

- **Open** - All year.
- **Beds** - 15: 1x8, 1x6, 1x1. All en suite & all single beds
- **Price/night** - £30pp. (Min 2 people, min cost £100). Heating by £1 coin meter.

CONTACT: Ivan
Tel: 01680 812043
info@craignure-bunkhouse.co.uk
www.craignure-bunkhouse.co.uk
Craignure, Isle Of Mull, Argyll And Bute, PA65 6AY

CONTACT: Nicola Welsh
Tel: 07514 195377
bookingsecretary.creichhall@gmail.com
visitmullandiona.co.uk/listings/creich-hall
Creich, Fionnphort, Isle of Mull, PA66 6BP

ULVA
HOSTEL

198a

Ulva hostel gives guests the unique opportunity to stay on a remote West coast island. The island of Ulva, lies just off the west coast of Mull and can be reached by foot passenger ferry from Mull. The hostel, originally a shooting lodge, sleeps 14 across 5 rooms. It has a fully equipped kitchen, large living room, dining room/workspace room and a sauna. There are also 2 family sized yurts and a camping area in the grounds.

DETAILS

- **Open** - 1st April to 31st October (Groups considered out of season).
- **Beds** - 18: Hostel 14: 2x4, 2x2 (dbl), 1x2 (twin). Yurts: 2 x 2/3. Plus camping
- **Price/night** - From £25pp. £63 Double. Yurts from £75. Enquire for sole use. .

CONTACT: Andrew & Yvette Primrose
Tel: 07538 969697
ulvahostel@gmail.com
ulvahostel.co.uk
Ardalum House, Isle of Ulva, Isle of Mull, Argyll. PA73 6LZ

ROSS OF MULL
BUNKROOMS

198b

Ross of Mull Bunkrooms are located less than a mile from the ferry link to Iona at Fionnphort. Ideal for exploring the superb wildlife, rich history & shell-sand beaches of the Ross of Mull, so loved by outdoor enthusiasts.

Perfect for day trips to Staffa, the Treshnish Isles & Iona.

There are two 4 bed bunk rooms, a well-equipped kitchen, woodburner and stunning views.

DETAILS

- **Open** - All year. Whole cottage only.
- **Beds** - 8: 2x4
- **Price/night** - Flexible rates from £50 - £160 depending on number of guests, time of year and length of stay.

CONTACT: Rachel Oliver
Tel: 07759 615200
info@rossofmullbunkrooms.co.uk
www.rossofmullbunkrooms.co.uk
Fionnphort, Isle of Mull PA66 6BL

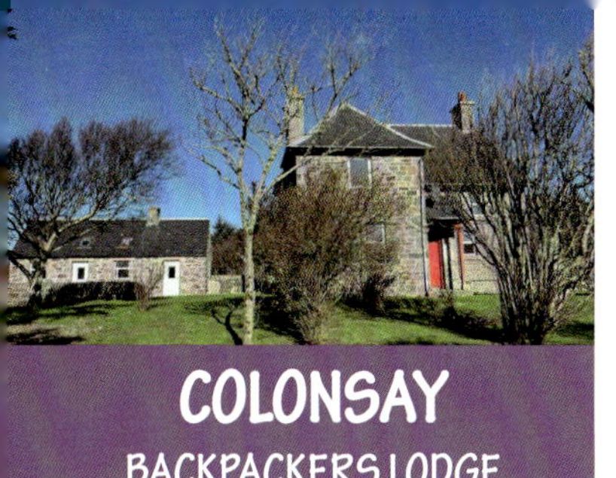

COLONSAY
BACKPACKERS LODGE
199a

Come to Colonsay Backpackers Lodge & savour the idyll of this Inner Hebridean island. Explore the magnificent sandy beaches, ancient forests & beautiful lochs.Wildlife abounds; spot dolphins, seals, otters & many rare birds. The pub, café & shop are 3 miles away. Or buy fresh lobster, crab & oysters from the fishing boats. The lodge is a refurbished gamekeeper's house with bothies. Centrally heated, it has 2 twin, 3 twin bunk & 2 three-bedded rooms.

DETAILS

- **Open** - April to October. 24 hours
- **Beds** - 18: 6x2, 2x3
- **Price/night** - From £40pp in self contained cabin with en suite; £35pp twin, £32pp bothy

CONTACT: The Manager
Tel: 01951 200211
cottages@colonsayholidays.co.uk
www.colonsayholidays.co.uk
Keepers Lodge, Colonsay Estate, Isle of Colonsay, Argyll, PA61 7YP

COLL
BUNKHOUSE
199b

This 5* self-catering hostel accommodation is a short hop from the ferry terminal & in the village next to local amenities. Ideal for groups, families (cot available) or individuals. Short or longer stays. A half hour from the mainland by plane, under 3 hours by ferry. This beautiful Hebridean island is ideal for walking, stargazing, wildlife, cycling, water sports or chilling amidst stunning scenery. Visit quiet and beautiful spaces and beaches and enjoy fine island hospitality. A warm welcome awaits you.

DETAILS

- **Open** - All year. 24 hours
- **Beds** - 14: 1x3(dbl), 1x5(dbl), 1x6
- **Price/night** - From £30pp with exclusive use rooms. Enquire for whole hostel hire rates.

CONTACT:
Tel: 01879 230217
collbunkhouse@developmentcoll.org.uk
www.collbunkhouse.com
Arinagour, Isle of Coll, Argyll, PA78 6SY

MILLHOUSE
HOSTEL
200a

Tiree is an idyllic Hebridean island surrounded by white beaches and clear, turquoise seas. Perfect for outdoor pursuits & wildlife enthusiasts, Millhouse Hostel sleeps 10 across 3 rooms. The Byre is a holiday let for groups of 10-16 people.   The hostel welcomes short or long stays. The Byre is normally let by the week, but short stays of 2 or more nights may be available.

DETAILS

- **Open** - Open all day. Check in 4pm. Check out 10am.
- **Beds** - 26:   Hostel: 10 : 3 x dbl + bunks . The Byre 16: 2x3, 2x5
- **Price/night** - Dorm bed £30. Private room £90 (for up to 4 people). The Byre: £1800 per week (plus £20pp over 10 people), enquire for short stays.

CONTACT:
Tel: 07598 946878
info@tireemillhouse.com
tireemillhouse.com
Cornaigmore, Isle of Tiree, PA77 6XA.

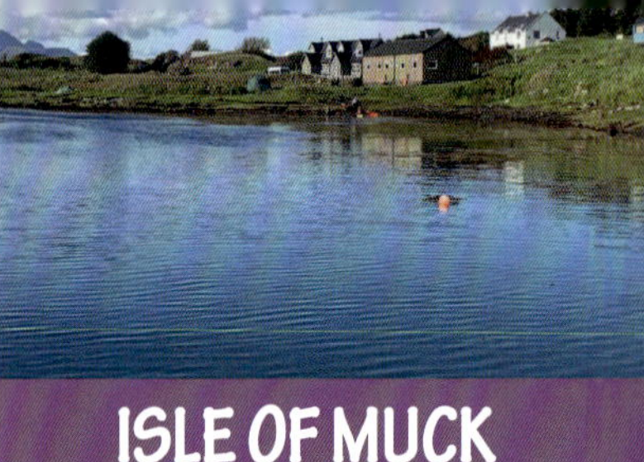

ISLE OF MUCK
BUNKHOUSE
200b

This self-catering bunkhouse can be booked as a hostel, or like a holiday cottage. It overlooks the ferry port of Port Mor & is near to The Tearoom and the island's Community Hall. The Isle of Muck is just 2 miles long by 1 mile wide and has a population of 40 people. With a rich cultural heritage & amazing wildlife, Muck is the perfect place to unwind.
BYO towel or hire. Bring your own food supplies (no shop on Muck).

DETAILS

- **Open** - All year. Reasonable (exclusive use) monthly lets available out of season.
- **Beds** - 8: 3x2 (bunks) 1x2 (double)
- **Price/night** - £30pp, under 16s £25pp (min 2 nights). Sole use £140/night (min 2 nights.) Weekly rate: £700. All rates include bed linen.

CONTACT:
muckbunkhouse@outlook.com
www.isleofmuck.com
Port Mor, Isle of Muck, PH41 2RP

GLEBE BARN

201a

Glebe Barn offers 4* homely accommodation on the extraordinary Isle of Eigg. It is situated within 1 mile of the island shop & café/restaurant. The main building sleeps up to 22 in a twin room, two triple rooms, and two dormitory rooms, with capacity for an additional 2 people in a private apartment. Perfect for individuals, families or groups. Sea views from every room.

DETAILS

■ **Open** - Groups all year; individuals from April to October. Open 24 hours.
■ **Beds** - 24: 2x2, 2x3, 1x6, 1x8
■ **Price/night** - £30pp (1-6 nights), £28 (7+ nights). Twin room £58 (1-6 nights), £54 (7+nights). Triple £85 (1-7 nights), £78 (7+ nights). Contact for group quote.

CONTACT: Tamsin McCarthy
Tel: 07951 785531 or 07535 652286
mccarthy@glebebarn.co.uk
www.glebebarn.co.uk
Glebe Barn, Isle of Eigg, Inner Hebrides, PH42 4RL

SHEENAS
BACKPACKERS LODGE

201b

The Backpackers Lodge, the oldest croft house in Mallaig, offers a homely base from which to explore the Inner Hebrides, the famous white sands of Morar and the remote peninsula of Knoydart. Mallaig is a working fishing village with all the excitement of the boats landing. You can see the seals playing in the harbour and take whale and dolphin watching trips. The hostel provides excellent budget accommodation with central heating, a well equipped kitchen/common room and free WiFi. Hot water and heating provided by renewable energy.

DETAILS

■ **Open** - All year. 9am-8pm
■ **Beds** - 8: 2x4
■ **Price/night** - From £40 pp. Please phone for price and availability

CONTACT: Ashley or Fraser
Tel: 01687 462764
backpackers@btinternet.com
www.mallaigbackpackers.co.uk
Harbour View, Mallaig, PH41 4PU

KNOYDART
BUNKHOUSE

202a

Welcome to the homely comfort of the Knoydart Foundation Bunkhouse on the stunningly remote peninsula of Knoydart in the west coast of Scotland, reachable only by boat or a long hike.

Community run, the Bunkhouse uses hydro electricity & promotes responsible tourism. Set amid wild, remote terrain, 20 mins' walk from pub, PO, shop & ferry at Inverie. Three mixed dorm rooms & a comfy communal lounge, kitchen and dining room, drying room and bathrooms.

DETAILS

- **Open** - All year.
- **Beds** - 26: 1x7, 1x8, 1x11
- **Price/night** - From: £29 adult, £15 under 16s. Sole use £600. Dogs £5/night.

CONTACT: Jenny
Tel: 01687 347422 or 01687 462242
stay@knoydart.org
knoydart.org/knoydart-bunkhouse/
Inverie, Knoydart, By Mallaig, Inverness-shire PH41 4PL

KINTAIL
OUTDOOR CENTRE

202b

Kintail Outdoor Centre (National Trust for Scotland) is set beneath the dramatic Five Sisters of Kintail and Ben Attow, just minutes from the A87, with Skye and Glenelg nearby. Sleeps 8–20 in 5 bunkrooms across two wings, each with showers. Facilities include a lounge with log burner, self-catering kitchen, dining area, drying room and laundry. An ideal base for hillwalking, adventures and field studies in one of Scotland's most spectacular landscapes.

DETAILS

- **Open** - All Year
- **Beds** -   20: Wing1 10:1x2,2x4   Wing2 10:1x4,1x6
- **Price/night** - £224 per wing (includes 8 guests) plus £28 for each extra person.

CONTACT: Holidays Department
Tel: 0131 458 0305 or 01599 511231
holidays@nts.org.uk
www.nts.org.uk
Morvich Farm, Inverinate, Ross-shire IV40 8HQ

SKYE
BACKPACKERS

203a

Whether your visit to Skye is to tackle the mighty mountains, meet the legendary faeries or simply to chill out, Skye Backpackers is the place for you. Located in the fishing village of Kyleakin surrounded by mountains and sea, the hostel has dorm, double and twin rooms. All beds come with sheets, duvets and 2 pillows. There is a fully equipped self-catering kitchen, a sunny dining area, as much free tea, coffee & hot chocolate as you can drink, free WiFi, a cosy lounge with a real fire and spectacular views.

DETAILS

- **Open** - Apr to Oct. 7am-12 noon then 5pm-10pm
- **Beds** - 53
- **Price/night** - From £23pp. ID required for check in.

CONTACT: Receptionist
Tel: 01599 534510
info@skyebackpackers.com
scotlandstophostels.com
Kyleakin, Isle of Skye, IV41 8PH

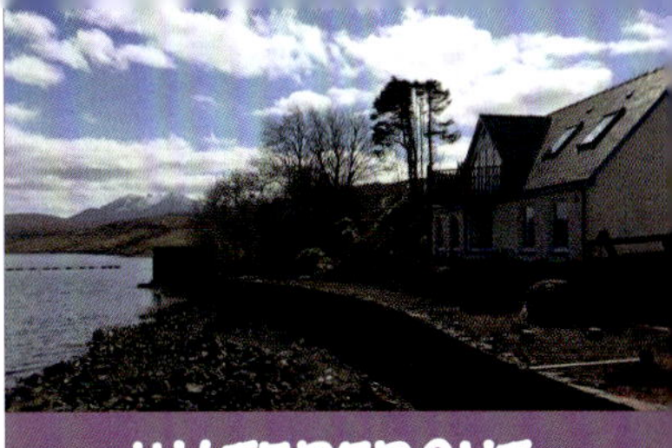

WATERFRONT
BUNKHOUSE

203b

Feet from the edge of Loch Harport, Isle of Skye, with breathtaking views of the Cuillins, this purpose built, stylish & comfortable bunkhouse is an ideal base for hill walkers or sightseers. There is spectacular scenery and abundant wildlife in the surrounding hills and glens. The bunkhouse has a kitchen and common room with a balcony overlooking the loch and 5 bunkrooms, one en suite. The Old Inn, a traditional highland pub provides breakfast, lunch and dinner if required.

DETAILS

- **Open** - 7 days a week. Usually closed throughout January.
- **Beds** - 24: 2x6, 2x4, 1x4 en suite.
- **Price/night** - £35pp. En suite £40pp. Sole use £650. Booking essential.

CONTACT: Elaine
Tel: 01478 640205
enquiries@theoldinnskye.co.uk
www.theoldinnskye.co.uk
The Old Inn, Carbost, Skye, IV47 8SR

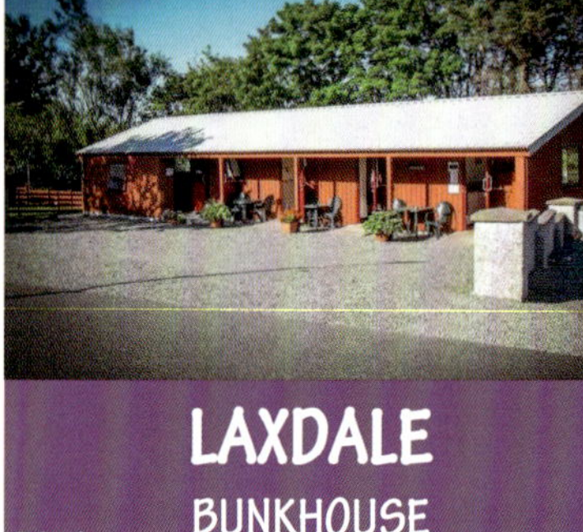

HEB
HOSTEL

204a

The Heb Hostel is a family-run backpackers hostel in the heart of Stornoway on the enchanting Isle of Lewis. It's ideal for travellers visiting the Hebrides. Cyclists, walkers, surfers, families & groups are all welcome. Clean, comfortable, friendly & relaxed, Heb Hostel aims to provide a quality stay at budget prices. There are many facilities, including a self catering kitchen, coin operated laundry and a bike shed!

DETAILS

■ **Open** - March - October. Open all day but may need to phone for access code.
■ **Beds** - 30: 1x8, 2x7,1x4 (family), 2x2.
■ **Price/night** - Dorm £25pp. Family room £90/£110. Twin/double from £70. Shepherds hut from £80.

CONTACT: Christine Macintosh
Tel: 01851 709889
christine@hebhostel.com
www.hebhostel.com
25 Kenneth St, Stornoway, Isle of Lewis, HS1 2DR

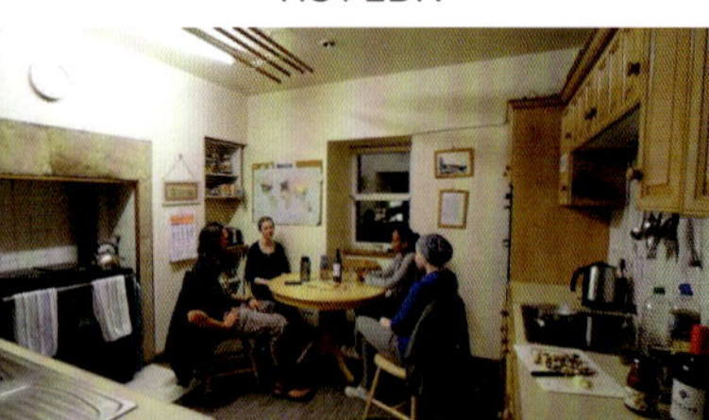

LAXDALE
BUNKHOUSE

204b

Laxdale Bunkhouse, on the Isle of Lewis, lies within Laxdale Holiday Park, a small family-run park set in peaceful leafy surroundings. Just 1.5 miles away from the town of Stornoway, it's an ideal base for exploring the island. Built in 1998, the bunkhouse has four rooms of four bunks. There is a drying room, a spacious fully equipped dining kitchen, a comfortable TV lounge and BBQ area. Toilets/ showers are located in the building & are suitable for the disabled. Wigwams are also available.

   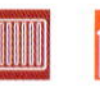        

DETAILS

■ **Open** - March to Nov. 9am - 10pm.
■ **Beds** - 16: 4x4.
■ **Price/night** - £24 adult, £20 child, £85 room (3 or less people) £365 sole use.

CONTACT: Gordon Macleod
Tel: 01851 706966 or 07786 392679
info@laxdaleholidaypark.com
www.laxdaleholidaypark.com
Laxdale Holiday Park, 6 Laxdale Lane, Stornoway, Isle of Lewis, HS2 0DR

GEARRANNAN
HOSTEL & BUNKHOUSE
205a

Part of the Gearrannan Blackhouse Village on the Isle of Lewis, the Gearrannan Hostel has been refurbished to sleep 13 including a 3-bed family room. Warm and cosy it has a well equipped kitchen & two modern shower rooms. The bunkhouse (groups only) sleeps 14 in bunks. The perfect base for many local attractions from surfing to country walks, archaeology to cycling. There are also 3 holiday cottages.

DETAILS

■ **Open** - All year. No Sunday arrivals.
■ **Beds** - Hostel: 13: 1x6, 1x4, 1x3. Bunkhouse: 14: 2x6 1x2. Black houses: 1x2, 2x3-5
■ **Price/night** - Hostel: from £35pp, family room from £95.

CONTACT: Mairi
Tel: 01851 643416
info@gearrannan.com
www.gearrannan.com
5a Gearrannan Carloway Isle of Lewis
HS2 9AL

GRINNEABHAT
HOSTEL
205b

Friendly community-owned hostel in a beautifully renovated school on the west coast of Lewis. Grinneabhat also houses a gallery and community room. It runs regular events, classes and workshops which guests are welcome to join. Perfect for visitors interested in exploring a biodiverse and culturally rich environment where Gaelic is still the living language of the community.

All rooms are ensuite and bed linen and towels are provided.

DETAILS

■ **Open** - All year
■ **Beds** - 12: 2x4, 2x2
■ **Price/night** - Bunks £30 - £40. Rooms £50 - £140. Family rooms £100 - £140. Whole hostel £300 - £450

CONTACT: Reception
Tel: 01851 710210
info@bragararnol.org
www.grinneabhat.com
North Bragar, Isle of Lewis. HS2 9DA

RAVENSPOINT
HOSTEL

206a

On the unspoilt Isle of Lewis, Ravenspoint Hostel sits on the shores of Loch Erisort, providing comfortable accommodation in a traditional crofting community where Gaelic is still spoken on a daily basis. Whether travelling by bike, bus, car or on foot, look out for white-tailed eagles, otters & deer. Enjoy exploring the community-owned Pairc Estate on where the hostel sits alongside a small shop, tea room, & museum

DETAILS

- **Open** - All Year. Winter stays (1November - 31March) require a minimum of 2 nights for dorm bookings.
- **Beds** - 9: 1xdbl, 1xtwin, 1x5 bunks
- **Price/night** - Private double or twin room £70. Shared dorm room £28pp.

CONTACT: Shop
Tel: 01851 880236
hostel@ravenspoint.net
ravenspoint.net
Kershader, South Lochs, Isle of Lewis, HS2 9QA

NUNTON HOUSE
HOSTEL

206b

Nunton House Hostel is situated on the enchanting Isle of Benbecula in the Outer Hebrides close to the beautiful beach of Culla Bay. Furnished to a very high standard, Nunton House Hostel sleeps 16 in 4 en suite rooms of 4. You can book by bunk, the room or sole use of the hostel. With beautiful beaches, stunning views, great moorland walks and causeway access to neighbouring islands, Nunton House Hostel makes the perfect base for a Hebridean adventure.

DETAILS

- **Open** - All year.
- **Beds** - 16: 4x4 (all en suite)
- **Price/night** - £35pp, private rooms £90 for 2 people, £120 for 3 people, £140 for 4 people.

CONTACT: Donald MacPhee
Tel: 01870 602017 or 07786158304
nuntonhousehostel@hotmail.co.uk
nuntonhousehostel.com
Nunton, Isle of Benbecula, Outer Hebrides, HS7 5LU

MOL MOR
TORRIDON

207a

Mol Mor Bunkhouse offers simple, comfortable accommodation for up to ten guests in the heart of the Torridon Estate.

With a well-equipped kitchen, cosy lounge with wood-burning stove, central heating,and breathtaking mountain scenery on the doorstep, it's the perfect base for walking clubs, schools, families, and friends—available for exclusive-use bookings with a minimum two-night stay.

        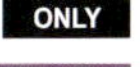

DETAILS

- **Open** - All year
- **Beds** - 10: 1x2, 2x4
- **Price/night** - Exclusive use £135 (£130 in 2025) for groups of five and under, larger groups £27 per person. Minimum of two nights stay.

CONTACT: Holidays Department
Tel: 0131 458 0305 or 01445 791368
holidays@nts.org.uk
www.nts.org.uk
The Mains, Torridon, Achnasheen, Ross-shire IV22 2EZ

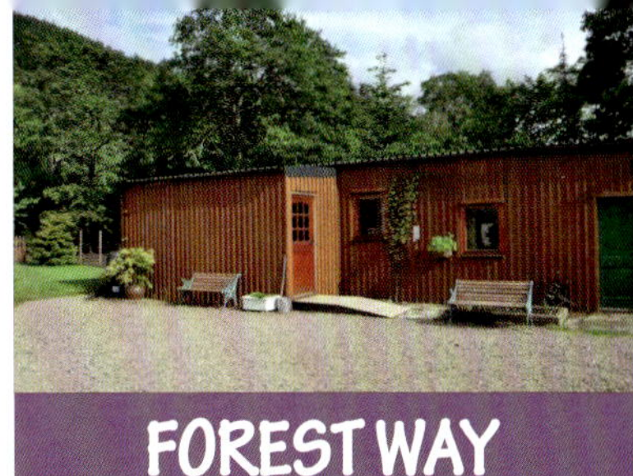

FOREST WAY
BUNKHOUSE

207b

Close to the idyllic fishing village of Ullapool in a peaceful rural setting with lots of wildlife. A perfect base for climbers & walkers with 22 Munros and many other hills in the area.

Next to Lael Forest Gardens which is renowned for its wildlife. The bunkhouse is ideally located for touring the North West Highlands with easy access to the areas of Torridon and up to Assynt.

DETAILS

- **Open** - All year.
- **Beds** - 11: 2x4 both en suite
- **Price/night** - From £25pp, £100 per room, £200 for the whole hostel. Discounts for stays of more than 1 night (see website for more info).

CONTACT: Iain
Tel: 07912 177419
bookings@forestway.co.uk
www.forestway.co.uk
Lael, Lochbroom, IV23 2RS

THE CEILIDH PLACE
BUNKHOUSE

208a

The Ceilidh Place, in the centre of Ullapool, has a music venue, restaurant, hotel, bar, bookshop, coffee shop, gallery and bunkhouse. There are regular ceilidhs, concerts & plays. The bunkhouse does not have self-catering facilities but the coffee shop is open from 8am til evening. Rooms also available in the hotel. The village of Ullapool is a small exciting port and fishing town, with ferries from the Outer Hebrides. Hill walkers and families love staying here.

DETAILS

■ **Open** - April to the end of October.
■ **Beds** - 32: 1xdb, 3x2, 3x4, 3xfamily
■ **Price/night** - From £30pp based on full occupancy (i.e 2 people in a 2 bed room, 4 people in a 4 bed room). Single occupancy starts from £40.

CONTACT: Reception
Tel: 01854 612103
stay@theceilidhplace.com
www.theceilidhplace.com
14 West Argyle St. Ullapool, IV26 2TY

BADRALLACH
BOTHY & CAMPSITE

208b

On the tranquil shores of Little Loch Broom overlooking one of Scotland's finest mountain ranges, Badrallach Bothy and Campsite offer a fine base for walking or relaxing. Fish in the nearby lochs or simply enjoy the flora and fauna. Hot showers, a great price and the feeling of remoteness make the Bothy and Campsite a firm favourite. There is also a holiday cottage for hire.

DETAILS

■ **Open** - All year: April-Sept 9am-8pm; Oct-Mar 10am-6pm
■ **Beds** - 12: (area is for sleeping mats and bags - no beds)
■ **Price/night** - £12.50pp, £2.50 per vehicle. £125 sole use. See facebook page for camping/cottage fees.

CONTACT: Chris Davidson
Tel: 07719 536870
mail@badrallach.com
www.badrallach.com
Croft No 9, Badrallach, Dundonnell, Ross-shire, IV23 2QP

INCHNADAMPH
LODGE

209a

Inchnadamph Explorers Lodge is a grand house tastefully converted to provide a variety of accommodation in the Scottish Highlands.

Choose from private rooms, dorms, a self-catering cottage, shepherd huts and steading studio apartments.

Located at the foot of Ben More Assynt, overlooking Loch Assynt, it is a great base to explore one of the wildest areas in the Highlands. On North Coast 500 classic road route.

DETAILS

- **Open** - Mid March to End Oct. All day
- **Beds** - 50
- **Price/night** - From £33pp.

CONTACT: Host
Tel: 01571 822218
team@inchnadamph.com
www.inchnadamph.com
Inchnadamph, Elphin, Sutherland.
IV27 4HL

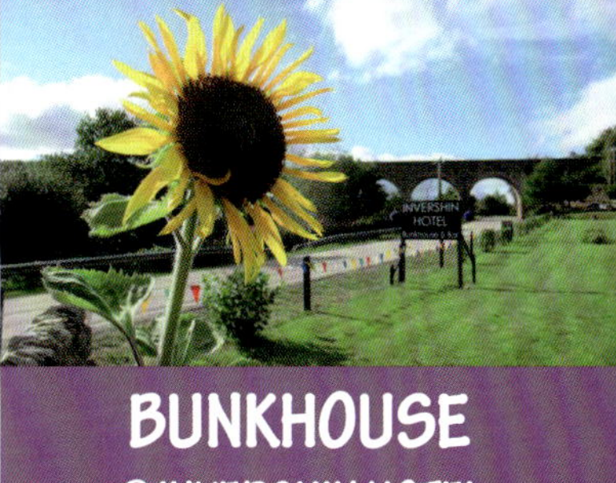

BUNKHOUSE
@ INVERSHIN HOTEL

209b

Situated within a small hotel in the north Highlands, the bunkhouse consists of 4 rooms with a shared shower room & toilet. Guests can enjoy the hotel facilities; comfortable reception area, cosy bar with real fire, real ale and regular music sessions. Cyclists, walkers, bikers, fishermen, Munro baggers, families and individuals are all welcome. The bunkhouse is just off the North Coast 500 road route. No self-catering facilities but breakfast & evening meals are available.

DETAILS

- **Open** - April-end Sept. Check in 4pm.
- **Beds** - 10: 2x twin, 2x triple (bunkbeds)
- **Price/night** - From £35pp. Breakfast optional extra.

CONTACT: Angus or Cheryl
Tel: 01549 421202
bunkhouse@invershin.com
www.invershin.com
Invershin Hotel, Lairg, Sutherland,
IV27 4ET

HELMSDALE
LODGE HOSTEL

210a

Set in the scenic coastal village of Helmsdale, on both the NC500 and the Land's End to John O'Groats routes. The Lodge offers ensuite rooms, a self-catering kitchen, a comfortable lounge with a log-burning stove, a garden, and a lockable bike shed. It is popular with 'end-to-enders' and walkers exploring the far-north Marilyn hills. A perfect stop-over en route to Orkney. Pets welcome on request. Groups welcome.

DETAILS

■ **Open** - All year. Advanced bookings only from Nov-March. Check in 4-8pm.
■ **Beds** - 24: 6x4 (all ensuite)
■ **Price/night** - Adults from £35. Children from £15. Private ensuite room from £80. Dog £10 per stay.

CONTACT: Marie
Tel: 07971 922356 or 07971 516287
stay@helmsdalehostel.co.uk
www.helmsdalehostel.co.uk
Stafford Street, Helmsdale, Sutherland,
KW8 6JR

CORNMILL

210b

Cornmill is situated on a traditional croft.

The mill was built in the early 1800s and was active until 1920s.

It was a 4 star bunkhouse for many years and has recently been converted into comfortable self catering cottage, ideal for families.

It is an historic building and one of the bedrooms has a patio door looking onto the workings of the old mill with its large wooden cog driving wheels.

DETAILS

■ **Open** - All year.
■ **Beds** - 8: 1x2 (en suite),1x6
■ **Price/night** - Please enquire for prices

CONTACT: Sandy Murray
Tel: 01641 571219 or 07592 510896
sandy.murray2@btinternet.com
Achumore, Strathhalladale, Sutherland,
KW13 6YT

KYLE OF TONGUE
HOSTEL AND CAMPSITE 211a

The Kyle of Tongue Hostel & Campsite is a stone lodge & campsite, situated on the shores of a sea loch on the Scottish North Coast. Furnished like a boutique hotel, but with all the friendliness of a hostel. There are comfortable private bedrooms, a relaxing cafe bar, a lounge/dining room and a well stocked shop. The campsite is fully equipped and has panoramic views of Castle Varich, Ben Hope & Ben Loyal. Holiday cottage and static caravan are also available.

DETAILS

- **Open** - April to October. Check in from 2pm
- **Beds** - 19 in hostel, plus cottage, static caravan and a large campsite.
- **Price/night** - Private rooms from £75. Contact for other prices.

CONTACT: Carol Mackay
Tel: 01847 611789
kothostelandhp@btinternet.com
www.tonguehostelandholidaypark.co.uk
Tongue, By Lairg, Sutherland, IV27 4XH

BROWNS
HOSTEL & HOUSES 211b

Self-catering accommodation in the captivating small town of Stromness, Orkney. Within walking/cycling distance of the ancient Maeshowe, Ring of Brodgar & Skara Brae. Stromness has a museum, art centre, festivals, scuba diving, sea angling etc. Facilities include fully equipped kitchen, single, double, twin, triple & family bedrooms, some with wash basins, others en suite. Towels & bedding inclusive. Free car park.

DETAILS

- **Open** - All year. All day. No curfew.
- **Beds** - 28: 3x1, 4x2, 3x3, 2x4
- **Price/night** - Twin/triple room from £30pp Single room from £35. Family en suite from £90. Twin or double occupancy ensuite rooms from £70.

CONTACT: Sylvia Brown
Tel: 01856 850661 or 07765 271009
info@brownsorkney.co.uk
www.brownsorkney.co.uk
45/47 Victoria Street, Stromness, Orkney, KW16 3BS

HOY
CENTRE

212a

Surrounded by magnificent scenery, the Hoy Centre is perfect for a peaceful & relaxing holiday. It's also ideal for walking, outdoor education, weddings, workshops, clubs or family gatherings. Offering 4* accommodation, the centre has a well-equipped kitchen, comfortable lounge & large dining hall. All rooms are en suite with twin beds & one set of bunks. Hoy is an RSPB reserve with 3,500ha of upland heath & cliffs & a large variety of wildlife including arctic hares.

DETAILS

- **Open** - All year. (not Xmas & New Year)
- **Beds** - 32: 8x4 (2 singles & bunks). All en suite
- **Price/night** - Please phone for prices for singles, families or groups including whole hostel bookings.

CONTACT: Customer Services
Tel: 01856 850907 or 01856 873535
stromnesscs@orkney.gov.uk
orkney.com
Moaness, Hoy, Orkney. KW16 3NJ

RACKWICK
HOSTEL

212b

Situated in the north of Hoy, breeding ground for many birds, including puffins, & site of famous 137m sea stack, The Old Man of Hoy. Wild flowers and bird life make this a must-visit location for naturalists.

Overlooking Rackwick Bay (one of the most beautiful places in Orkney), Rackwick Hostel sleeps 8 across 2 bunk rooms. There's a small kitchen with a good range of utensils & separate dining area. Bedding provided. Free car parking and bike storage.

DETAILS

- **Open** - All year.
- **Beds** - 8: 2x4
- **Price/night** - For prices please check accommodation's website or phone.

CONTACT: Customer Services
Tel: 01856 850907 or 01856 873535
stromnesscs@orkney.gov.uk
orkney.com
Rackwick Hostel, Rackwick, Hoy, Orkney, KW16 3NJ

BIRSAY
HOSTEL

213a

Birsay Hostel in the northwest corner of the Orkney mainland offers comfortable accommodation to groups of up to 26 in 5 bedrooms. An ideal venue for outdoor education trips, clubs or family gatherings. It has a well equipped kitchen, dining area, drying room, disabled access and all bed linen is provided. There is a campsite in the extensive grounds. Close to spectacular coast, RSPB reserves, early settlements and UNESCO heritage sites.

DETAILS

■ **Open** - April to September. Out of season booking may be available by arrangement for large bookings.
■ **Beds** - 26: 2x4, 1x2, 1x6, 1x10 + camping.
■ **Price/night** - Prices on enquiry.

CONTACT: Customer Services
Tel: 01856 850907 or 01856 873535
stromnesscs@orkney.gov.uk
orkney.com
Birsay, Orkney, KW17 2LY

ROUSAY
HOSTEL

213b

The island of Rousay is a walker's and birdwatcher's paradise with many footpaths and theTrumland RSPB reserve. Often called 'the Egypt of the North', Rousay contains some of the best preserved archaeological sites in the north of Scotland, set in spectacular scenery rich in wildlife, and flowers.

The small, friendly community creates a unique welcome for visitors to this beautiful island. Rousay Hostel is within walking distance of the shop, bike hire and pier.

DETAILS

■ **Open** - All year. All day
■ **Beds** - 11
■ **Price/night** - £20 per person (£23 with bed linen). Camping £10 per person.

CONTACT: Carol or Eric
Tel: 01856 821252 Mob: 07545 374029
trumland@btopenworld.com
Trumland Organic Farm, Rousay,
Orkney, KW17 2PU

AYRES ROCK
HOSTEL

214a

Sanday is the perfect place to take time out, with long stretches of unspoilt sandy beaches, an abundance of birds, seals and other wildlife, glittering seas, clear air and spectacular skies. Those lucky enough to live here enjoy a rare quality of life in a small, friendly and safe community. Ayres Rock is a small friendly hostel with twin/dbl rooms, a 1-bed cottage, pods and a campsite. Credited 4 Stars VisitScotland

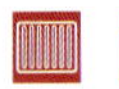

DETAILS

- **Open** - All year. 8am to 10pm.
- **Beds** - 16 + camping. Hostel 8:2x2 (twin),1x2(dbl). Cottage 2. Pods: 3x2 .
- **Price/night** - Twin room from £50. Double from £60. Pods from £35. Please enquire for sole use and camping.

CONTACT: Claire
Tel: 01857 600410
sandayhostel@gmail.com
ayres-rock-hostel-orkney.co.uk
Ayre, Coo Road, Sanday, Orkney
KW17 2AY

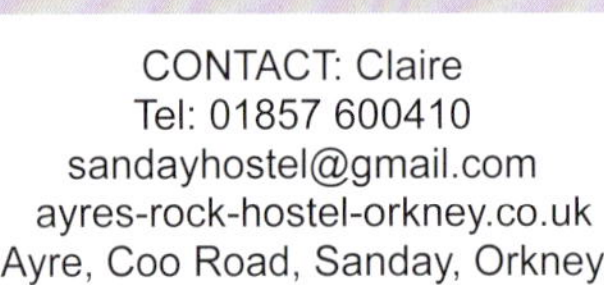

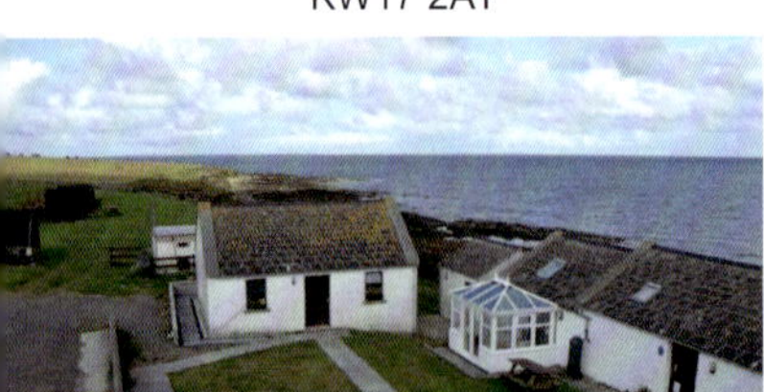

OBSERVATORY
HOSTEL

214b

On a 34 acre croft managed by the North Ronaldsay Bird Observatory on the most northern isle of Orkney. Adjacent to a shell sand beach visited by seals and unique seaweed-eating sheep. Spectacular bird migration and outstanding views. Ideal accommodation for those interested in wildlife but welcomes all. The hostel sleeps 10 in three dormitories with a self-catering kitchen. Lounge bar and meals available in the Observatory Guest House.

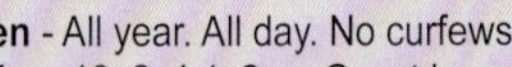

DETAILS

- **Open** - All year. All day. No curfews.
- **Beds** - 10: 2x4,1x2 + Guest house.
- **Price/night** - Hostel: £25, half board from £58. Guest house: private rooms £75 - £100 half board.

CONTACT: Duty Warden
Tel: 01857 633200
enquiries@nrbo.org.uk
www.nrbo.org.uk
NRBO, North Ronaldsay, Orkney
Islands, KW17 2BE

ISLESBURGH HOUSE
HOSTEL

215a

Islesburgh House 5 star Hostel offers top quality hostel style accommodation in Lerwick, the thriving main town on the Shetland Isles.

You are assured of a comfortable stay in bright and spacious surroundings. There is a choice of private rooms with 2, 4, 6 or 8 beds, a well equipped kitchen, a large dining room and a comfortable lounge. Situated next to the community centre where there is a daytime cafe and cultural events.

 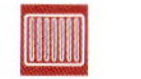    

DETAILS

- **Open** - Jan-Nov
- **Beds** - 62: dorms & private rooms
- **Price/night** - Please enquire

CONTACT: Reception
Tel: 01595 745100
islesburgh@shetland.gov.uk
shetland.gov.uk
King Harald Street, Lerwick, Shetland.
ZE1 0EQ

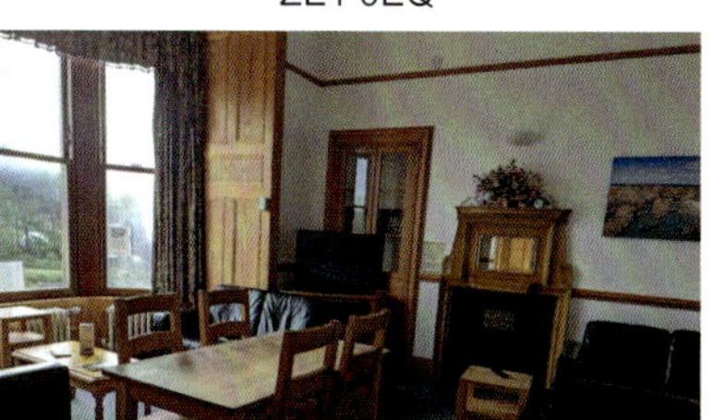

GARDIESFAULD
HOSTEL

215b

Gardiesfauld Hostel is on Unst, the most northerly of the Shetland Isles with spectacular cliffs sculpted by the Atlantic Ocean on the west and secluded, sandy beaches on the east with rocky outcrops where seals and otters appear.

On the picturesque shore at Uyeasound, this refurbished hostel has good facilities and a relaxed atmosphere. There is a kitchen, dining room, lounge, conservatory and rooms with en suite facilities as well as a garden where you can pitch a tent or park your caravan.

DETAILS

- **Open** - April to October. Groups only in winter. Open all day.
- **Beds** - 35: 1 x 10, 3 x 6, 1 x 5, 1 x 2
- **Price/night** - Adults £25, U16's £10. Camping £10, U16s £3. Hook ups £25.

CONTACT: Warden
Tel: 07900 597951 or 01957 755279
alisonhunter379@btinternet.com
Uyeasound, Unst, Shetland, ZE2 9DW

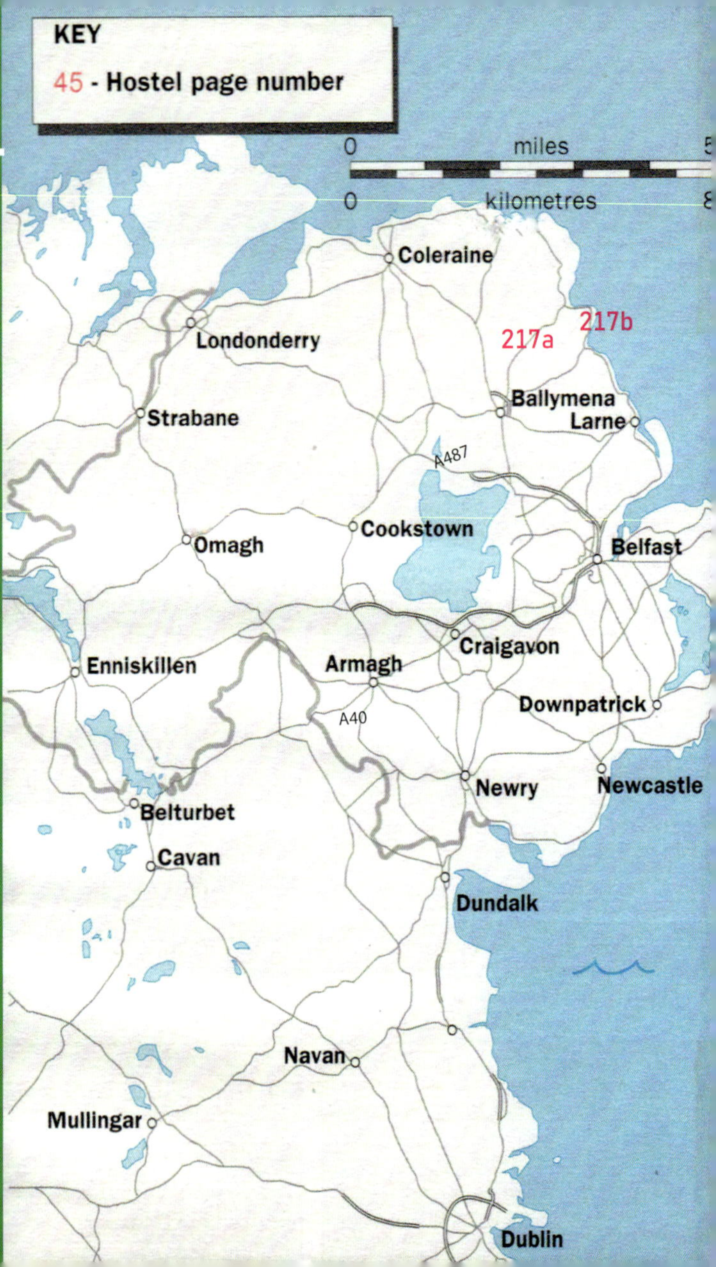
KEY
45 - Hostel page number
0 miles 5
0 kilometres 8
Coleraine
217b
217a
Londonderry
Ballymena
Larne
Strabane
A487
Cookstown
Belfast
Omagh
Craigavon
Armagh
Enniskillen
Downpatrick
A40
Newry
Newcastle
Belturbet
Cavan
Dundalk
Navan
Mullingar
Dublin

BALLYEAMON
BARN
217a

On the Antrim Coast & Glens National Landscape, a choice of accommodation in this stunning part of Northern Ireland. A traditional hostel offering accommodation in bunks in a large spacious dorm, and a Loft apartment sleeping up to 6 in double or futon beds, ideal for families or friends. Both share the same kitchen. The hostel has it's own 'session house' where local musicians & storytellers meet and entertain guests and a workshop space available to hire.

  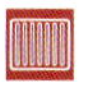      

DETAILS
- **Open** - Mar - Nov. Groups all year.
- **Beds** - 20: Hostel: 1x14. Loft 6: 2 doubles + 2 futons
- **Price/night** - Barn: £20pp. Loft from £100. Please enquire for sole use.

CONTACT: Liz Weir
Tel: 07703 440558
liz@lizweir.net
www.ballyeamonbarn.com
127 Ballyemon Road, Cushendall, County Antrim, N Ireland. BT44 0QP

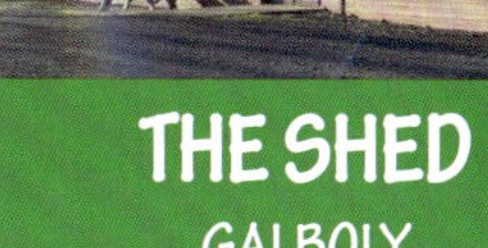

THE SHED
GALBOLY
217b

This newly opened hostel sits on the world famous Antrim Coast Road, close to the Hidden Village of Galboly used in Game of Thrones. The NCN 93 and The Ulster Way run past the doorstep. There are stunning coastal views around every corner and plenty of attractions. The Shed sleeps 6 in 3 rooms, it has a breakfast bar area, communal kitchen and a cosy sitting room. Book by the room or book sole use for your family or friends. Dogs welcome.

DETAILS
- **Open** - All year
- **Beds** - 6: 2x2 (bunks), 1x2 (double)
- **Price/night** - Bunk room: £65. Double room £80. Sole use from £420 for 2 nights.

CONTACT: Jonny Davies
Tel: 07540 186731
Jonathan.davies@email.com
theshedgalboly.com
80 Garron Road, Carnlough, Co Antrim, N Ireland, BT44 0JU

INDEX

1912 Centre	57a	Bossington Bunkhouse	44b
3 Peaks Bunkbarn	89a	Boswinger Hostel	39b
Aite Cruinnichidh	193a	Bradwell War Memorial Hall	75b
Abersoch Sgubor Unnos	157b	Braich Goch Bunkhouse	148b
Aberystwyth Uni Bunkhouse	147a	Brecon Bunkhouse	131b
Ackers Adventure	65b	Bretton Hostel	73b
All Stretton Bunkhouse	63b	Bridges Youth Hostel	63a
Almond Lodge Brecon B	135a	Bristol Wing, The	48b
Almond Lodge Helvellyn	101a	Broadrake Bunkbarn	88b
Alnwick Youth Hostel	119a	Brompton on Swale Bunkb.	94a
Alston Youth Hostel	110a	Bron-y-Gader Bunkhouse	159b
Alstonefield Camping Barn	69a	Browns Hostel & Houses	211b
Anglesey Outdoor Centre	167a	Brynkir Coach House	157a
Ardentinny Outdoor Centre	178b	Bunker Portland, The	45b
Argyll Backpackers	180a	Bunkhouse@Invershin Hotel	209b
Ashbourne Gateway Lodge	68b	Bunkorama	150b
Auchlishie Bunkhouse	185a	Butterton Camping Barns	69b
Ayres Rock Hostel	214a	Bwthyn Bach Bunkhouse	145b
Aysgill Camping Barn	89b	By the Way Hostel	182a
Bachelors Hall	40b	Caban Caron Hostel	143a
Badrallach Bothy	208b	Caban Cysgu Bunkhouse	161a
Bala Backpackers	151a	Caerhafod Lodge	140a
Ballater Hostel	186b	Caldbeck Glamping Barns	104b
Ballyeamon Barn	217a	Calvert Devon Lodges	42b
Balmaha Bunkhouse	181a	Camp Hillcrest Bunkhouse	59b
Bank House Farm Hostel	95a	Campbeltown Backpackers	179b
Barholm Accommodation	172b	Capel Tanrallt Self Catering	166a
Barrington Bunkhouse	111b	Cardiff Residential Centre	128a
Base Camp Hathersage	76b	Carrs Farm Bunkhouse	112a
Base Camp Snowdonia	154a	Carrshield Camping Barn	110b
Bath YMCA	47b	Castle Rock Hostel	177b
Beili Neuadd Bunkhouse	144b	Ceilidh Place Bunkhouse	208a
Bell Heath Centre	65a	CellB	155a
Bells Bothy Bunkhouse	176b	Ceunant Isaf Bunkhouse	164b
Ben Lomond Bunkhouse	181b	Chapel Gallery Bunkhouse	90a
Birsay Hostel	213a	Chartners Farm	118a
Blacksmiths Bunkhouse	193b	Chase the Wild Goose Hostel	194a
Blakebeck Farm Camping B.	104a	Chellington Centre	56a
Blakedean Scout Hostel	83a	Cleikum Mill Lodge	175b
Bluebell Farm Bunkbarn	122b	Clun Mill Hostel	62a
Boarshurst Centre	81a	Clyngwyn Bunkhouse	134a
Borth Youth Hostel	147b	Coed Owen Bunkhouse	133b

INDEX